ENGLISH
FOR EVERYONE

EVERYDAY ENGLISH

 FREE AUDIO
website and app
www.dkefe.com

ENGLISH
FOR EVERYONE

EVERYDAY ENGLISH

Project Editor Amanda Eisenthal
Senior Art Editor Gilda Pacitti
Editors Andrea Mills, Laura Sandford, Rona Skene, James Smart
Designers Karen Constanti, Ali Scrivens, Anna Scully
Illustrator Gus Scott
Managing Editor Carine Tracanelli
Managing Art Editor Anna Hall
Jacket Designer Juhi Sheth
DTP Designer Deepak Mittal
Senior Jackets Coordinator Priyanka Sharma Saddi
Jackets Design Development Manager Sophia MTT
Senior Production Editor Andy Hilliard
Senior Production Controller Meskerem Berhane
Publisher Andrew Macintyre
Managing Director, DK Learning Hilary Fine

First published in Great Britain in 2024 by
Dorling Kindersley Limited
DK, One Embassy Gardens, 8 Viaduct Gardens,
London, SW11 7BW

The authorised representative in the EEA is
Dorling Kindersley Verlag GmbH. Arnulfstr. 124,
80636 Munich, Germany

Copyright © 2024 Dorling Kindersley Limited
A Penguin Random House Company
10 9 8 7 6 5 4 3
003-329222-Aug/2024

A CIP catalogue record for this book
is available from the British Library.
ISBN: 978-0-2415-6613-8

Printed and bound in China

www.dk.com

Contents

ON HOLIDAY

HEALTH AND MEDICINE

MEDIA AND COMMUNICATIONS

How to use this book

English for Everyone: Everyday English will help you learn, understand, and practise common and useful British English phrases for a wide range of everyday situations. Most units in the book consist of conversation modules, with illustrated dialogues to place the phrases in context, and practice exercises. Listen to the audio on the website or app, repeat the words and phrases out loud, then complete the exercises to reinforce what you've learned. The answers to the exercises are at the back of the book.

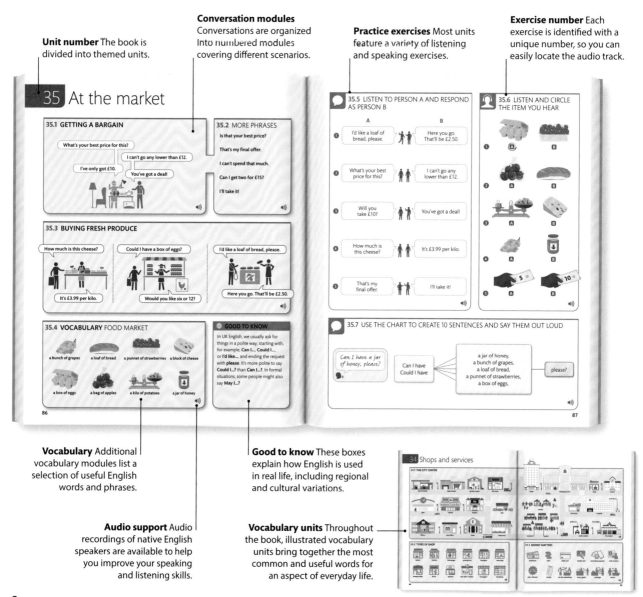

Unit number The book is divided into themed units.

Conversation modules Conversations are organized into numbered modules covering different scenarios.

Practice exercises Most units feature a variety of listening and speaking exercises.

Exercise number Each exercise is identified with a unique number, so you can easily locate the audio track.

Vocabulary Additional vocabulary modules list a selection of useful English words and phrases.

Good to know These boxes explain how English is used in real life, including regional and cultural variations.

Audio support Audio recordings of native English speakers are available to help you improve your speaking and listening skills.

Vocabulary units Throughout the book, illustrated vocabulary units bring together the most common and useful words for an aspect of everyday life.

Practice exercises

The conversation modules are followed by listening and speaking exercises.
Work through the exercises to test your understanding of the dialogues, fix the new phrases in your memory, and improve your speaking fluency. Answers are provided for the speaking exercises and the listening exercises.

Listening exercise This symbol indicates that you should listen to an audio track in order to answer the questions in the exercise.

Listening and speaking exercise This exercise allows you to simply listen to and repeat the dialogues.

Listen to Person A Listen to the first part of the conversation in the audio track.

Respond as Person B In response to Person A, read the text for Person B out loud. Cover the dialogues to challenge yourself!

Speaking exercise This symbol indicates that you should say your answers out loud.

Fill in the gaps In these speaking exercises, the gaps are a prompt to find the missing word from the panel and say the whole phrase out loud.

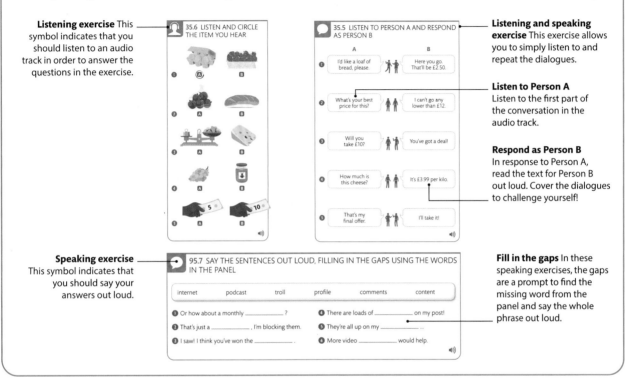

Audio

This book offers extensive supporting audio resources. Each word and phrase in the conversation and vocabulary modules is recorded, and can be played, paused, and repeated as often as you like.

 SUPPORTING AUDIO This symbol indicates that extra audio material to support a module or exercise is available for you to listen to.

 LISTENING EXERCISES This symbol indicates that you should listen to an audio track in order to answer the questions in the exercise.

 FREE AUDIO website and app **www.dkefe.com**

To access the audio, download the app or go online, then choose the **British English** option when prompted.

Answers

Answers are provided for most of the exercises, so you can see how well you have understood and remembered the phrases and expressions you have learned.

Answers The answers to the exercises are at the back of the book.

Exercise numbers Match these numbers to the unique module number at the top-left corner of each exercise.

Audio This symbol indicates that the answers can also be listened to.

01 Greetings

1.1 INFORMAL GREETINGS

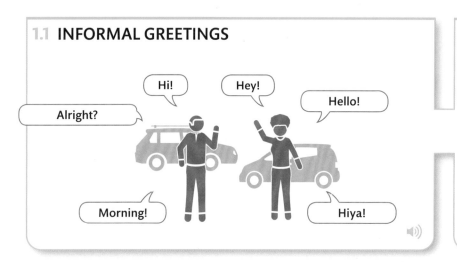

Alright?

Hi!

Hey!

Hello!

Morning!

Hiya!

1.2 MORE PHRASES

Hello there!

Evening all!

Hey, everyone!

Long time no see!

It's been ages!

1.3 FORMAL GREETINGS

Good morning.

Hello.

How do you do?

It's good to meet you.

1.4 MORE PHRASES

Good afternoon.

Good evening.

It's a pleasure to meet you.

It's lovely to meet you all.

It's nice to meet face to face!

1.5 EXCHANGING GREETINGS

How are you doing?

I'm good! How've you been?

Hey, Jay, how's it going?

Hey, good to see you. Been too long!

🌐 GOOD TO KNOW

In informal English, you will often hear greetings in their abbreviated form, such as **How've you been?**, which flows more naturally than its long form, **How have you been?** It's also common to omit **It's** before phrases like **Good to see you**, **Nice to meet you**, and **Been too long!**

1.6 LISTEN TO PERSON A AND RESPOND AS PERSON B

A   **B**

1 How're you doing?   I'm good! How've you been?

2 Hey, Jay, how's it going?   Hey, good to see you. Been too long!

3 Morning!   Hiya!

4 Good morning.   Hello.

5 It's good to meet you.   How do you do?

1.7 LISTEN AND NUMBER THE SENTENCES IN THE ORDER YOU HEAR THEM

A Morning! ☐

B Evening all! ☐

C It's lovely to meet you all. ☐

D Long time no see! ☐

E How do you do? ☐

F It's been ages! ☐

G Hello there! 1

H It's a pleasure to meet you. ☐

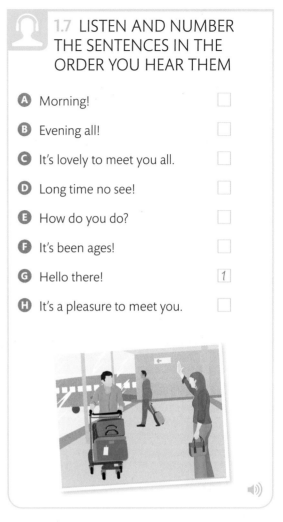

1.8 SAY THE SENTENCES OUT LOUD, FILLING IN THE GAPS USING THE WORDS IN THE PANEL

| doing | afternoon | time | meet | Hey | going | Good | do |

1 How do you _____ ?

2 _____ evening.

3 It's good to _____ you.

4 Good _____ .

5 Hey, Jay, how's it _____ ?

6 _____ , everyone!

7 How're you _____ ?

8 Long _____ no see!

11

02 Making introductions

2.1 INTRODUCING YOURSELF INFORMALLY

Hey, I'm Tao.

How's it going? I'm Joe.

Hi, my name's Karim.

I'm Eva. Lovely to meet you.

You, too!

I don't think we've met. I'm Sofia.

I'm Jasmine, a friend of Jack's.

Really nice to meet you.

2.2 INTRODUCING YOURSELF FORMALLY

Hello, I'm Daniyal Ali.

It's a pleasure to meet you, Mr Ali.

Good morning, my name's Levi.

Pleased to meet you. I'm Maria.

Good to meet you, Maria.

We have a new starter! Would you like to introduce yourself?

Of course. I'm Samantha, but you can call me Sam.

2.3 INTRODUCING OTHER PEOPLE

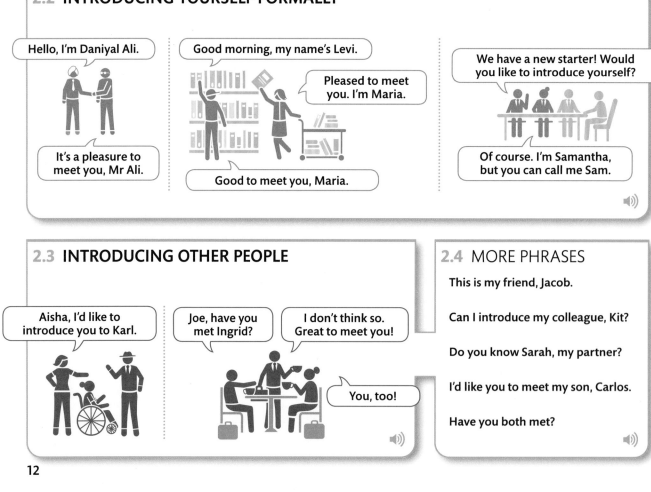

Aisha, I'd like to introduce you to Karl.

Joe, have you met Ingrid?

I don't think so. Great to meet you!

You, too!

2.4 MORE PHRASES

This is my friend, Jacob.

Can I introduce my colleague, Kit?

Do you know Sarah, my partner?

I'd like you to meet my son, Carlos.

Have you both met?

2.5 LISTEN TO PERSON A AND RESPOND AS PERSON B

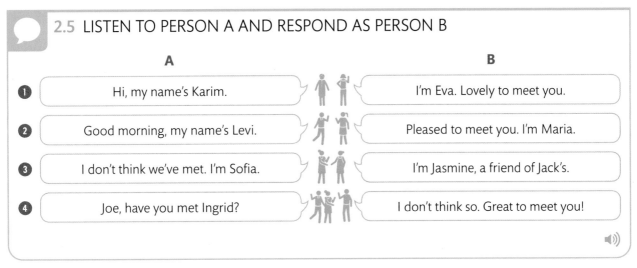

	A		B
❶	Hi, my name's Karim.		I'm Eva. Lovely to meet you.
❷	Good morning, my name's Levi.		Pleased to meet you. I'm Maria.
❸	I don't think we've met. I'm Sofia.		I'm Jasmine, a friend of Jack's.
❹	Joe, have you met Ingrid?		I don't think so. Great to meet you!

2.6 USE THE CHART TO CREATE NINE SENTENCES AND SAY THEM OUT LOUD

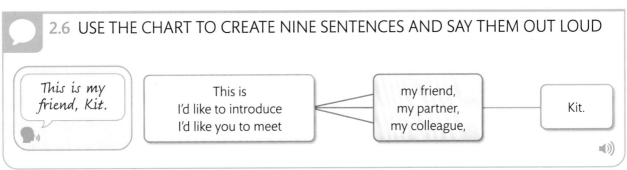

This is my friend, Kit.

This is	my friend,	Kit.
I'd like to introduce	my partner,	
I'd like you to meet	my colleague,	

2.7 RESPOND OUT LOUD TO THE AUDIO, FILLING IN THE GAPS USING THE WORDS IN THE PANEL

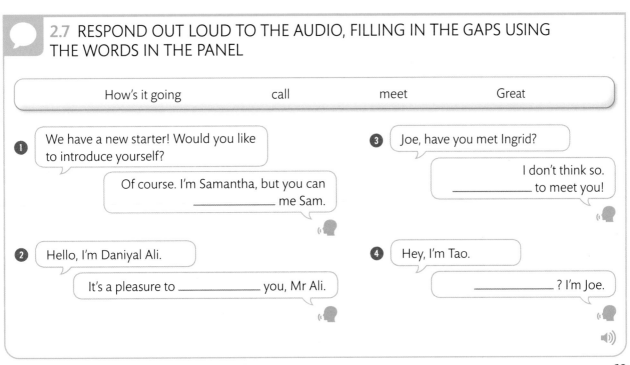

| How's it going | call | meet | Great |

❶ We have a new starter! Would you like to introduce yourself?

Of course. I'm Samantha, but you can _____ me Sam.

❷ Hello, I'm Daniyal Ali.

It's a pleasure to _____ you, Mr Ali.

❸ Joe, have you met Ingrid?

I don't think so. _____ to meet you!

❹ Hey, I'm Tao.

_____ ? I'm Joe.

03 Conversation fillers

3.1 STARTING A SENTENCE

Right, let's get started!

Okay, I'll weigh the sugar and you whisk the eggs.

So, do you like these trousers?

Well, I love the colour, but I think they're a bit too short.

3.2 IN THE MIDDLE OF A SENTENCE

What did you think of the play?

I **kind of** liked it, but it was a bit long.

How's the new puppy?

He's, **like**, really cute but super naughty!

You must be disappointed with the result.

Yeah, but, **you know**, the team did their best.

3.3 AT THE END OF A SENTENCE

How was your pasta?

It was okay, **I guess**.

I hate rush hour! I'm thinking of moving to the countryside.

That's not a bad idea, **actually**.

Are you coming to Sam's party tonight?

I'm a bit too tired, **to be honest**.

3.4 TAG QUESTIONS

George plays the guitar, **doesn't he?**

Yeah, **he does.**

You haven't seen my keys, **have you?**

No, **I haven't**, sorry.

He's really upset, **isn't he?**

Yeah, **he is.**

3.5 SHOWING YOU'RE LISTENING

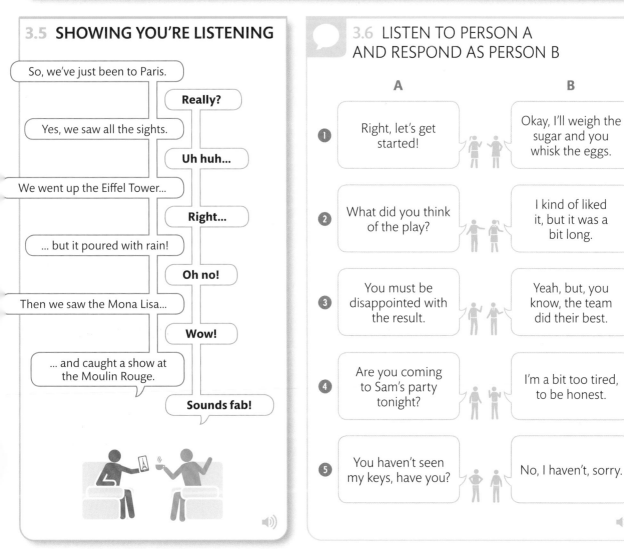

So, we've just been to Paris.

Really?

Yes, we saw all the sights.

Uh huh...

We went up the Eiffel Tower...

Right...

... but it poured with rain!

Oh no!

Then we saw the Mona Lisa...

Wow!

... and caught a show at the Moulin Rouge.

Sounds fab!

3.6 LISTEN TO PERSON A AND RESPOND AS PERSON B

	A		B
1	Right, let's get started!		Okay, I'll weigh the sugar and you whisk the eggs.
2	What did you think of the play?		I kind of liked it, but it was a bit long.
3	You must be disappointed with the result.		Yeah, but, you know, the team did their best.
4	Are you coming to Sam's party tonight?		I'm a bit too tired, to be honest.
5	You haven't seen my keys, have you?		No, I haven't, sorry.

15

Saying you don't understand

4.1 WAYS TO SAY YOU DON'T UNDERSTAND

Sorry, I'm not with you.

Sorry, I don't understand. My English isn't great.

I'm not quite sure what you mean.

4.2 SAYING YOU CAN'T HEAR SOMEONE

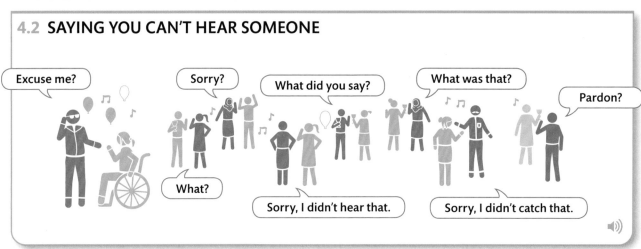

Excuse me?

Sorry?

What did you say?

What was that?

Pardon?

What?

Sorry, I didn't hear that.

Sorry, I didn't catch that.

4.3 ASKING SOMEONE TO REPEAT

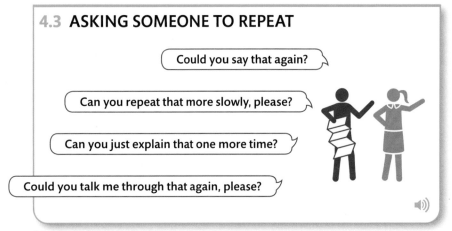

Could you say that again?

Can you repeat that more slowly, please?

Can you just explain that one more time?

Could you talk me through that again, please?

🌐 GOOD TO KNOW

Saying **What?** is a simple way to ask someone to repeat what they just said. However, it can sound blunt to English speakers, especially in the UK, so is best saved for friends. **Excuse me?** or **Sorry, I didn't catch that** are more polite alternatives when speaking to someone you don't know well.

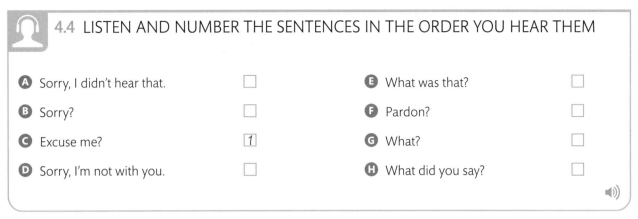

4.4 LISTEN AND NUMBER THE SENTENCES IN THE ORDER YOU HEAR THEM

A Sorry, I didn't hear that. ☐

B Sorry? ☐

C Excuse me? 1

D Sorry, I'm not with you. ☐

E What was that? ☐

F Pardon? ☐

G What? ☐

H What did you say? ☐

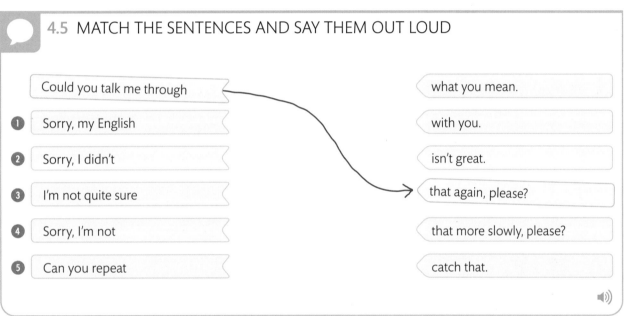

4.5 MATCH THE SENTENCES AND SAY THEM OUT LOUD

Could you talk me through — that again, please?

1 Sorry, my English — isn't great.

2 Sorry, I didn't — catch that.

3 I'm not quite sure — what you mean.

4 Sorry, I'm not — with you.

5 Can you repeat — that more slowly, please?

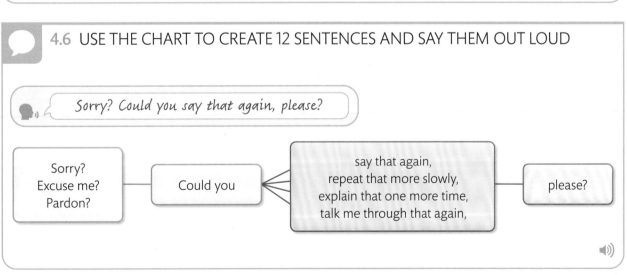

4.6 USE THE CHART TO CREATE 12 SENTENCES AND SAY THEM OUT LOUD

Sorry? Could you say that again, please?

| Sorry? Excuse me? Pardon? | Could you | say that again, repeat that more slowly, explain that one more time, talk me through that again, | please? |

17

05 Opinions and preferences

5.1 SAYING WHAT YOU LIKE

I quite like these boots... What do you think?

I absolutely love them!

This soup is great, isn't it?

Yeah, it's pretty good!

Are you off hiking again?

Yes, I'm really into it at the moment!

5.2 SAYING WHAT YOU DON'T LIKE

Do you fancy going out for a curry tonight?

Hmm... I'm not much of a curry fan.

We're heading to the skate park – wanna come?

No, I'm good. Skateboarding isn't really my thing.

Are you into horror films?

No way! I can't stand them.

5.3 MORE PHRASES

I'm a big fan!

It's so my thing!

I've always loved it.

I'm just not really into it.

I'm not that keen on it.

I couldn't think of anything worse!

5.4 LISTEN TO PERSON A AND RESPOND AS PERSON B

A **B**

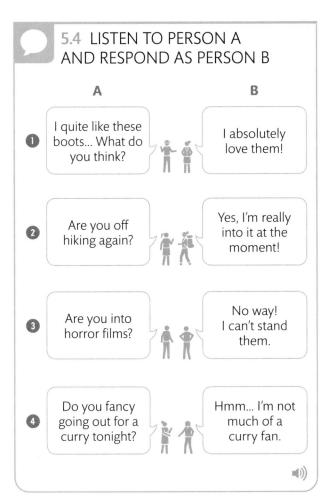

1 I quite like these boots... What do you think? | I absolutely love them!

2 Are you off hiking again? | Yes, I'm really into it at the moment!

3 Are you into horror films? | No way! I can't stand them.

4 Do you fancy going out for a curry tonight? | Hmm... I'm not much of a curry fan.

5.5 SAY THE SENTENCES OUT LOUD, FILLING IN THE GAPS USING THE WORDS IN THE PANEL

think   fan   great   into
always   love   thing   pretty

1 Yes, I'm really _____ it at the moment!

2 I absolutely _____ them!

3 I've _____ loved it.

4 I'm a big _____ !

5 Yeah, it's _____ good!

6 It's so my _____ !

7 This soup is _____ , isn't it?

8 What do you _____ ?

5.6 MATCH THE SENTENCES AND SAY THEM OUT LOUD

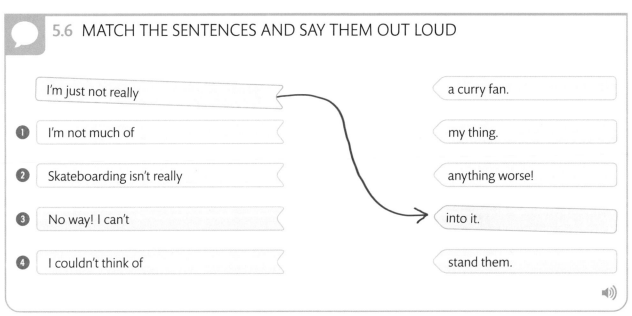

I'm just not really   →   into it.

1 I'm not much of   a curry fan.

2 Skateboarding isn't really   my thing.

3 No way! I can't   anything worse!

4 I couldn't think of   stand them.

19

5.7 GIVING OPINIONS FORMALLY

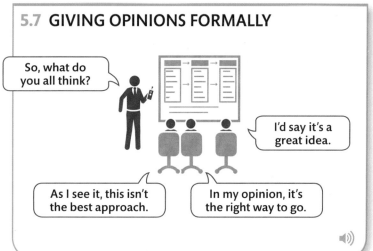

5.8 MORE PHRASES

What's your view?

What's your opinion on this?

How do you feel about it?

I feel like...

As far as I'm concerned...

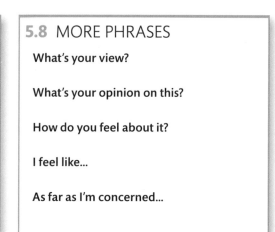

5.9 EXPRESSING PREFERENCES

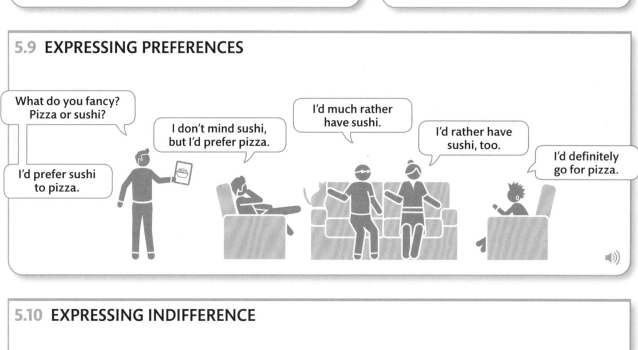

5.10 EXPRESSING INDIFFERENCE

5.11 LISTEN TO PERSON A AND RESPOND AS PERSON B

	A		B
❶	So, what do you all think?		I'd say it's a great idea.
❷	How do you feel about it?		As I see it, this isn't the best approach.
❸	What do you fancy? Pizza or sushi?		I don't mind sushi, but I'd prefer pizza.
❹	I'd much rather have sushi.		I'd rather have sushi, too.
❺	Which would you rather – bowling or ice skating?		I don't really mind. Happy either way.

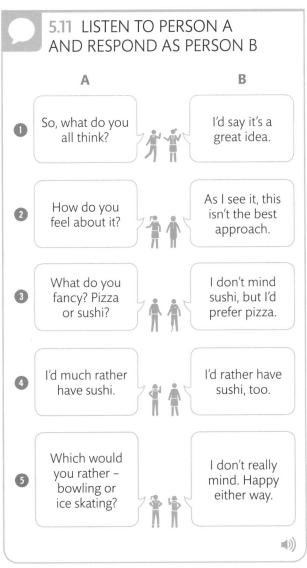

5.12 LISTEN AND NUMBER THE SENTENCES IN THE ORDER YOU HEAR THEM

Ⓐ What's your opinion on this? ☐

Ⓑ I'd say it's a great idea. ☐

Ⓒ I don't really mind. ☐

Ⓓ What's your view? 1

Ⓔ I'd definitely go for pizza. ☐

Ⓕ How do you feel about it? ☐

Ⓖ In my opinion, it's the right way to go. ☐

Ⓗ As far as I'm concerned... ☐

Ⓘ I'm not fussed. Both are okay with me. ☐

Ⓙ As I see it, this isn't the best approach. ☐

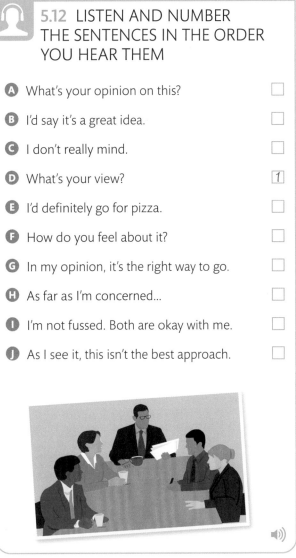

5.13 USE THE CHART TO CREATE EIGHT SENTENCES AND SAY THEM OUT LOUD

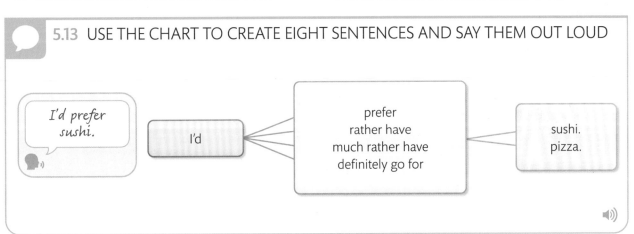

I'd prefer sushi.

I'd

prefer
rather have
much rather have
definitely go for

sushi.
pizza.

06 Agreeing and disagreeing

6.1 AGREEING WITH OPINIONS

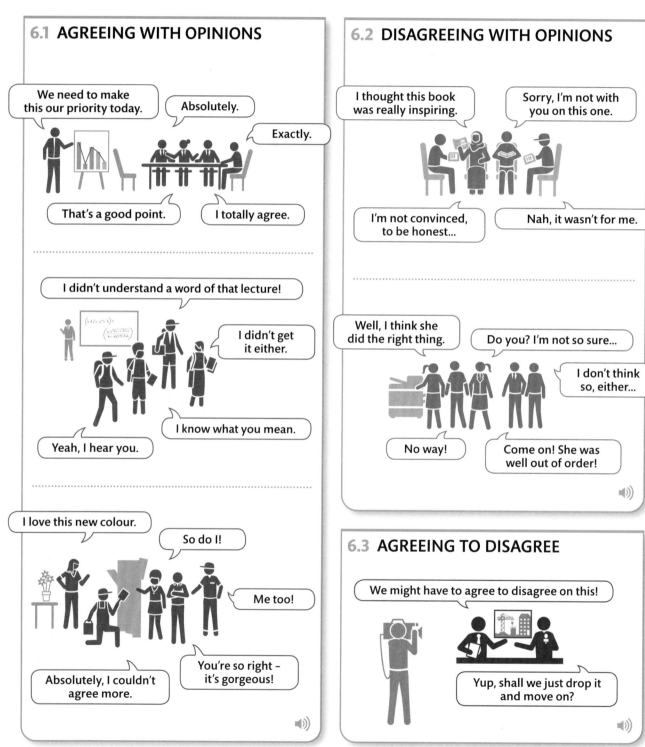

We need to make this our priority today.

Absolutely.

Exactly.

That's a good point.

I totally agree.

I didn't understand a word of that lecture!

I didn't get it either.

I know what you mean.

Yeah, I hear you.

I love this new colour.

So do I!

Me too!

You're so right – it's gorgeous!

Absolutely, I couldn't agree more.

6.2 DISAGREEING WITH OPINIONS

I thought this book was really inspiring.

Sorry, I'm not with you on this one.

I'm not convinced, to be honest...

Nah, it wasn't for me.

Well, I think she did the right thing.

Do you? I'm not so sure...

I don't think so, either...

No way!

Come on! She was well out of order!

6.3 AGREEING TO DISAGREE

We might have to agree to disagree on this!

Yup, shall we just drop it and move on?

6.4 LISTEN TO PERSON A AND RESPOND AS PERSON B

	A		B
❶	We need to make this our priority today.		I totally agree.
❷	I didn't understand a word of that lecture!		I know what you mean.
❸	I thought this book was really inspiring.		Nah, it wasn't for me.
❹	Well, I think she did the right thing.		Do you? I'm not so sure...

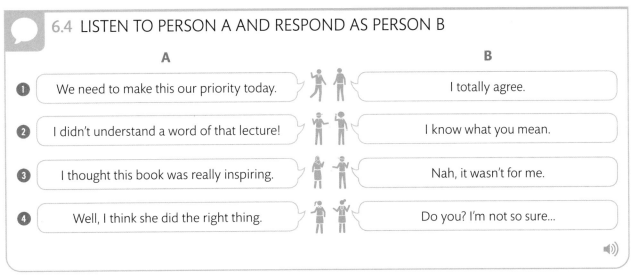

6.5 USE THE CHART TO CREATE 12 SENTENCES AND SAY THEM OUT LOUD

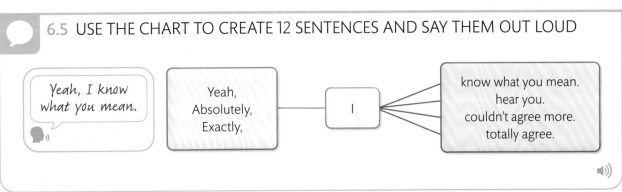

Yeah, I know what you mean.

| Yeah, Absolutely, Exactly, | I | know what you mean. hear you. couldn't agree more. totally agree. |

6.6 MATCH THE SENTENCES AND SAY THEM OUT LOUD

I'm not convinced, → to be honest...

		agree more.	
❶	Absolutely, I couldn't	to disagree on this!	
❷	I don't think	what you mean.	
❸	I know	to be honest...	
❹	We might have to agree	with you on this one.	
❺	Sorry, I'm not	so, either...	

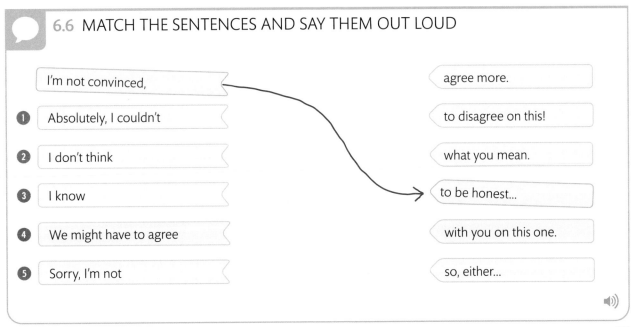

23

07 Making suggestions

7.1 MAKING PLANS

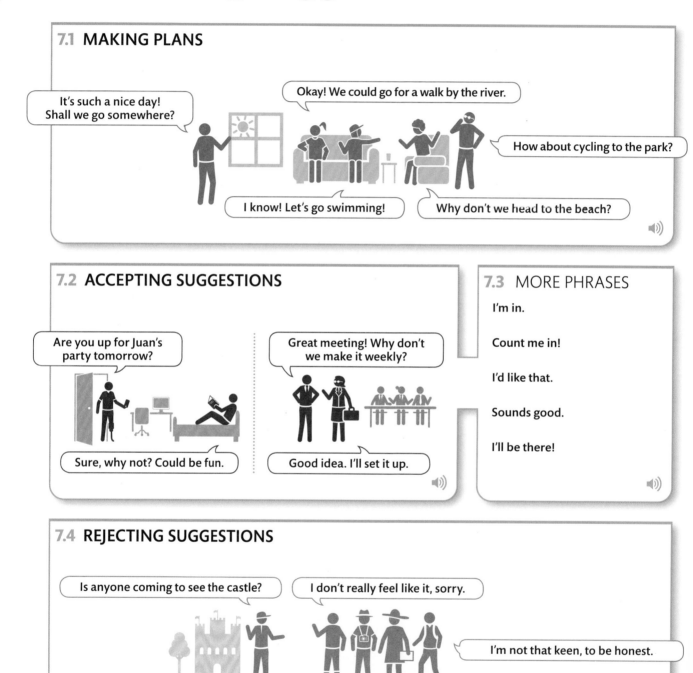

It's such a nice day! Shall we go somewhere?

Okay! We could go for a walk by the river.

How about cycling to the park?

I know! Let's go swimming!

Why don't we head to the beach?

7.2 ACCEPTING SUGGESTIONS

Are you up for Juan's party tomorrow?

Sure, why not? Could be fun.

Great meeting! Why don't we make it weekly?

Good idea. I'll set it up.

7.3 MORE PHRASES

I'm in.

Count me in!

I'd like that.

Sounds good.

I'll be there!

7.4 REJECTING SUGGESTIONS

Is anyone coming to see the castle?

I don't really feel like it, sorry.

I'm not that keen, to be honest.

I think I'll give it a miss.

Hmm... I'd rather not, if you don't mind.

7.5 LISTEN TO PERSON A AND RESPOND AS PERSON B

	A		B
1	It's such a nice day! Shall we go somewhere?		Okay! We could go for a walk by the river.
2	Are you up for Juan's party tomorrow?		Sure, why not? Could be fun.
3	Great meeting! Why don't we make it weekly?		Good idea. I'll set it up.
4	Is anyone coming to see the castle?		I'm not that keen, to be honest.
5	How about cycling to the park?		I know! Let's go swimming.

7.6 SAY THE SENTENCES OUT LOUD, FILLING IN THE GAPS USING THE WORDS IN THE PANEL

feel	think	How	keen
Sounds	Count	Let's	like

1 _____ about cycling to the park?

2 I _____ I'll give it a miss.

3 _____ me in!

4 I know! _____ go swimming!

5 I'd _____ that.

6 I'm not that _____ , to be honest.

7 _____ good.

8 I don't really _____ like it, sorry.

7.7 USE THE CHART TO CREATE NINE SENTENCES AND SAY THEM OUT LOUD

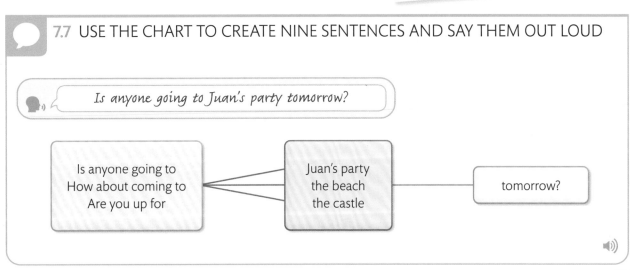

Is anyone going to Juan's party tomorrow?

Is anyone going to How about coming to Are you up for	Juan's party the beach the castle	tomorrow?

08 Saying thank you

8.1 WAYS TO THANK PEOPLE

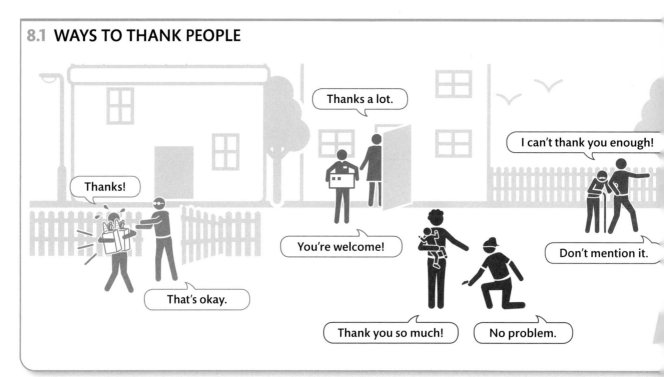

8.3 LISTEN TO PERSON A AND RESPOND AS PERSON B

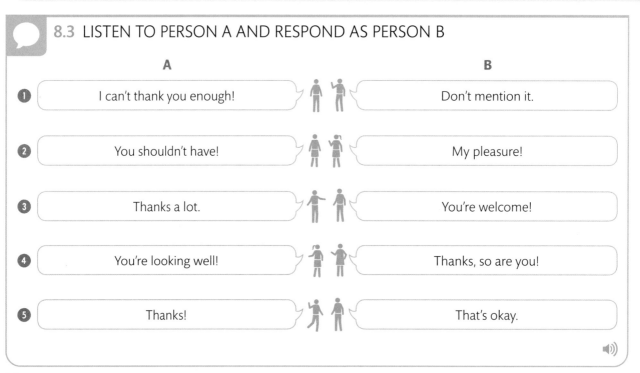

	A		B
❶	I can't thank you enough!		Don't mention it.
❷	You shouldn't have!		My pleasure!
❸	Thanks a lot.		You're welcome!
❹	You're looking well!		Thanks, so are you!
❺	Thanks!		That's okay.

You shouldn't have!

My pleasure!

You're looking well!

Thanks, so are you!

8.2 MORE PHRASES

Thanks a million!

Thank you, I really appreciate it.

That's so kind!

I owe you one!

Thanks for having me over!

Cheers.

Any time!

No worries!

8.4 LISTEN AND NUMBER THE SENTENCES IN THE ORDER YOU HEAR THEM

A Cheers. ☐

B Any time! ☐

C No problem. 1

D You shouldn't have! ☐

E Thanks a million! ☐

F No worries! ☐

G I owe you one! ☐

H That's so kind! ☐

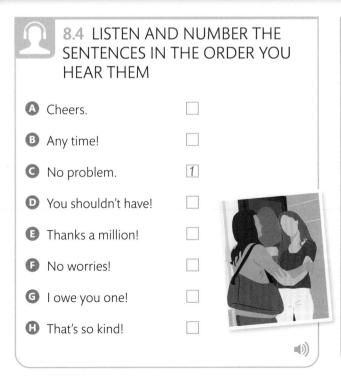

8.5 SAY THE SENTENCES OUT LOUD, FILLING IN THE GAPS USING THE WORDS IN THE PANEL

enough	pleasure	much
appreciate	mention	

1 Don't _____ it.

2 Thank you so _____ !

3 My _____ !

4 I can't thank you _____ !

5 Thank you, I really _____ it.

09 Saying sorry

9.1 MAKING AND ACCEPTING APOLOGIES

Oops! Sorry!

No worries!

I'm really sorry I forgot your birthday!

No big deal!

Oh no, your top! I've messed up, sorry!

It's okay, it'll come out in the wash.

9.2 MORE PHRASES

My bad!

I'm sorry to bother you.

I owe you an apology.

I feel awful.

That's okay, it was nothing.

No problem, I'm happy to help.

You don't have to apologize!

Thank you, that means a lot.

9.3 EXPRESSING SYMPATHY

I was sorry to hear you've been in hospital.

Thank you. I'm feeling much better now.

I'm sorry for your loss.

Thanks, I appreciate you saying that.

🌐 GOOD TO KNOW

Sorry is a word with many uses. In UK English, people sometimes say **sorry** instead of **excuse me**. You might say **sorry** to ask someone to move in a crowded place or to apologize for bumping into them. UK English also uses **sorry** to ask someone to repeat what they just said: **Sorry? I didn't quite catch that...**

9.4 LISTEN TO PERSON A AND RESPOND AS PERSON B

A   **B**

1. Oops! Sorry! — No worries!

2. Oh no, your top! I've messed up, sorry. — It's okay, it'll come out in the wash.

3. I'm really sorry I forgot your birthday! — No big deal!

4. My bad! — That's okay, it was nothing.

5. I'm sorry for your loss. — Thanks, I appreciate you saying that.

9.5 LISTEN AND NUMBER THE SENTENCES IN THE ORDER YOU HEAR THEM

A I'm sorry for your loss. ☐

B I owe you an apology. ☐

C I was sorry to hear you've been in hospital. ☐ 1

D I feel awful. ☐

E Oh no, your top! I've messed up, sorry! ☐

F No problem, I'm happy to help. ☐

G I'm sorry to bother you. ☐

H You don't have to apologize! ☐

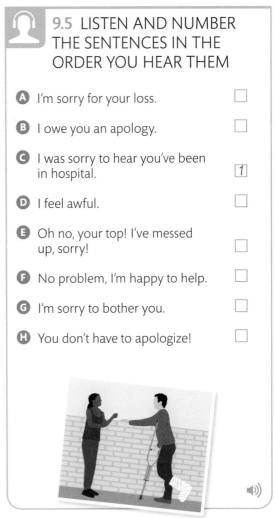

9.6 MATCH THE SENTENCES AND SAY THEM OUT LOUD

I was sorry to hear → you've been in hospital.

1. Thanks, I appreciate — you saying that.

2. That's okay, — it was nothing.

3. I'm really sorry — I forgot your birthday!

4. Thank you, that — means a lot.

29

10 Saying goodbye

10.1 INFORMAL GOODBYES

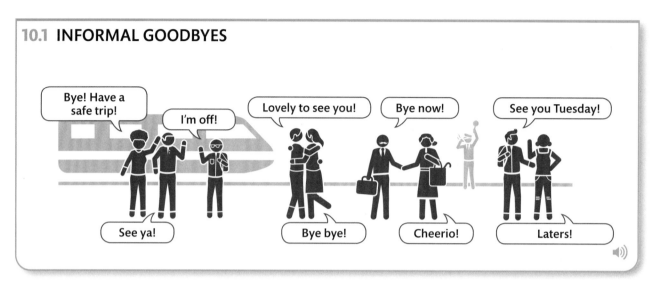

Bye! Have a safe trip!

I'm off!

Lovely to see you!

Bye now!

See you Tuesday!

See ya!

Bye bye!

Cheerio!

Laters!

10.2 FORMAL GOODBYES

Goodbye.

Look forward to seeing you again soon.

It was a pleasure meeting you.

All the best.

Speak to you soon.

Good talking with you.

Thank you for your time.

10.3 MAKING FUTURE PLANS

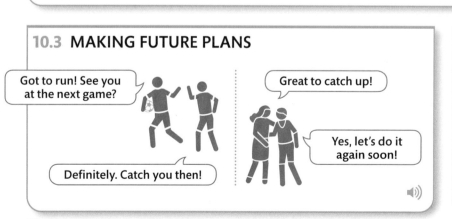

Got to run! See you at the next game?

Great to catch up!

Yes, let's do it again soon!

Definitely. Catch you then!

GOOD TO KNOW

When it comes to saying goodbye, English has many regional and cultural variations. **Ta-ra!** is often used in the north of England and Wales, while **See ya!**, **Laters!** or **I'm outta here!** are common among younger speakers.

10.4 LISTEN AND NUMBER THE SENTENCES IN THE ORDER YOU HEAR THEM

A Goodbye. ☐

B See you Tuesday! 1

C Speak to you soon. ☐

D See ya! ☐

E All the best. ☐

F I'm off! ☐

G Laters! ☐

H Bye now! ☐

10.5 MATCH THE SENTENCES AND SAY THEM OUT LOUD

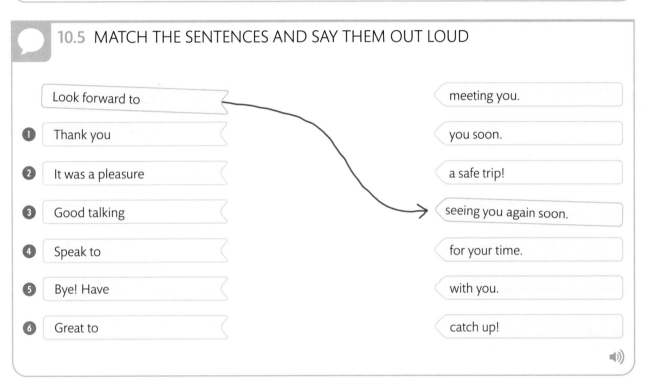

Look forward to — seeing you again soon.

1 Thank you

2 It was a pleasure

3 Good talking

4 Speak to

5 Bye! Have

6 Great to

meeting you.

you soon.

a safe trip!

seeing you again soon.

for your time.

with you.

catch up!

10.6 USE THE CHART TO CREATE NINE SENTENCES AND SAY THEM OUT LOUD

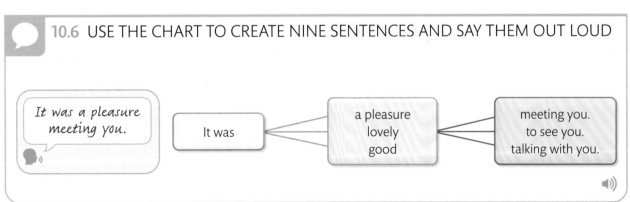

It was a pleasure meeting you.

It was | a pleasure / lovely / good | meeting you. / to see you. / talking with you.

11 Dates, time, and weather

11.1 DISCUSSING DATES

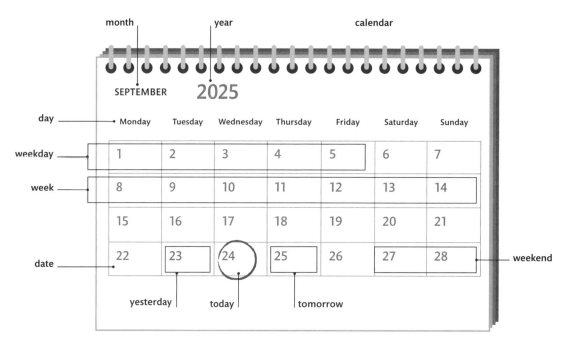

11.2 TELLING THE TIME

one o'clock / 1pm

five past one

ten past one

quarter past one

twenty past one

twenty-five past one

one thirty /
half (past) one

twenty-five to two

twenty to two

quarter to two

ten to two

five to two

What time does it start?

At 6pm.

second

minute

half hour

hour

1st	2nd	3rd	4th	5th	6th
first	second	third	fourth	fifth	sixth

7th	8th	9th	10th	20th	21st
seventh	eighth	ninth	tenth	twentieth	twenty-first

once a week	twice a week	three times a week	every day	every week	every month

1900	1901	1910	2000	2001	2033
nineteen hundred	nineteen oh-one	nineteen ten	two thousand	two thousand and one	twenty thirty-three

11.3 DESCRIBING THE WEATHER

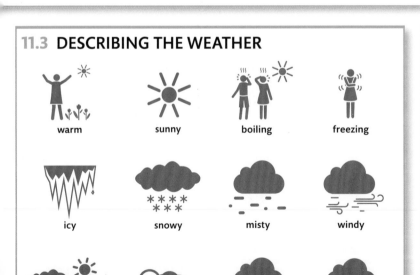

warm   sunny   boiling   freezing

icy   snowy   misty   windy

cloudy   overcast   pouring   foggy

11.4 EXTREME WEATHER

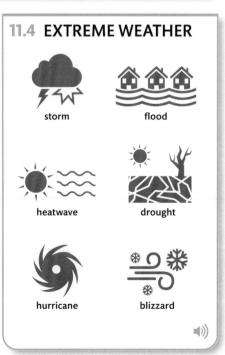

storm   flood

heatwave   drought

hurricane   blizzard

12 Making arrangements

12.1 TIMES

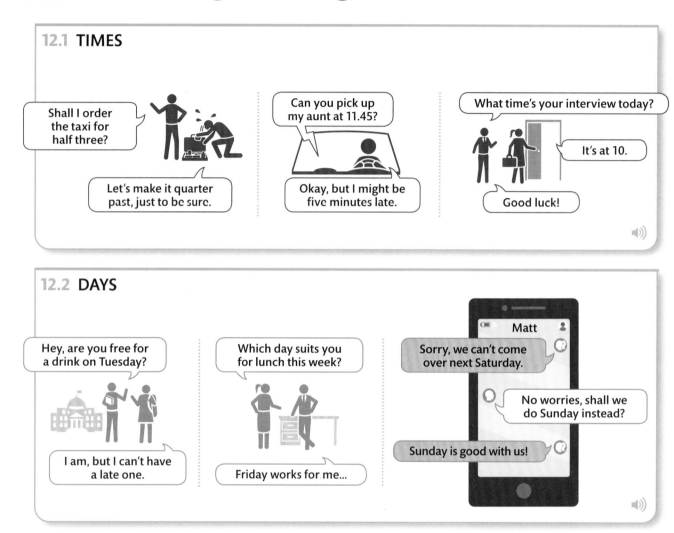

12.2 DAYS

12.3 DATES

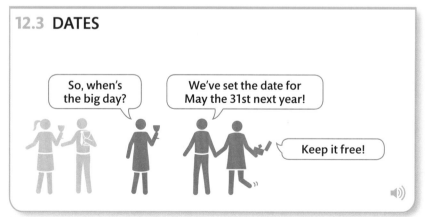

GOOD TO KNOW

UK English uses different language to talk about dates depending on whether it is written or spoken. Written English usually expresses a date as a cardinal number followed by a month (e.g. **31 May**), but spoken English would express this date as **May the 31st**, **May 31st**, or **the 31st of May**.

12.4 LISTEN TO THE AUDIO AND MATCH THE CORRECT RESPONSE

Can you pick up my aunt at 11.45?

1 Sorry, we can't come over next Saturday.

2 Shall I order the taxi for half three?

3 Which day suits you for lunch this week?

4 What time's your interview today?

No worries, shall we do Sunday instead?

Let's make it quarter past, just to be sure.

It's at 10.

Okay, but I might be five minutes late.

Friday works for me...

12.5 LISTEN TO PERSON A AND RESPOND AS PERSON B

A	B
1 Hey, are you free for a drink on Tuesday?	I am, but I can't have a late one.
2 Which day suits you for lunch this week?	Friday works for me...
3 So, when's the big day?	We've set the date for May the 31st next year!
4 What time's your interview today?	It's at 10.

12.6 SAY THE SENTENCES OUT LOUD, FILLING IN THE GAPS USING THE WORDS IN THE PANEL

works   on Tuesday   next   three

May the 31st   free   suits

1 Which day _____ you for lunch this week?

2 Friday _____ for me...

3 Shall I order the taxi for half _____ ?

4 Hey, are you free for a drink _____ ?

5 Sorry, we can't come over _____ Saturday.

6 Keep it _____ !

7 We've set the date for _____ next year!

13 Talking about the weather

13.1 DESCRIBING THE WEATHER

What's the weather like out there?

It's boiling! Over 30 degrees every day.

How was the weather on your holiday?

A bit mixed – the usual sunshine and showers!

It's a bit chilly today, isn't it?

Yes, the weather's turned, hasn't it?

13.2 MORE PHRASES

What's the temperature like?

It's freezing outside!

It's really windy!

Lovely weather, isn't it?

It's blowing a gale out there!

It's absolutely pouring!

13.3 THE WEATHER FORECAST

Here's the forecast for tomorrow...

... it will be mainly cloudy...

... with a few sunny spells...

... and a slight chance of a shower...

... with temperatures a little below normal.

13.4 MORE PHRASES

Today we'll see scattered showers.

Mist and fog will form later.

There'll be plenty of warm sunshine.

Snow is expected.

Temperatures are above average for the time of year.

13.5 LISTEN TO PERSON A AND RESPOND AS PERSON B

A   **B**

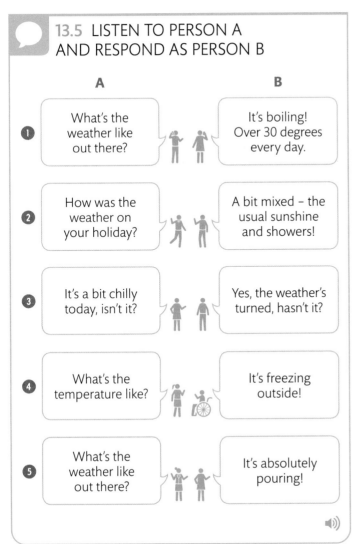

1. A: What's the weather like out there?
   B: It's boiling! Over 30 degrees every day.

2. A: How was the weather on your holiday?
   B: A bit mixed – the usual sunshine and showers!

3. A: It's a bit chilly today, isn't it?
   B: Yes, the weather's turned, hasn't it?

4. A: What's the temperature like?
   B: It's freezing outside!

5. A: What's the weather like out there?
   B: It's absolutely pouring!

13.6 LISTEN AND NUMBER THE PICTURES IN THE ORDER THEY ARE DESCRIBED

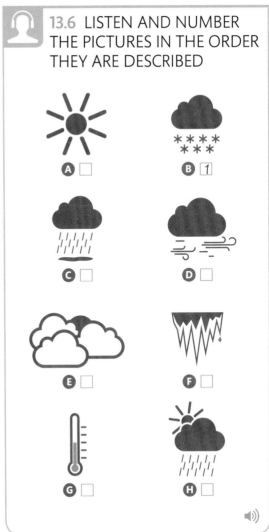

A ☐
B 1
C ☐
D ☐
E ☐
F ☐
G ☐
H ☐

13.7 USE THE CHART TO CREATE 10 SENTENCES AND SAY THEM OUT LOUD

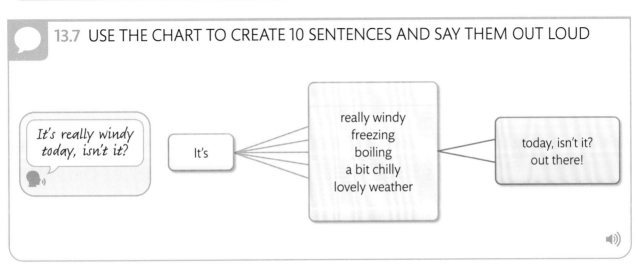

It's really windy today, isn't it?

It's | really windy / freezing / boiling / a bit chilly / lovely weather | today, isn't it? / out there!

14 Family and relationships

14.1 MY FAMILY

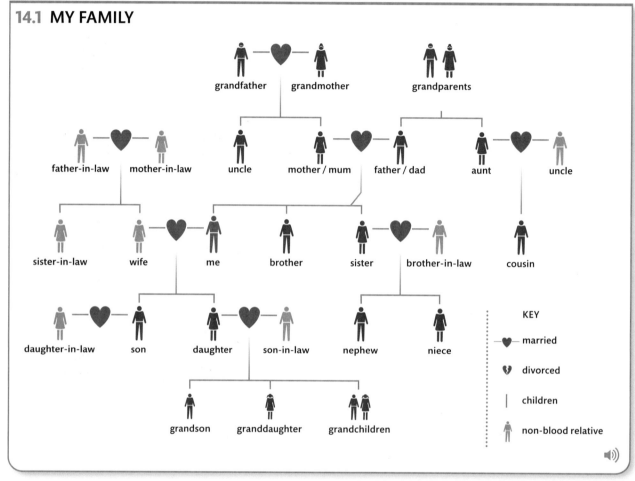

KEY
- ❤ married
- 💔 divorced
- | children
- non-blood relative

14.2 MY STEPFAMILY

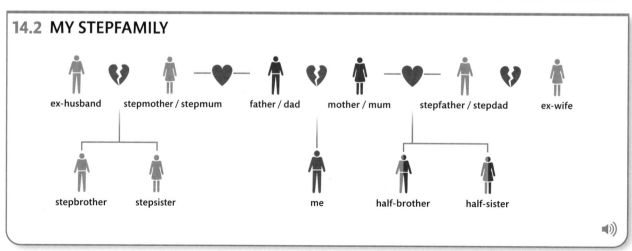

14.3 RELATIONSHIPS

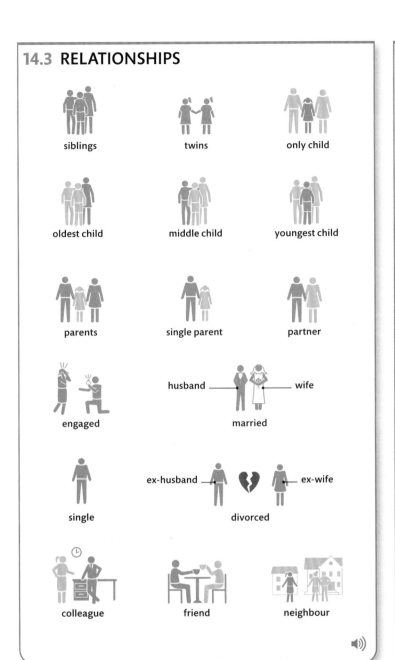

siblings

twins

only child

oldest child

middle child

youngest child

parents

single parent

partner

engaged

husband — wife

married

single

ex-husband — ex-wife

divorced

colleague

friend

neighbour

14.4 LIFE EVENTS

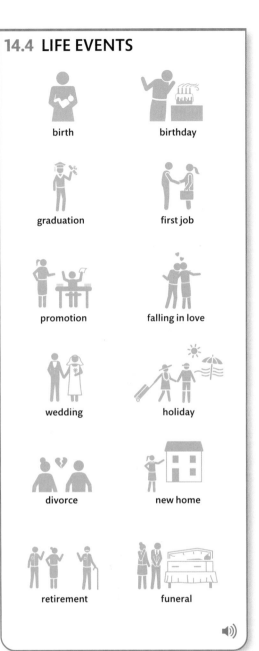

birth

birthday

graduation

first job

promotion

falling in love

wedding

holiday

divorce

new home

retirement

funeral

14.5 GROWING UP

baby

toddler

girl   boy

children

teenagers

woman   man

adults

senior citizens

15 Talking about family

15.1 IMMEDIATE FAMILY

Have you got any brothers or sisters, Tarik?

Yes, I've got a brother and two stepsisters.

I'm the youngest.

Are you close to your family, Chloe?

Yeah, I speak to my parents nearly every day.

But I don't see my sister much. She's moved to India.

So, have you got any kids?

Yes, two daughters. How about you?

I've got a toddler, and baby number two on the way!

🌐 GOOD TO KNOW

Members of the family may be known by different names. **Mum** or **Mummy** and **Dad** or **Daddy** are common in the UK, particularly in the south. **Mam** is popular in parts of northern England, Northern Ireland and Wales, while **Mom** and **Pop** are used in US English.

15.2 EXTENDED FAMILY

Don't forget we're visiting Grandma today.

Auntie Dot will be there, too.

Oh, and cousin Henry!

How many grandchildren have you got?

Two grandsons and a granddaughter. I adore them!

15.3 MORE PHRASES

I'm the oldest.

I'm the middle child.

I'm an only child.

I've got two younger sisters.

We grew up in Birmingham.

15.4 LISTEN AND NUMBER THE PICTURES IN THE ORDER THEY ARE DESCRIBED

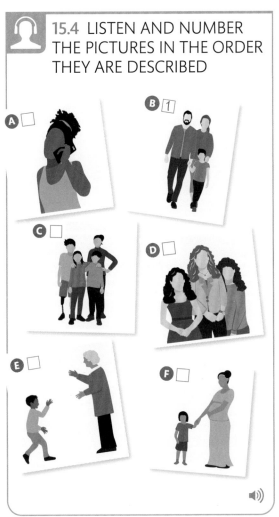

A ☐
B ☐ 1
C ☐
D ☐
E ☐
F ☐

15.5 LISTEN TO PERSON A AND RESPOND AS PERSON B

A	B
① Have you got any brothers or sisters, Tarik?	Yes, I've got a brother and two stepsisters.
② Don't forget we're visiting Grandma today.	Auntie Dot will be there, too.
③ So, have you got any kids?	Yes, two daughters. How about you?
④ Are you close to your family, Chloe?	Yeah, I speak to my parents nearly every day.
⑤ How many grandchildren have you got?	Two grandsons and a granddaughter. I adore them!

15.6 MATCH THE SENTENCES AND SAY THEM OUT LOUD

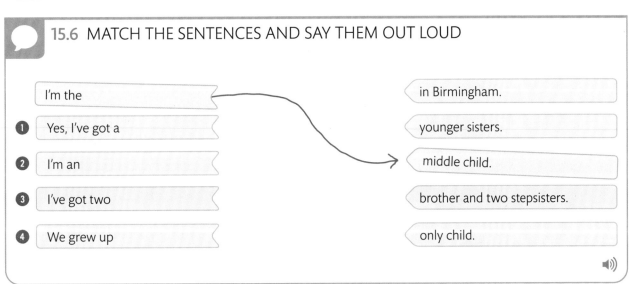

I'm the → middle child.

in Birmingham.

① Yes, I've got a — younger sisters.

② I'm an — brother and two stepsisters.

③ I've got two — only child.

④ We grew up

16 Life events

16.1 CELEBRATIONS

Happy birthday!
What presents did you get?

I hear congratulations are in order?
Yes, I got the promotion!

Here's to the newlyweds!
Thanks, everyone!

16.2 MILESTONES

Congrats on the birth of your baby boy!
Isn't he beautiful!

Well done!
Happy graduation!
We're really proud of you!

Welcome to my new home!
Your very own place at last!

16.3 OTHER EVENTS

Happy anniversary! Here's to another 30 years!
Oh, they're gorgeous! Thank you!

All the best for your retirement.
I'll miss you all!

I'm so sorry for your loss.
Let me know if there's anything I can do.

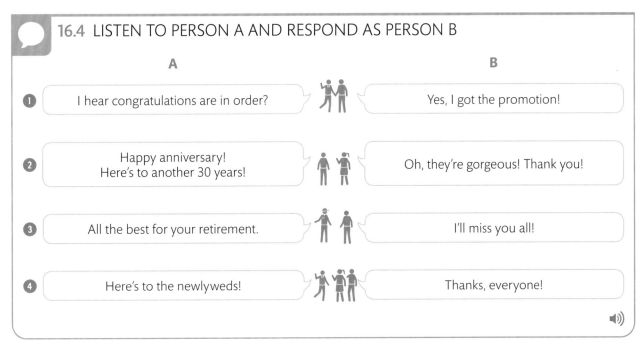

16.4 LISTEN TO PERSON A AND RESPOND AS PERSON B

A

B

1. I hear congratulations are in order? — Yes, I got the promotion!

2. Happy anniversary! Here's to another 30 years! — Oh, they're gorgeous! Thank you!

3. All the best for your retirement. — I'll miss you all!

4. Here's to the newlyweds! — Thanks, everyone!

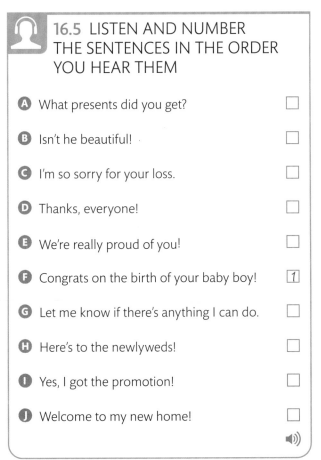

16.5 LISTEN AND NUMBER THE SENTENCES IN THE ORDER YOU HEAR THEM

A What presents did you get? ☐

B Isn't he beautiful! ☐

C I'm so sorry for your loss. ☐

D Thanks, everyone! ☐

E We're really proud of you! ☐

F Congrats on the birth of your baby boy! ☐1

G Let me know if there's anything I can do. ☐

H Here's to the newlyweds! ☐

I Yes, I got the promotion! ☐

J Welcome to my new home! ☐

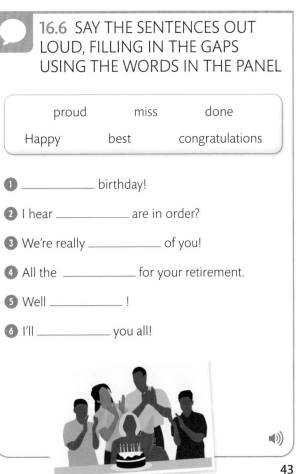

16.6 SAY THE SENTENCES OUT LOUD, FILLING IN THE GAPS USING THE WORDS IN THE PANEL

> proud   miss   done
>
> Happy   best   congratulations

1 _____ birthday!

2 I hear _____ are in order?

3 We're really _____ of you!

4 All the _____ for your retirement.

5 Well _____ !

6 I'll _____ you all!

17 Socializing

17.1 AT A PARTY

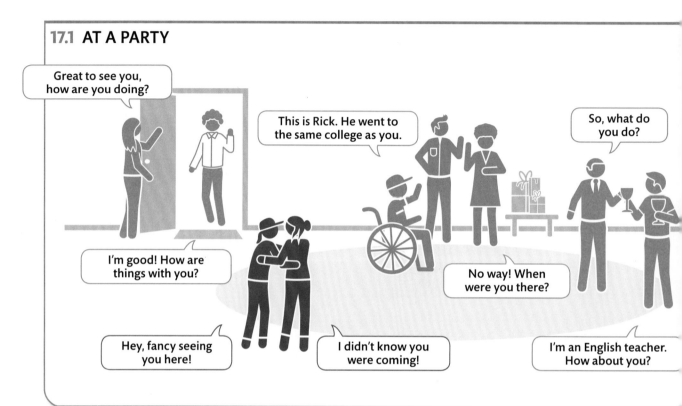

17.3 LISTEN TO THE AUDIO AND MATCH THE CORRECT RESPONSE

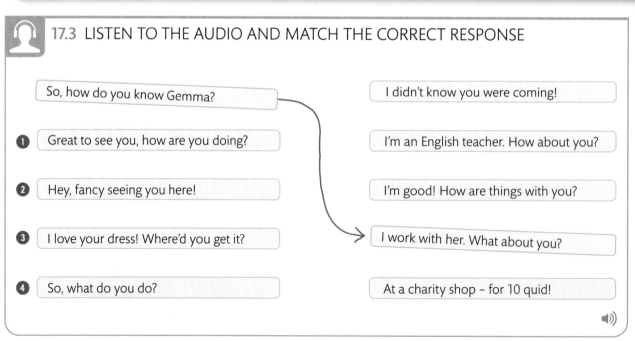

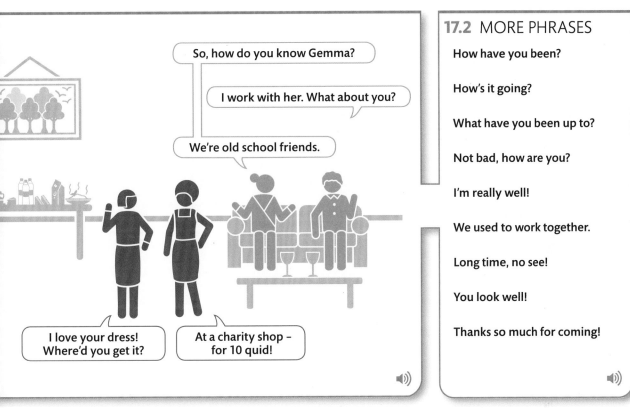

So, how do you know Gemma?

I work with her. What about you?

We're old school friends.

I love your dress! Where'd you get it?

At a charity shop – for 10 quid!

17.2 MORE PHRASES

How have you been?

How's it going?

What have you been up to?

Not bad, how are you?

I'm really well!

We used to work together.

Long time, no see!

You look well!

Thanks so much for coming!

17.4 LISTEN TO PERSON A AND RESPOND AS PERSON B

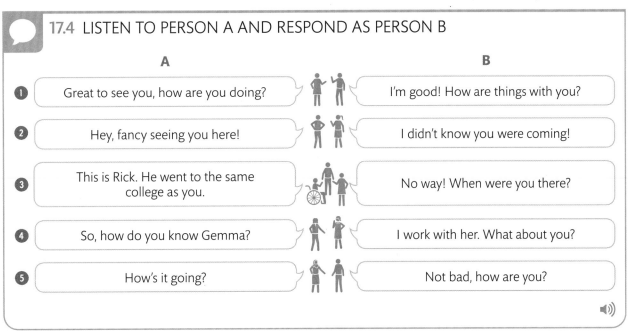

	A		B
❶	Great to see you, how are you doing?		I'm good! How are things with you?
❷	Hey, fancy seeing you here!		I didn't know you were coming!
❸	This is Rick. He went to the same college as you.		No way! When were you there?
❹	So, how do you know Gemma?		I work with her. What about you?
❺	How's it going?		Not bad, how are you?

18 Dating and romance

18.1 ASKING SOMEONE ON A DATE

I was wondering if you'd like to go out this Saturday?

I'd love to! Pick me up at 7?

Do you fancy going for a coffee next week?

Yeah, I'd like that. Next Friday, maybe?

We should meet up sometime.

Saturday afternoon?

Sure, sounds good.

Cool, I'll message you.

18.2 MORE WAYS TO SAY YES

Sounds great!

That would be really nice.

Sure, why not?

I was hoping you'd ask me.

You took your time!

I thought you'd never ask!

18.3 TURNING DOWN A DATE

I'd love to take you out tonight.

That's really kind, but I already have plans.

Another night, maybe?

Thanks, but I'm not dating right now.

18.4 MORE WAYS TO SAY NO

I'm not looking for a relationship, sorry.

I just like you as a friend.

Thanks, but I'm actually already seeing someone.

It was lovely to meet you, but I'm not really feeling a connection.

18.5 LISTEN TO PERSON A AND RESPOND AS PERSON B

	A		B
1	Do you fancy going for a coffee next week?		Yeah, I'd like that. Next Friday, maybe?
2	We should meet up sometime.		Sure, sounds good.
3	I'd love to take you out tonight.		That's really kind, but I already have plans.
4	Another night, maybe?		Thanks, but I'm not dating right now.

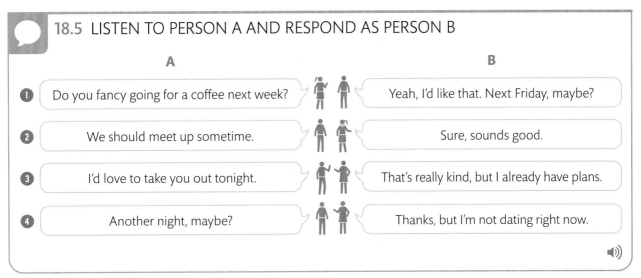

18.6 USE THE CHART TO CREATE 12 SENTENCES AND SAY THEM OUT LOUD

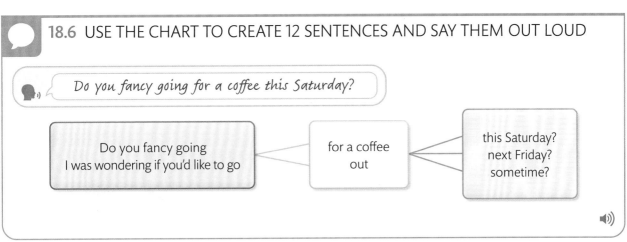

Do you fancy going for a coffee this Saturday?

Do you fancy going / I was wondering if you'd like to go	for a coffee / out	this Saturday? / next Friday? / sometime?

18.7 MATCH THE SENTENCES AND SAY THEM OUT LOUD

	I'm not looking	you'd ask me.
1	I was hoping	as a friend.
2	You took	for a relationship, sorry.
3	That would be	your time!
4	I just like you	really nice.

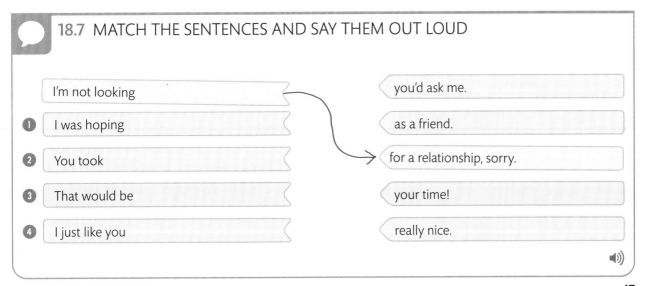

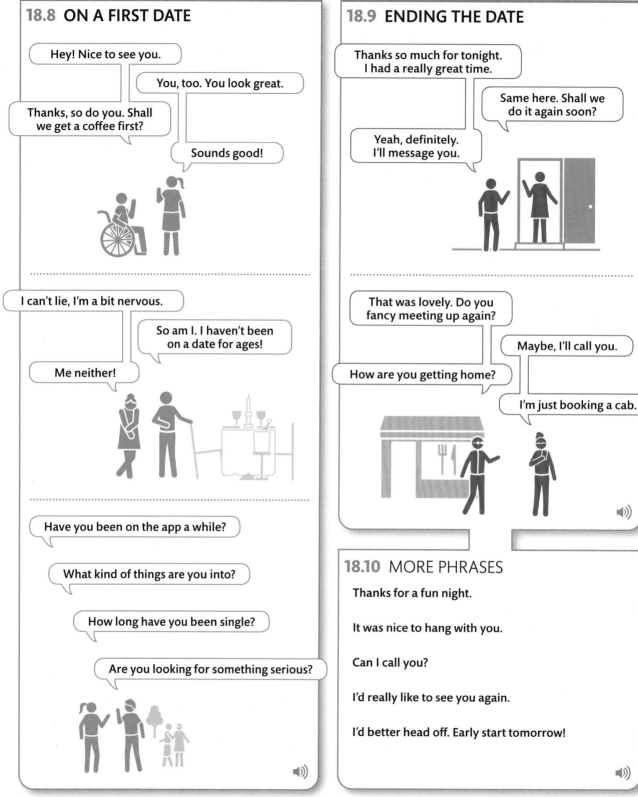

18.8 ON A FIRST DATE

Hey! Nice to see you.

You, too. You look great.

Thanks, so do you. Shall we get a coffee first?

Sounds good!

I can't lie, I'm a bit nervous.

So am I. I haven't been on a date for ages!

Me neither!

Have you been on the app a while?

What kind of things are you into?

How long have you been single?

Are you looking for something serious?

18.9 ENDING THE DATE

Thanks so much for tonight. I had a really great time.

Same here. Shall we do it again soon?

Yeah, definitely. I'll message you.

That was lovely. Do you fancy meeting up again?

Maybe, I'll call you.

How are you getting home?

I'm just booking a cab.

18.10 MORE PHRASES

Thanks for a fun night.

It was nice to hang with you.

Can I call you?

I'd really like to see you again.

I'd better head off. Early start tomorrow!

18.11 LISTEN TO PERSON A AND RESPOND AS PERSON B

A		B
1 Hey! Nice to see you.		You, too. You look great.
2 I can't lie, I'm a bit nervous.		So am I. I haven't been on a date for ages!
3 How are you getting home?		I'm just booking a cab.
4 Thanks so much for tonight. I had a really great time.		Same here. Shall we do it again soon?

🔊

18.12 LISTEN AND NUMBER THE SENTENCES IN THE ORDER YOU HEAR THEM

A Can I call you? ☐

B Thanks, so do you. Shall we get a coffee first? ☐1☐

C Are you looking for something serious? ☐

D Thanks for a fun night. ☐

E Have you been on the app a while? ☐

F Yeah, definitely. I'll message you. ☐

G That was lovely. Do you fancy meeting up again? ☐

H I can't lie, I'm a bit nervous. ☐

I Maybe, I'll call you. ☐

J How long have you been single? ☐

🔊

18.13 SAY THE SENTENCES OUT LOUD, FILLING IN THE GAPS USING THE WORDS IN THE PANEL

single	again	into
booking	head	hang

1 It was nice to _____ with you.

2 What kind of things are you _____ ?

3 I'd really like to see you _____ .

4 I'd better _____ off. Early start tomorrow!

5 How long have you been _____ ?

6 I'm just _____ a cab.

🔊

49

19 Showing support

19.1 BEING ENCOURAGING

I'm so stressed. My exams are in two weeks!

Hang in there, sweetheart. I know you can do it!

We're never going to finish on time...

Come on, we've got this!

I don't know whether to try out for the team.

Go on, it's worth a shot!

Yeah, you're a great player!

19.2 OFFERING SUPPORT

I know things are tough, but we're here for you.

Thanks, guys, you're the best!

You can talk to me any time. My door's always open.

Thank you, I really appreciate it.

It's good to have you back! Anything you need, just ask.

That's really kind. I will!

19.3 MORE PHRASES

Let me know if I can do anything.

I know this hasn't been easy.

We've got your back.

You've been a lot of help.

That means a lot.

I'm very grateful.

19.4 LISTEN AND NUMBER THE SENTENCES IN THE ORDER YOU HEAR THEM

A We've got your back. ☐

B Thank you, I really appreciate it. ☑

C I know things are tough, but we're here for you. ☐

D You can talk to me any time. My door's always open. ☐

E That means a lot. ☐

F I'm very grateful. ☐

G Go on, it's worth a shot! ☐

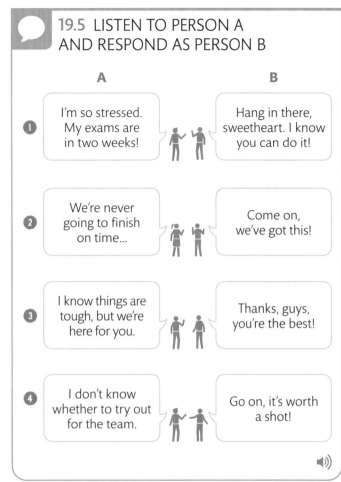

19.5 LISTEN TO PERSON A AND RESPOND AS PERSON B

	A	B
1	I'm so stressed. My exams are in two weeks!	Hang in there, sweetheart. I know you can do it!
2	We're never going to finish on time...	Come on, we've got this!
3	I know things are tough, but we're here for you.	Thanks, guys, you're the best!
4	I don't know whether to try out for the team.	Go on, it's worth a shot!

19.6 SAY THE SENTENCES OUT LOUD, FILLING IN THE GAPS USING THE WORDS IN THE PANEL

kind	tough	help	appreciate
easy	ask	grateful	anything

1 Anything you need, just _____ .

2 Let me know if I can do _____ .

3 I know things are _____ , but we're here for you.

4 You've been a lot of _____ .

5 That's really _____ . I will!

6 I'm very _____ .

7 I know this hasn't been _____ .

8 Thank you, I really _____ it.

20 Eating and drinking

20.1 COFFEES, TEAS, AND SOFT DRINKS

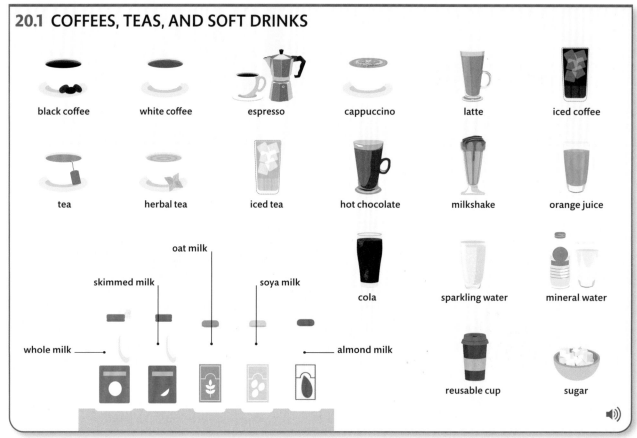

black coffee   white coffee   espresso   cappuccino   latte   iced coffee

tea   herbal tea   iced tea   hot chocolate   milkshake   orange juice

oat milk

skimmed milk

soya milk

cola   sparkling water   mineral water

whole milk

almond milk

reusable cup   sugar

20.2 VERBS

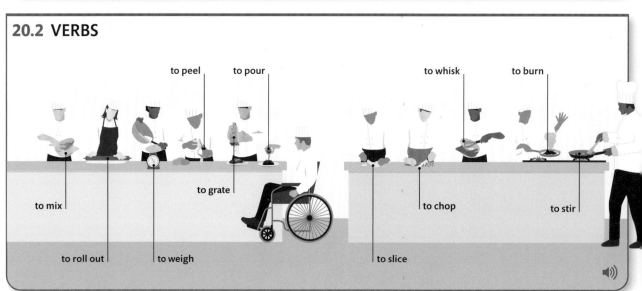

to peel   to pour   to whisk   to burn

to grate

to mix   to chop   to stir

to roll out   to weigh   to slice

20.3 KITCHEN EQUIPMENT

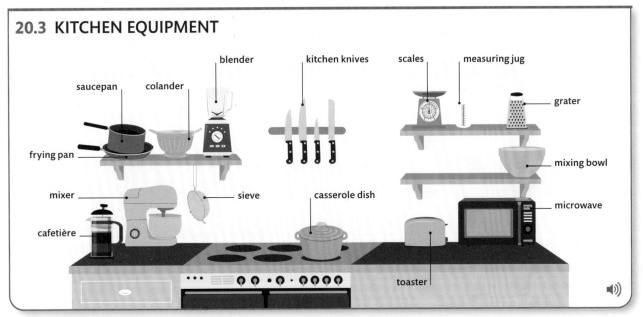

saucepan · colander · blender · kitchen knives · scales · measuring jug · grater · frying pan · mixer · sieve · casserole dish · mixing bowl · microwave · cafetière · toaster

20.4 FOOD PREPARATION

fried · stir-fried · deep-fried

poached · boiled · stewed

roasted · baked · grilled

marinated · steamed · smoked

20.5 EATING OUT

starter · main course · side order

dessert / pudding · to book a table · to order

bill · 50% to split the bill 50% · gluten-free

vegan · vegetarian · dairy-free

53

21 Cafés and coffee shops

21.1 AT THE COFFEE SHOP

Hi, what can I get you?

This sandwich is vegan, right?

That's right. Would you like it toasted?

To have in or take away?

To take away, please.

Two black coffees and an orange juice, please.

Excuse me, what's the Wi-Fi code?

It's right here, on this sign.

21.2 MORE PHRASES

An iced coffee to go, please.

Could I have a skinny latte?

I brought my own cup.

Any milk or sugar?

Have you got a loyalty card?

Regular or large?

Take a seat and I'll bring your drinks over to you.

21.3 LISTEN AND CIRCLE THE ITEM YOU HEAR

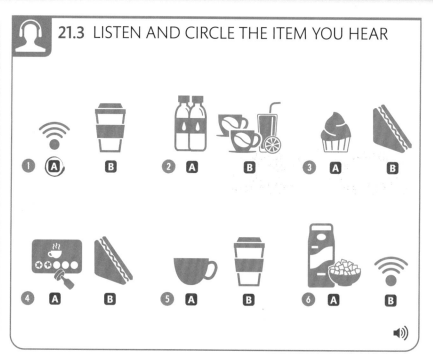

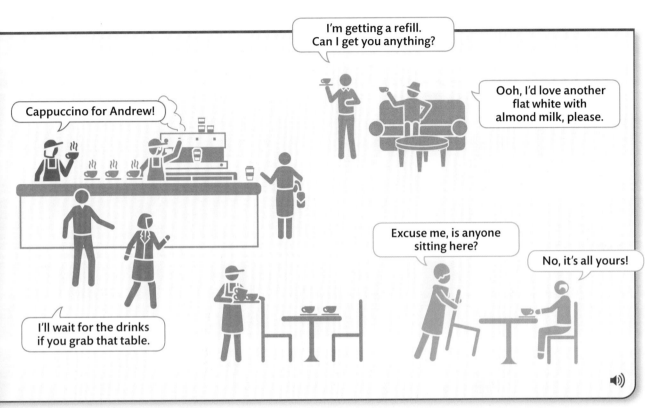

21.4 LISTEN TO PERSON A AND RESPOND AS PERSON B

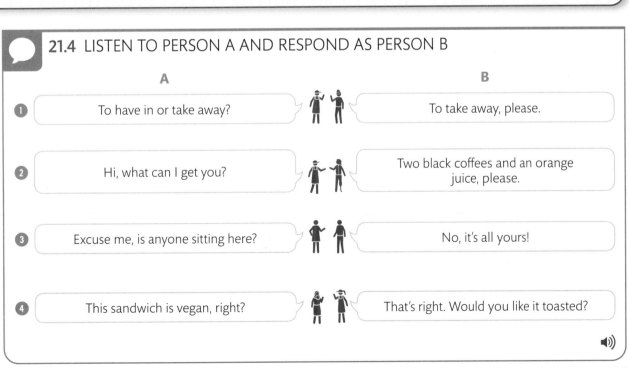

22 Takeaway and delivery

22.1 GETTING A TAKEAWAY

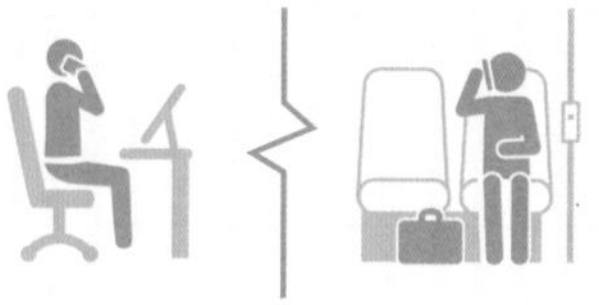

Shall we get a takeaway curry tonight?

Good idea. I'll pick it up on my way home.

Two burgers to go, please.

Do you want fries with that?

I've come to pick up my order.

Can I take your name, please?

22.2 ORDERING A DELIVERY

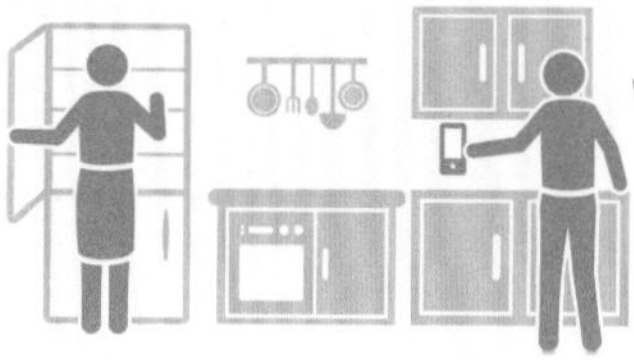

We've got no food. Let's get a pizza in!

Okay, I'll order it on the app.

Can I check if you deliver to this address?

Of course. What's your postcode?

Our fried chicken order still hasn't arrived.

Sorry about that. Let me check what's happening.

22.3 VOCABULARY TAKEAWAY MEALS

curry

noodles

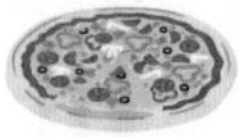

pizza

sushi

tacos

kebab

burgers

fried chicken

fries

nachos

takeaway

delivery

22.4 LISTEN TO PERSON A AND RESPOND AS PERSON B

	A		**B**
1	Shall we get a takeaway curry tonight?		Good idea. I'll pick it up on my way home.
2	We've got no food. Let's get a pizza in!		Okay, I'll order it on the app.
3	Can I check if you deliver to this address?		Of course. What's your postcode?
4	Two burgers to go, please.		Do you want fries with that?
5	I've come to pick up my order.		Can I take your name, please?

22.5 LISTEN AND NUMBER THE PICTURES IN THE ORDER THEY ARE DESCRIBED

A ☐   B 1   C ☐   D ☐   E ☐   F ☐

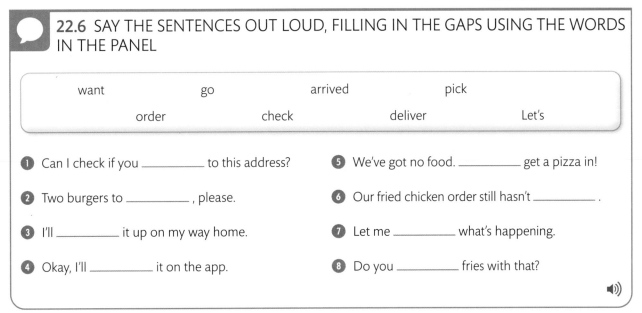

22.6 SAY THE SENTENCES OUT LOUD, FILLING IN THE GAPS USING THE WORDS IN THE PANEL

want	go	arrived	pick
order	check	deliver	Let's

1. Can I check if you _____ to this address?

2. Two burgers to _____ , please.

3. I'll _____ it up on my way home.

4. Okay, I'll _____ it on the app.

5. We've got no food. _____ get a pizza in!

6. Our fried chicken order still hasn't _____ .

7. Let me _____ what's happening.

8. Do you _____ fries with that?

23 Bars and pubs

23.1 BUYING DRINKS

Hi, can I get two gin and tonics, please?

Sure. Would you like ice and lemon with that?

It's my round! What's everyone drinking?

A pint of lager for me, please!

What dry white wine can you recommend?

We have a large selection – check out our wine list.

23.2 MORE QUESTIONS

What lagers have you got on tap?

Have you got a bar menu?

Do you serve mocktails?

What soft drinks are there?

Do we pay at the bar?

What time do you stop serving?

23.3 LAST ORDERS

Last orders, please! We close in 10 minutes.

Can we have the same again, please?

🌐 GOOD TO KNOW

In UK English, **Can I get...?** is an increasingly common way to ask for things in shops, cafés, or restaurants.

23.4 VOCABULARY DRINKS

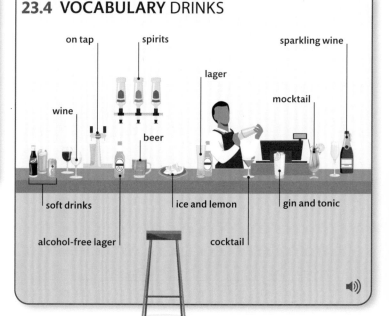

on tap · spirits · sparkling wine · lager · mocktail · wine · beer · soft drinks · ice and lemon · gin and tonic · alcohol-free lager · cocktail

23.5 LISTEN TO PERSON A AND RESPOND AS PERSON B

A		B
1 Last orders, please! We close in 10 minutes.		Can we have the same again, please?
2 It's my round! What's everyone drinking?		A pint of lager for me, please!
3 What dry white wine can you recommend?		We have a large selection – check out our wine list.
4 Hi, can I get two gin and tonics, please?		Sure. Would you like ice and lemon with that?

🔊

23.6 LISTEN AND NUMBER THE SENTENCES IN THE ORDER YOU HEAR THEM

A Have you got a bar menu? ☐

B What time do you stop serving? ☐

C Hi, can I get two gin and tonics, please? ☐

D It's my round! What's everyone drinking? ☑ *1*

E Can we have the same again, please? ☐

F We have a large selection – check out our wine list. ☐

G What lagers have you got on tap? ☐

H Do we pay at the bar? ☐

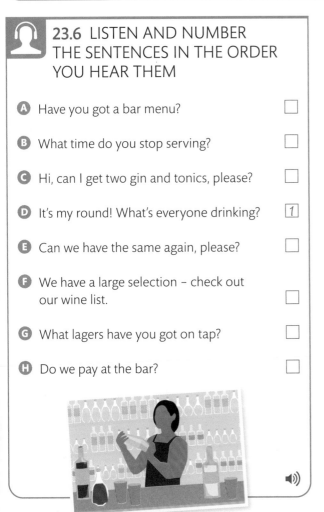

🔊

23.7 SAY THE SENTENCES OUT LOUD, REPLACING THE PICTURES WITH WORDS

1 Can I get a [🍺] , please? 🗣

2 Do you serve [🍹🍹] ? 🗣

3 A glass of [🍷] for me, please! 🗣

4 What [🍸🍸] can you recommend? 🗣

5 What [🥤🥤] are there? 🗣

🔊

59

24 At the restaurant

24.1 BOOKING A TABLE

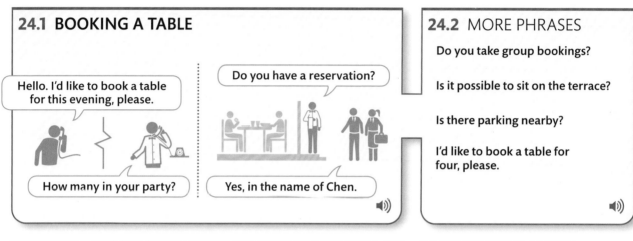

Hello. I'd like to book a table for this evening, please.

Do you have a reservation?

How many in your party?

Yes, in the name of Chen.

24.2 MORE PHRASES

Do you take group bookings?

Is it possible to sit on the terrace?

Is there parking nearby?

I'd like to book a table for four, please.

24.3 ORDERING YOUR MEAL

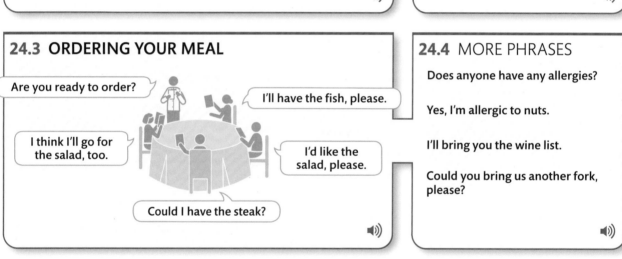

Are you ready to order?

I'll have the fish, please.

I think I'll go for the salad, too.

I'd like the salad, please.

Could I have the steak?

24.4 MORE PHRASES

Does anyone have any allergies?

Yes, I'm allergic to nuts.

I'll bring you the wine list.

Could you bring us another fork, please?

24.5 VOCABULARY A RESTAURANT TABLE

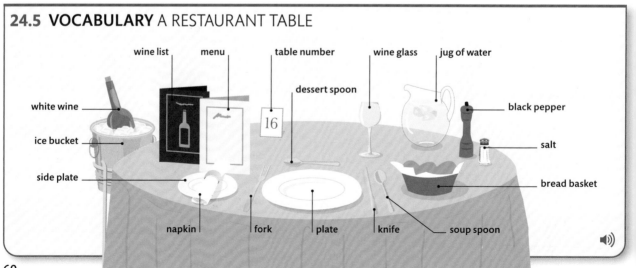

wine list · menu · table number · wine glass · jug of water · dessert spoon · white wine · black pepper · ice bucket · salt · side plate · bread basket · napkin · fork · plate · knife · soup spoon

24.6 LISTEN TO PERSON A AND RESPOND AS PERSON B

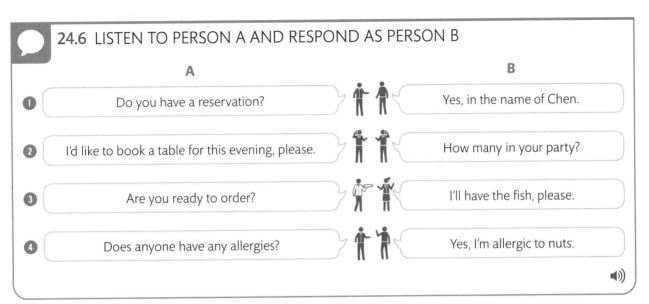

	A		B
1	Do you have a reservation?		Yes, in the name of Chen.
2	I'd like to book a table for this evening, please.		How many in your party?
3	Are you ready to order?		I'll have the fish, please.
4	Does anyone have any allergies?		Yes, I'm allergic to nuts.

24.7 LISTEN AND NUMBER THE PICTURES IN THE ORDER THEY ARE DESCRIBED

A ☐   B ☐   C 1   D ☐   E ☐   F ☐

24.8 SAY THE SENTENCES OUT LOUD, REPLACING THE PICTURES WITH WORDS

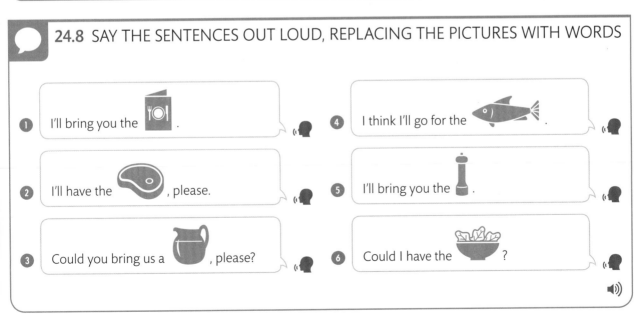

1 I'll bring you the [menu] .

2 I'll have the [steak] , please.

3 Could you bring us a [jug] , please?

4 I think I'll go for the [fish] .

5 I'll bring you the [pepper] .

6 Could I have the [salad] ?

24.9 DISCUSSING YOUR MEAL

How's your soup?

Really tasty. How's yours?

It's really good. Want to try some?

Your chicken looks delicious.

It's a bit too salty, actually.

How's your steak?

Nothing special, to be honest. I should've ordered the salad!

🌐 GOOD TO KNOW

We often use **actually** or **to be honest** at the beginning or end of a sentence to give an opinion, show we disagree with someone, or correct a misunderstanding.

24.10 MAKING COMPLAINTS

Sorry, but...

... this pasta is a bit cold.

... I didn't order red wine. I ordered white.

... this glass is dirty.

24.11 PAYING THE BILL

Would you like to see the dessert menu?

Not for me, thanks. I'm completely full!

Just the bill, please.

Shall we split the bill?

No, I'll get this. It's your birthday, after all!

24.12 MORE PHRASES

How would you like to pay?

We'll pay half each.

Can we pay by cash?

Let's split it three ways.

Would you like a receipt?

It's on me!

24.13 LISTEN AND CIRCLE THE ITEM YOU HEAR

1. Ⓐ B
2. A B
3. A B
4. A B

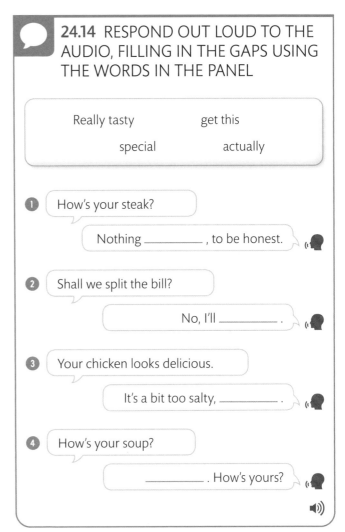

24.14 RESPOND OUT LOUD TO THE AUDIO, FILLING IN THE GAPS USING THE WORDS IN THE PANEL

Really tasty   get this

special   actually

1. How's your steak?

   Nothing _____, to be honest.

2. Shall we split the bill?

   No, I'll _____.

3. Your chicken looks delicious.

   It's a bit too salty, _____.

4. How's your soup?

   _____. How's yours?

24.15 USE THE CHART TO CREATE EIGHT SENTENCES AND SAY THEM OUT LOUD

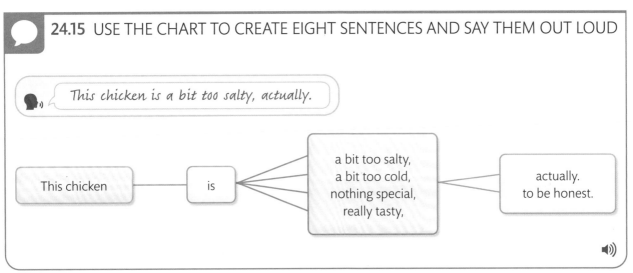

This chicken is a bit too salty, actually.

| This chicken | is | a bit too salty, a bit too cold, nothing special, really tasty, | actually. to be honest. |

63

25 Cooking and eating

25.1 FOLLOWING A RECIPE

What are you making?

I'm trying a new recipe for brownies. Fancy helping?

Sure, love to! I'll start weighing the flour.

How long does the bread need in the oven?

It says to check it after 30 minutes.

Okay, I'll set the timer!

So what do we do next?

Let's see... Peel and slice the apples.

25.3 COOKING METHODS

How are you cooking the broccoli?

I'm steaming it to keep the flavour.

I've brought the soup to the boil. What next?

Turn it down and simmer for 20 minutes.

Fancy eggs for lunch? Poached or scrambled?

Poached for me.

I'll have scrambled!

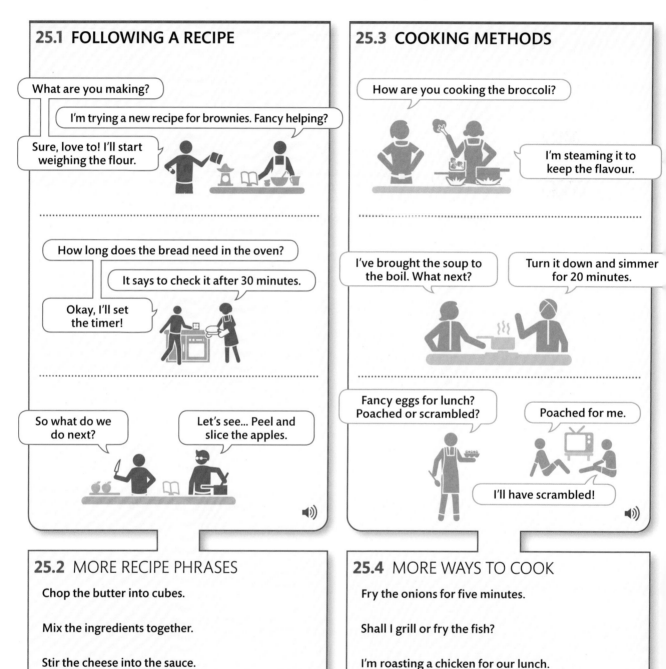

25.2 MORE RECIPE PHRASES

Chop the butter into cubes.

Mix the ingredients together.

Stir the cheese into the sauce.

Preheat the oven to 250°C (480°F).

25.4 MORE WAYS TO COOK

Fry the onions for five minutes.

Shall I grill or fry the fish?

I'm roasting a chicken for our lunch.

I've baked you a birthday cake!

25.5 LISTEN AND NUMBER THE PICTURES IN THE ORDER THEY ARE DESCRIBED

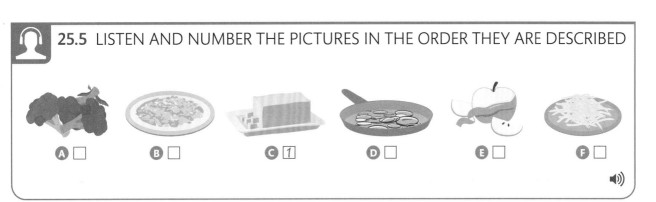

A ☐   B ☐   C 1   D ☐   E ☐   F ☐

🔊

25.6 LISTEN TO PERSON A AND RESPOND AS PERSON B

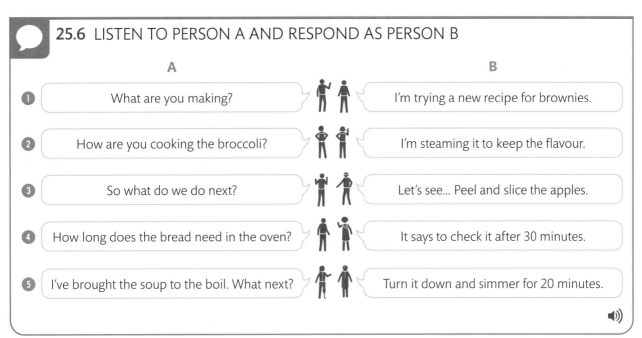

	A		B
1	What are you making?		I'm trying a new recipe for brownies.
2	How are you cooking the broccoli?		I'm steaming it to keep the flavour.
3	So what do we do next?		Let's see... Peel and slice the apples.
4	How long does the bread need in the oven?		It says to check it after 30 minutes.
5	I've brought the soup to the boil. What next?		Turn it down and simmer for 20 minutes.

🔊

25.7 SAY THE SENTENCES OUT LOUD, FILLING IN THE GAPS USING THE WORDS IN THE PANEL

Preheat	baked	set	Mix	weighing	simmer	Chop	roasting

1 I'll start _____ the flour.

2 _____ the butter into cubes.

3 _____ the oven to 250°C (480°F).

4 Turn it down and _____ for 20 minutes.

5 I'm _____ a chicken for our lunch.

6 _____ the ingredients together.

7 I've _____ you a birthday cake!

8 Okay, I'll _____ the timer!

🔊

25.8 COOKING TOGETHER

Who's cooking tonight?

It's my turn. I'm doing veggie lasagne.

Great! I love the way you make it.

Shall I do some garlic bread to go with it?

25.9 ENJOYING FOOD

This is so delicious.

It tastes amazing!

It's really tasty.

This is absolutely fantastic!

That was yummy.

25.10 HAVING A BARBECUE

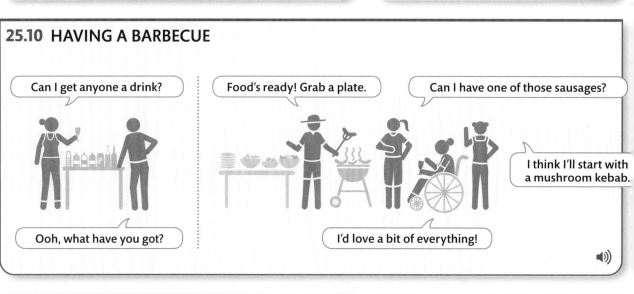

Can I get anyone a drink?

Food's ready! Grab a plate.

Can I have one of those sausages?

I think I'll start with a mushroom kebab.

Ooh, what have you got?

I'd love a bit of everything!

25.11 COOKING FOR FRIENDS

Thanks for having us over. Something smells good!

I've made a Thai green curry. Hope you like it!

25.12 DIETARY REQUIREMENTS

Is there anything you don't eat?

I don't eat pork.

I can't have things that contain gluten.

I'm vegetarian / vegan / pescatarian.

I'm allergic to shellfish.

I'm not so keen on peppers.

25.13 LISTEN AND NUMBER THE SENTENCES IN THE ORDER YOU HEAR THEM

A Food's ready! Grab a plate. ☐

B This is so delicious. ☐

C Who's cooking tonight? ☑ 1

D Can I get anyone a drink? ☐

E I've made a Thai green curry. ☐

F Is there anything you don't eat? ☐

G I can't have things that contain gluten. ☐

H Ooh, what have you got? ☐

🔊

25.14 MATCH THE SENTENCES AND SAY THEM OUT LOUD

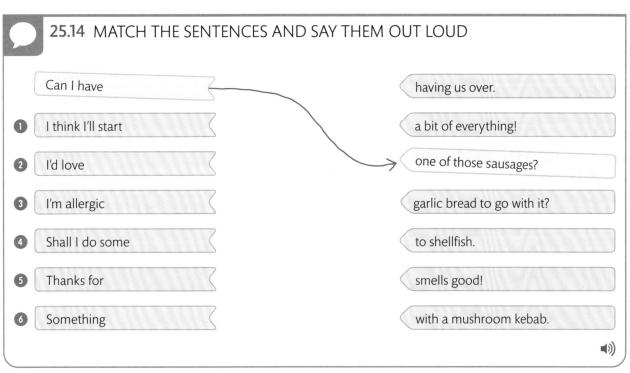

Can I have → one of those sausages?

1 I think I'll start — having us over.

2 I'd love — a bit of everything!

3 I'm allergic — garlic bread to go with it?

4 Shall I do some — to shellfish.

5 Thanks for — smells good!

6 Something — with a mushroom kebab.

🔊

25.15 USE THE CHART TO CREATE 12 SENTENCES AND SAY THEM OUT LOUD

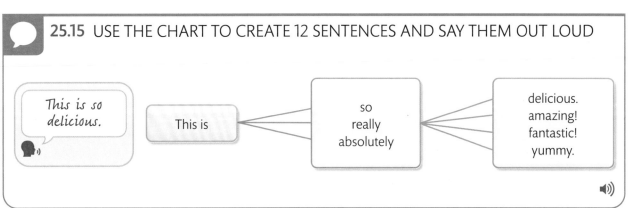

This is so delicious.

This is | so / really / absolutely | delicious. / amazing! / fantastic! / yummy.

🔊

26 Free time and hobbies

26.1 OUTDOOR ACTIVITIES

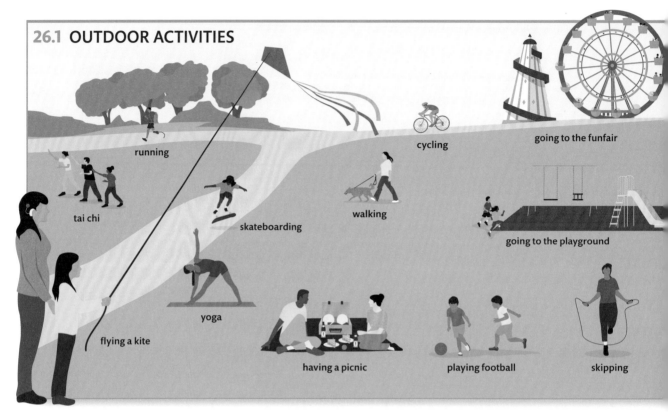

running

cycling

going to the funfair

tai chi

walking

going to the playground

skateboarding

yoga

flying a kite

having a picnic

playing football

skipping

26.2 GAMES

darts

board game

jigsaw puzzle

cards

gaming

dominoes

chess

chess pieces

chessboard

26.3 CREATIVE HOBBIES

painting

drawing

crafting

knitting

sewing

photography

pottery

baking

gardening

mountain biking

snowboarding

skiing

climbing

quad biking

sailing

hiking

fishing

swimming

orienteering

foraging

horse riding

birdwatching

camping

26.4 ENTERTAINMENT

theatre

cinema

nightclub

ballet

concert

festival

band

orchestra

choir

26.5 MUSIC GENRES

pop

rock

country

hip-hop

dance

bhangra

jazz

classical

opera

27 At the cinema

27.1 GETTING TICKETS

What time is the next screening?

It's at 2pm. We're just in time!

Three tickets for the 2pm screening, please.

27.2 OTHER QUESTIONS

How long is the film?

Which screen is it showing at?

Is there time to get popcorn?

Is the next screening sold out?

Can we have seats at the back?

27.3 ASKING QUESTIONS ABOUT ACCESS

Is the film okay for kids under 10?

It's a "U", so it's fine for all ages!

Can I get to Screen 2 this way?

Yes, just follow the ramps.

Is this the subtitled screening?

You need to go to Screen 5, just up the stairs.

27.4 DISCUSSING THE FILM

How good was that?

Those action scenes really blew me away!

The 3D glasses made it so realistic!

That was way too long!

The acting was rubbish.

I wasn't keen on the ending.

27.5 LISTEN TO PERSON A AND RESPOND AS PERSON B

A	B
1 What time is the next screening?	It's at 2pm. We're just in time!
2 Is the film okay for kids under 10?	It's a "U", so it's fine for all ages!
3 Can I get to Screen 2 this way?	Yes, just follow the ramps.
4 How good was that?	Those action scenes really blew me away!

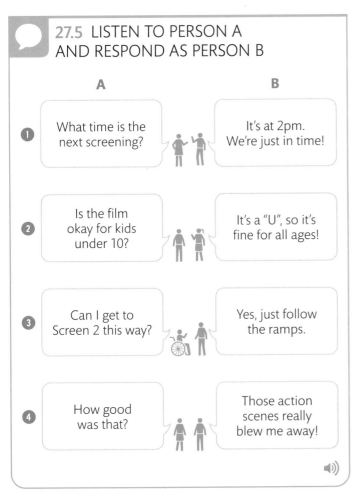

27.6 LISTEN AND NUMBER THE PICTURES IN THE ORDER THEY ARE DESCRIBED

27.7 SAY THE SENTENCES OUT LOUD, FILLING IN THE GAPS USING THE WORDS IN THE PANEL

film	keen	3D glasses	popcorn
kids	subtitled	seats	screen

1 The _____ made it so realistic!

2 Which _____ is it showing at?

3 Can we have _____ at the back?

4 I wasn't _____ on the ending.

5 Is there time to get _____ ?

6 How long is the _____ ?

7 Is this the _____ screening?

8 Is the film okay for _____ under 10?

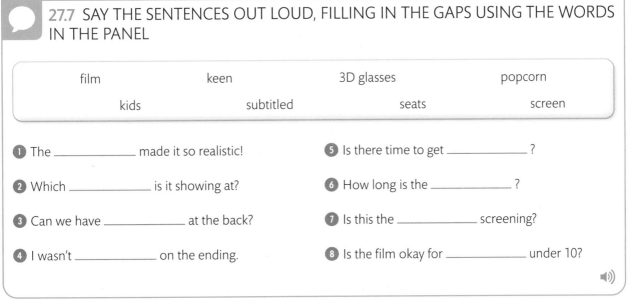

28 At the theatre

28.1 AT THE BOX OFFICE

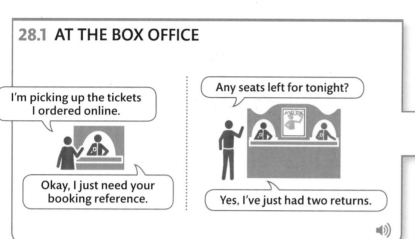

I'm picking up the tickets I ordered online.

Okay, I just need your booking reference.

Any seats left for tonight?

Yes, I've just had two returns.

28.2 MORE PHRASES

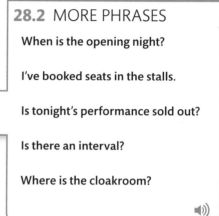

When is the opening night?

I've booked seats in the stalls.

Is tonight's performance sold out?

Is there an interval?

Where is the cloakroom?

28.3 BEFORE THE PERFORMANCE

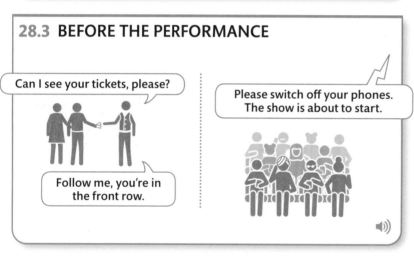

Can I see your tickets, please?

Follow me, you're in the front row.

Please switch off your phones. The show is about to start.

28.4 THE INTERVAL

How long is the interval?

It's 20 minutes. Time for a drink at the bar!

28.5 VOCABULARY INSIDE THE THEATRE

seat

performer

box

front row

audience

curtain

prop

set

stage

stalls

28.6 LISTEN AND CIRCLE THE ITEM YOU HEAR

28.7 MATCH THE SENTENCES AND SAY THEM OUT LOUD

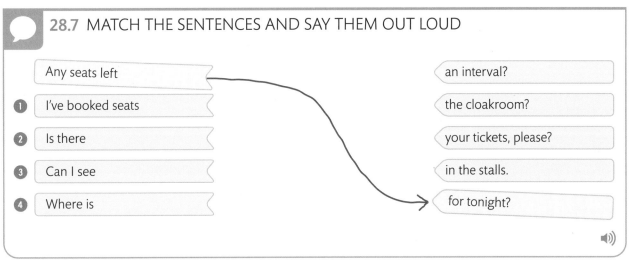

Any seats left — for tonight?

1. I've booked seats — in the stalls.
2. Is there — an interval?
3. Can I see — your tickets, please?
4. Where is — the cloakroom?

28.8 USE THE CHART TO CREATE SIX SENTENCES AND SAY THEM OUT LOUD

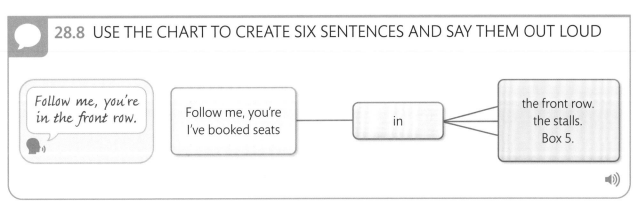

Follow me, you're in the front row.

Follow me, you're / I've booked seats — in — the front row. / the stalls. / Box 5.

73

29 Concerts and festivals

29.1 AT A CONCERT

What time does the main gig start?

9pm, but the support band has just come on.

Have your bags ready for inspection, please.

Sorry, you can't take bottles in.

Let's find the refreshment stand. I'm thirsty!

I'll meet you back in the main arena.

29.2 AT AN OPEN-AIR FESTIVAL

Who's playing on the main stage tonight?

Here's the line-up for the whole weekend. Enjoy!

29.3 MORE PHRASES

Is the campsite open yet?

I can't find my tent.

Can I see your wristband, please?

That food truck sells great burgers.

The toilet queue is too long!

29.4 AT A CLASSICAL CONCERT

There's a free classical concert at the park tonight.

Do we have to book tickets?

No, we can just turn up.

That was really impressive!

What an amazing performance!

Encore! Encore!

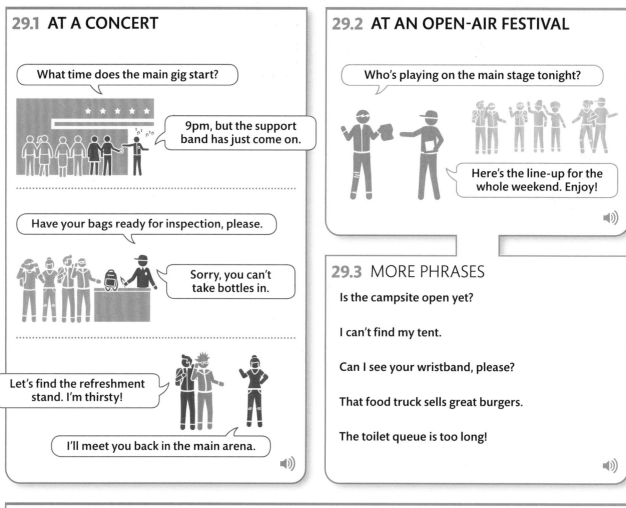
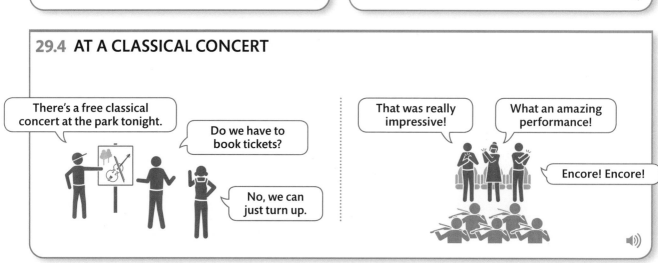

29.5 LISTEN AND NUMBER THE PICTURES IN THE ORDER THEY ARE DESCRIBED

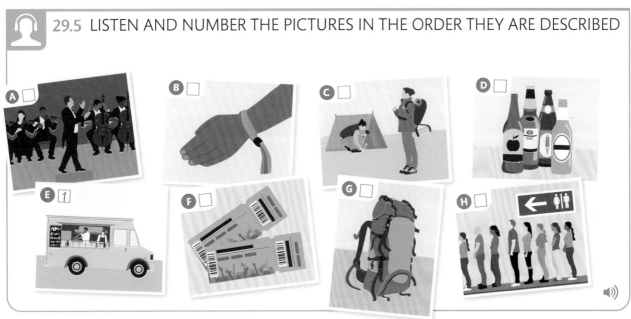

A ☐ B ☐ C ☐ D ☐

E ☑ F ☐ G ☐ H ☐

29.6 RESPOND OUT LOUD TO THE AUDIO, FILLING IN THE GAPS USING THE WORDS IN THE PANEL

turn up   the line-up

come on   performance

the main arena

1 Who's playing on the main stage tonight?

Here's _____ for the whole weekend.

2 Let's find the refreshment stand. I'm thirsty!

I'll meet you back in _____ .

3 Do we have to book tickets?

No, we can just _____ .

4 What time does the main gig start?

9pm, but the support band has just _____ .

5 That was really impressive!

What an amazing _____ !

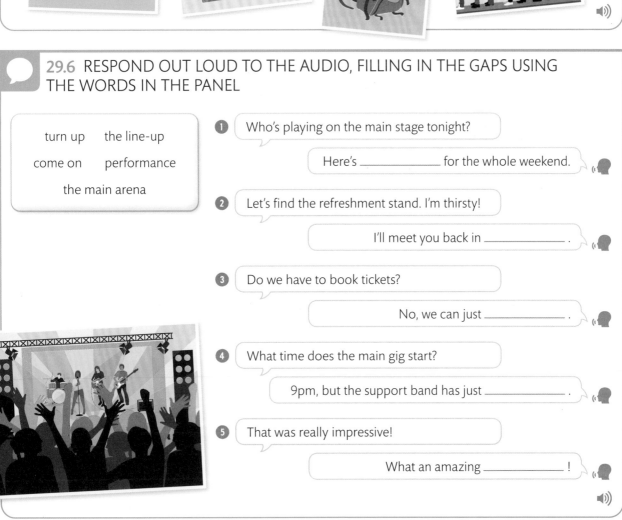

30 At the gym

30.1 JOINING A GYM

How much does it cost to join?

Here's our list of membership options.

Can I have a tour?

Yes, I'll show you round now.

So, what do you think?

It all looks great. Sign me up!

30.2 OTHER QUESTIONS TO ASK

What fitness classes do you run?

Would I need to pay extra for yoga classes?

Can I book a personal trainer?

Are there any women-only sessions?

30.3 ATTENDING A CLASS

Have you been to this fitness class before?

Yes, a few times. It's good fun!

Hi, I'm here for the spin class.

Great, grab a free bike and join in!

30.4 VOCABULARY AT THE GYM

personal trainer

to work out

weight training

spin class

yoga

Pilates

fitness class

HIIT

dance class

30.5 LISTEN TO PERSON A AND RESPOND AS PERSON B

A		B
1 How much does it cost to join?	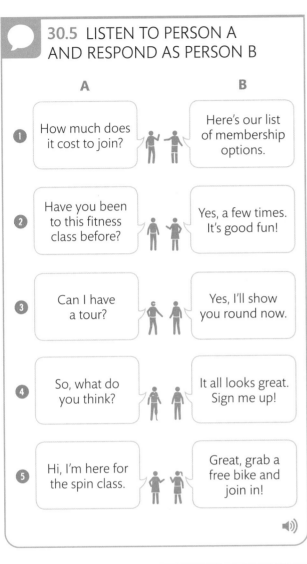	Here's our list of membership options.
2 Have you been to this fitness class before?		Yes, a few times. It's good fun!
3 Can I have a tour?		Yes, I'll show you round now.
4 So, what do you think?		It all looks great. Sign me up!
5 Hi, I'm here for the spin class.		Great, grab a free bike and join in!

🔊

30.6 LISTEN AND NUMBER THE SENTENCES IN THE ORDER YOU HEAR THEM

Ⓐ Can I have a tour? ☐

Ⓑ It all looks great. Sign me up! ☐

Ⓒ Can I book a personal trainer? ☐ 1

Ⓓ Here's our list of membership options. ☐

Ⓔ What fitness classes do you run? ☐

Ⓕ How much does it cost to join? ☐

Ⓖ Are there any women-only sessions? ☐

Ⓗ Would I need to pay extra for yoga classes? ☐

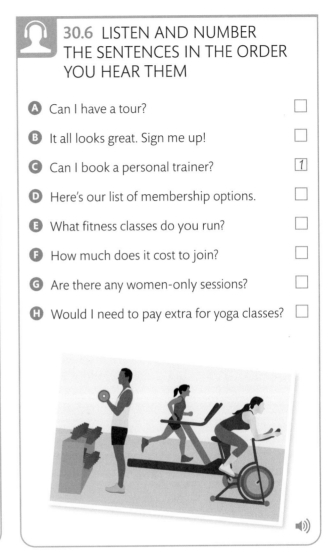

🔊

30.7 USE THE CHART TO CREATE FIVE SENTENCES AND SAY THEM OUT LOUD

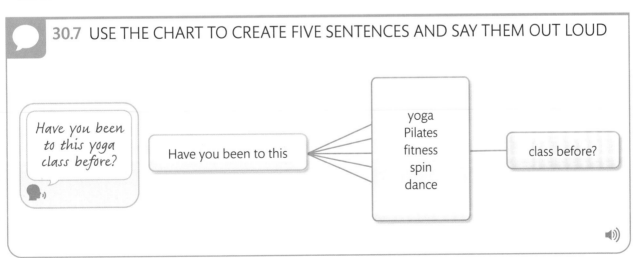

Have you been to this yoga class before?

| Have you been to this | yoga Pilates fitness spin dance | class before? |

🔊

77

31 Sporting activities

31.1 TEAM GAMES

Wanna join us for a game of baseball?

Yeah, I'm up for that.

Are you coming to basketball practice?

No, I sprained my ankle last week!

Pass it!

Over here!

Shoot!

Man on!

31.2 AT THE SPORTS CENTRE

Hi, do you give tennis lessons here?

Yes, we run them on Saturdays.

Can I book a swimming session, please?

Of course. What time would you like?

You look lost. Do you need any help?

I'm looking for the badminton court.

31.3 VOCABULARY SPORTS

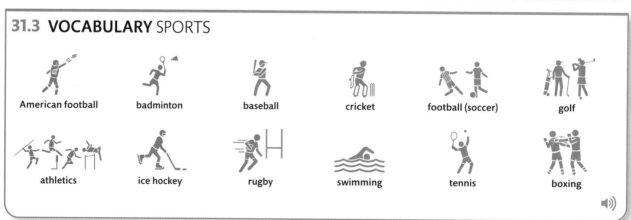

American football   badminton   baseball   cricket   football (soccer)   golf

athletics   ice hockey   rugby   swimming   tennis   boxing

31.4 LISTEN TO THE AUDIO AND MATCH THE CORRECT RESPONSE

Wanna join us for a game of baseball?

1 Hi, do you give tennis lessons here?

2 Can I book a swimming session, please?

3 Pass it!

4 Are you coming to basketball practice?

Of course. What time would you like?

No, I sprained my ankle last week!

Yes, we run them on Saturdays.

Yeah, I'm up for that.

Over here!

31.5 LISTEN TO PERSON A AND RESPOND AS PERSON B

A	B
1 Can I book a swimming session, please?	Of course. What time would you like?
2 Are you coming to basketball practice?	No, I sprained my ankle last week!
3 You look lost. Do you need any help?	I'm looking for the badminton court.
4 Wanna join us for a game of baseball?	Yeah, I'm up for that.

31.6 SAY THE SENTENCES OUT LOUD, REPLACING THE PICTURES WITH WORDS

1 Wanna join us for a game of  ?

2 Are you coming to ____ practice?

3 Do you give ____ lessons here?

4 I'd like to book a ____ lesson, please.

5 We run ____ practice on Mondays.

32 Sports events

32.1 BUYING TICKETS

Fancy going to watch the golf tournament?

Yes! When do tickets go on sale?

Tonight. I think they'll sell out fast!

Any seats left for the tennis final today?

Yes, there are a few. You're just in time!

32.2 OTHER QUESTIONS TO ASK

Have all the tickets sold out?

Can I buy a season ticket?

Is there a student discount?

Do you have seats for disabled spectators?

32.3 WATCHING SPORT

Are you watching the athletics?

You bet! It starts in half an hour.

Are you showing the football here?

Yes, we are. Tonight at 8.

Come on, guys!

You can do it!

Go, Tigers!

Keep going!

Keep it up!

32.4 LISTEN TO PERSON A AND RESPOND AS PERSON B

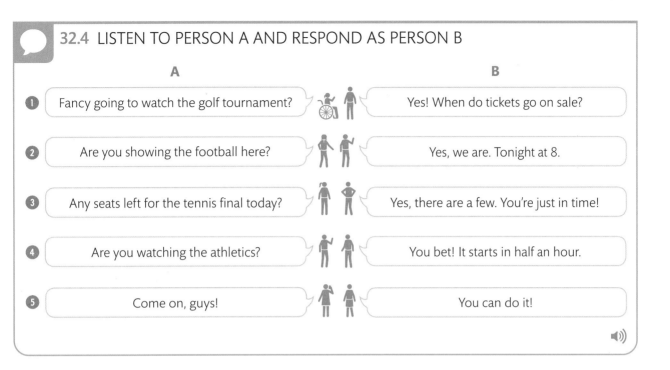

	A	B
1	Fancy going to watch the golf tournament?	Yes! When do tickets go on sale?
2	Are you showing the football here?	Yes, we are. Tonight at 8.
3	Any seats left for the tennis final today?	Yes, there are a few. You're just in time!
4	Are you watching the athletics?	You bet! It starts in half an hour.
5	Come on, guys!	You can do it!

32.5 LISTEN AND NUMBER THE PICTURES IN THE ORDER THEY ARE DESCRIBED

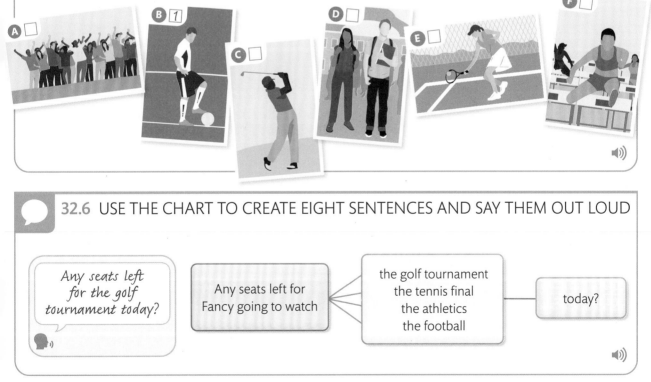

32.6 USE THE CHART TO CREATE EIGHT SENTENCES AND SAY THEM OUT LOUD

Any seats left for the golf tournament today?

Any seats left for	the golf tournament	today?
Fancy going to watch	the tennis final	
	the athletics	
	the football	

33 Hobbies

33.1 STARTING A NEW HOBBY

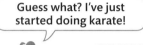 Guess what? I've just started doing karate!

No way! Good for you!

 Check this out... I'm giving knitting a go!

Wow! Maybe I'll have a go, too!

 I've taken up pottery recently.

That sounds fun – I might join you.

33.2 ASKING ABOUT HOBBIES

 Have you got any hobbies?

Yeah, I play tennis and I'm learning the guitar.

 So, what do you normally do in your free time?

I usually go swimming at the weekend. How about you?

 What do you do outside of work?

Gaming, mostly. And I'm writing a blog.

33.3 TALKING ABOUT HOBBIES

So how long have you all been playing?

The piano? Since I was 11.

 I've been playing the sax for 10 years!

 How about you?

 I only started learning the bass guitar three years ago.

33.4 LISTEN AND CIRCLE THE ITEM YOU HEAR

1. A / **B**
2. A / B
3. A / B
4. A / B
5. A / B

33.5 SAY THE SENTENCES OUT LOUD, REPLACING THE PICTURES WITH WORDS

1. I'm giving a go!
2. I've taken up recently.
3. I only started learning a year ago.
4. I usually play at the weekend.
5. I've just started learning the .
6. I've been playing the for six years.

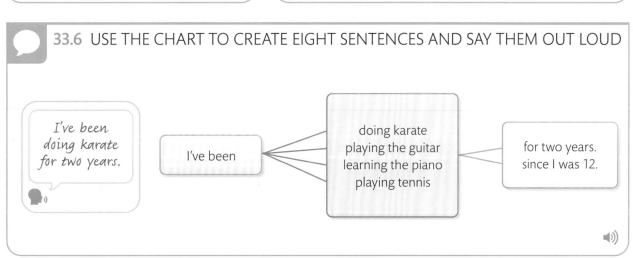

33.6 USE THE CHART TO CREATE EIGHT SENTENCES AND SAY THEM OUT LOUD

I've been doing karate for two years.

I've been

doing karate
playing the guitar
learning the piano
playing tennis

for two years.
since I was 12.

34 Shops and services

34.1 THE CITY CENTRE

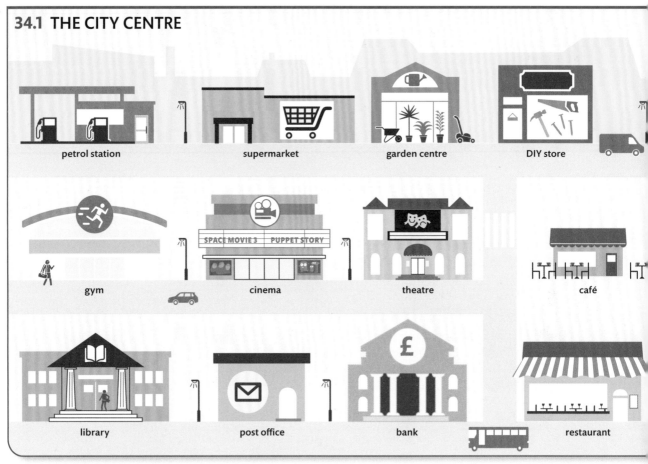

petrol station supermarket garden centre DIY store

gym cinema theatre café

library post office bank restaurant

34.2 TYPES OF SHOP

bakery butcher fishmonger greengrocer boutique shoe shop

antiques shop florist optician hair salon / barber newsagent bookshop

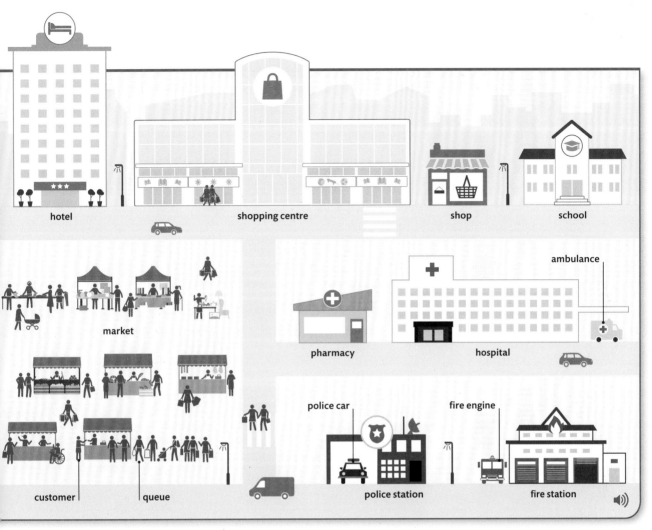

hotel

shopping centre

shop

school

market

pharmacy

hospital

ambulance

customer

queue

police car

police station

fire engine

fire station

34.3 MONEY MATTERS

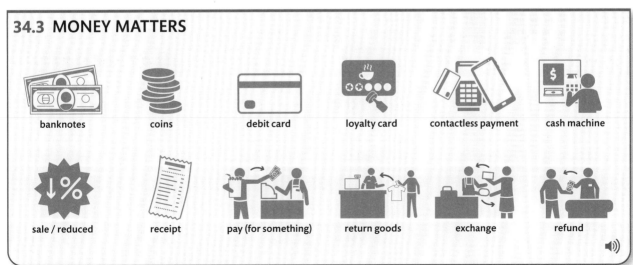

banknotes

coins

debit card

loyalty card

contactless payment

cash machine

sale / reduced

receipt

pay (for something)

return goods

exchange

refund

35 At the market

35.1 GETTING A BARGAIN

What's your best price for this?

I can't go any lower than £12.

I've only got £10.

You've got a deal!

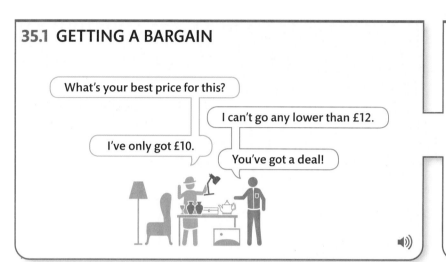

35.2 MORE PHRASES

Is that your best price?

That's my final offer.

I can't spend that much.

Can I get two for £15?

I'll take it!

35.3 BUYING FRESH PRODUCE

How much is this cheese?

It's £3.99 per kilo.

Could I have a box of eggs?

Would you like six or 12?

I'd like a loaf of bread, please.

Here you go. That'll be £2.50.

35.4 VOCABULARY FOOD MARKET

a bunch of grapes

a loaf of bread

a punnet of strawberries

a block of cheese

a box of eggs

a bag of apples

a kilo of potatoes

a jar of honey

GOOD TO KNOW

In UK English, we usually ask for things in a polite way, starting with, for example, **Can I...**, **Could I...**, or **I'd like...**, and ending the request with **please**. It's more polite to say **Could I...?** than **Can I...?**. In formal situations, some people might also say **May I...?**

35.5 LISTEN TO PERSON A AND RESPOND AS PERSON B

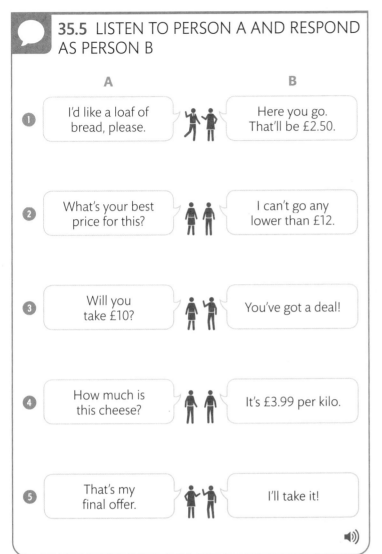

A

B

1. I'd like a loaf of bread, please. — Here you go. That'll be £2.50.

2. What's your best price for this? — I can't go any lower than £12.

3. Will you take £10? — You've got a deal!

4. How much is this cheese? — It's £3.99 per kilo.

5. That's my final offer. — I'll take it!

35.6 LISTEN AND CIRCLE THE ITEM YOU HEAR

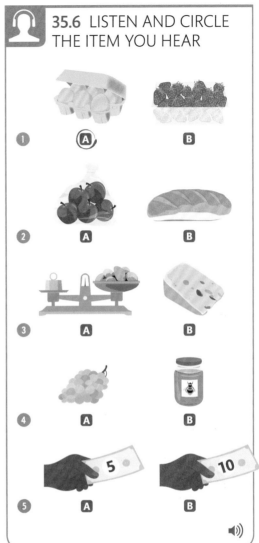

1. Ⓐ   B

2. A   B

3. A   B

4. A   B

5. A   B

35.7 USE THE CHART TO CREATE 10 SENTENCES AND SAY THEM OUT LOUD

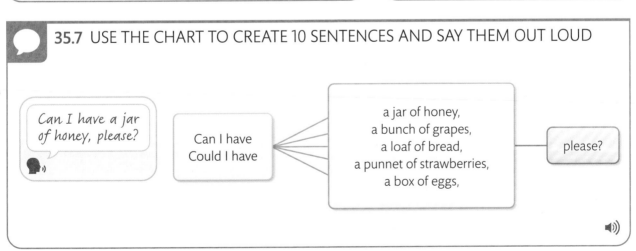

Can I have a jar of honey, please?

| Can I have Could I have | a jar of honey, a bunch of grapes, a loaf of bread, a punnet of strawberries, a box of eggs, | please? |

36 At the supermarket

36.1 ASKING FOR THINGS

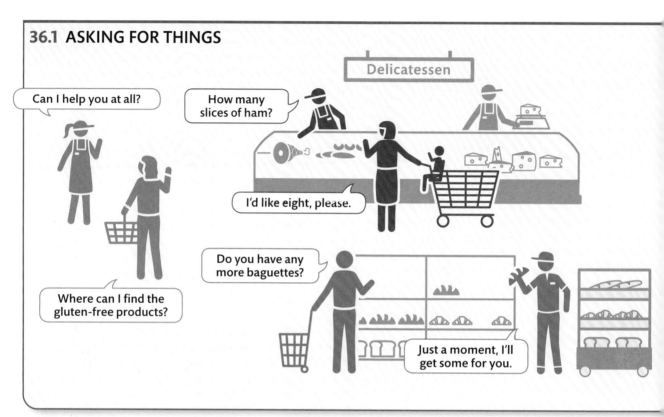

Delicatessen

Can I help you at all?

How many slices of ham?

I'd like eight, please.

Where can I find the gluten-free products?

Do you have any more baguettes?

Just a moment, I'll get some for you.

36.2 LISTEN AND NUMBER THE SENTENCES IN THE ORDER YOU HEAR THEM

A You'll find them in aisle 10. ☐

B I can't find the pet food. ☐

C Can I help you at all? 1

D How many slices of ham? ☐

E Do you stock oat milk here? ☐

F I'd like eight, please. ☐

36.3 LISTEN AND CIRCLE THE ITEM YOU HEAR

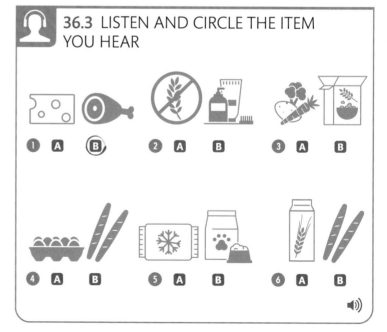

1 A **B**

2 A B

3 A B

4 A B

5 A B

6 A B

36.4 LISTEN TO PERSON A AND RESPOND AS PERSON B

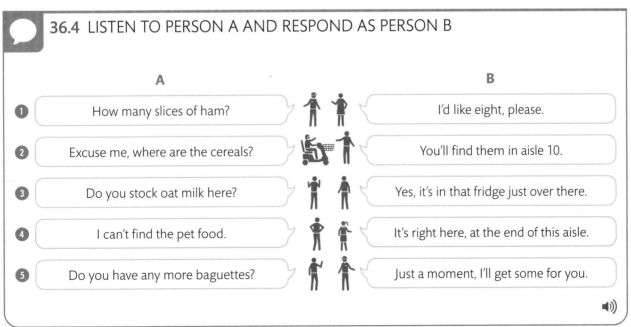

A		B
1 How many slices of ham?		I'd like eight, please.
2 Excuse me, where are the cereals?		You'll find them in aisle 10.
3 Do you stock oat milk here?		Yes, it's in that fridge just over there.
4 I can't find the pet food.		It's right here, at the end of this aisle.
5 Do you have any more baguettes?		Just a moment, I'll get some for you.

36.5 AT THE CHECKOUT

Do you need a bag?

No, I've brought my own, thanks.

That's £45.20. Have you got a loyalty card?

Yes, just a second...

That's all gone through. Would you like a receipt?

No, that's fine, thanks.

36.7 USING THE SELF-CHECKOUT

Excuse me, this milk carton is leaking.

No problem, I'll go and get another one.

This barcode won't scan.

Here. I'll give it a try.

Please tap or insert your card into the payment device.

36.8 VOCABULARY AISLES

bakery

fruit

vegetables

dairy products

meat and poultry

frozen food

gluten-free products

cereals

household products

pet food

health and beauty

baby products

deli

checkout

self-checkout

Would you like to use the self-checkout?

No, thanks. I'm happy to wait.

36.6 MORE PHRASES

Do you accept cash?

How much is it for a bag?

Could I have a receipt, please?

Could you scan my loyalty card, please?

I haven't got my loyalty card with me.

Can I use these vouchers?

36.9 LISTEN AND NUMBER THE SENTENCES IN THE ORDER YOU HEAR THEM

A Do you need a bag? ☐

B This barcode won't scan. ☐

C Would you like to use the self-checkout? ☐1

D No, thanks. I'm happy to wait. ☐

E That's £45.20. Have you got a loyalty card? ☐

F Can I use these vouchers? ☐

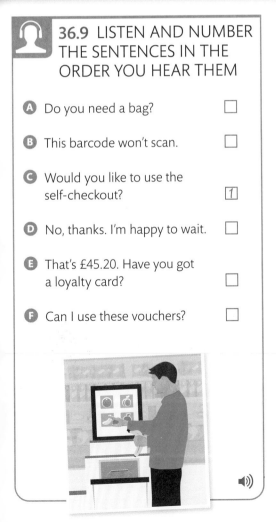

36.10 SAY THE SENTENCES OUT LOUD, REPLACING THE PICTURES WITH WORDS

1 Excuse me, where's the  aisle?

2 Would you like to use the ?

3 Where can I find the ?

4 Do you stock here?

5 I can't find the and .

91

37 At the garden centre

37.1 BUYING PLANTS

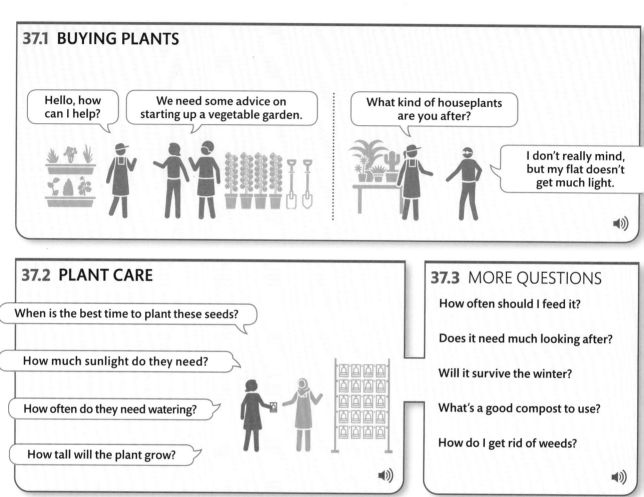

Hello, how can I help?

We need some advice on starting up a vegetable garden.

What kind of houseplants are you after?

I don't really mind, but my flat doesn't get much light.

37.2 PLANT CARE

When is the best time to plant these seeds?

How much sunlight do they need?

How often do they need watering?

How tall will the plant grow?

37.3 MORE QUESTIONS

How often should I feed it?

Does it need much looking after?

Will it survive the winter?

What's a good compost to use?

How do I get rid of weeds?

37.4 VOCABULARY GARDENING

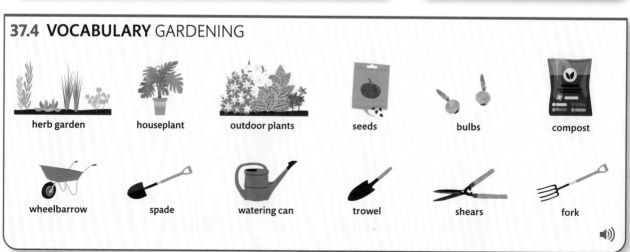

herb garden

houseplant

outdoor plants

seeds

bulbs

compost

wheelbarrow

spade

watering can

trowel

shears

fork

37.5 LISTEN AND NUMBER THE PICTURES IN THE ORDER THEY ARE DESCRIBED

Ⓐ ☐

Ⓑ 1

Ⓒ ☐

Ⓓ ☐

Ⓔ ☐

Ⓕ ☐

🔊

37.6 SAY THE SENTENCES OUT LOUD, FILLING IN THE GAPS USING THE WORDS IN THE PANEL

seeds   feed   sunlight

weeds   survive   looking

1 Will it _____ the winter?

2 When is the best time to plant these _____ ?

3 How much _____ do they need?

4 Does it need much _____ after?

5 How often should I _____ it?

6 How do I get rid of _____ ?

🔊

37.7 MATCH THE SENTENCES AND SAY THEM OUT LOUD

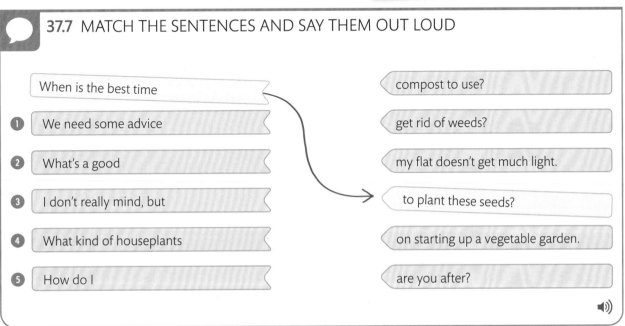

When is the best time

1 We need some advice

2 What's a good

3 I don't really mind, but

4 What kind of houseplants

5 How do I

compost to use?

get rid of weeds?

my flat doesn't get much light.

to plant these seeds?

on starting up a vegetable garden.

are you after?

🔊

38 At the DIY store

38.1 ASKING FOR ADVICE

What would you recommend for sanding a table?

What do I need for tiling my bathroom?

What's best for plastering walls?

What have you got for filling a crack?

38.2 MORE PHRASES

I'd like to remodel my bedroom.

I need to hang a picture.

What should I use for painting my kitchen?

I'm after some advice about plastering.

38.3 BUYING TOOLS

Can you show me to the tools section?

I'm looking for a hammer and nails.

Where can I find a saw?

Who can I ask about drills?

38.4 MORE PHRASES

Will I need ID to buy this saw?

Where are the screws?

What kind of screwdrivers do you sell?

Have you got any cordless power tools?

38.5 VOCABULARY TOOLS AND HOME IMPROVEMENTS

 hammer

 nail

 screwdriver

 screw

 saw

 drill

 to paint

 to plaster

 to sand

 to tile

 to fill

 to hang

38.6 LISTEN AND NUMBER THE SENTENCES IN THE ORDER YOU HEAR THEM

A What's best for plastering walls? ☐

B What do I need for tiling my bathroom? ☐

C What should I use for painting my kitchen? ☑ 1

D Where can I find a saw? ☐

E What have you got for filling a crack? ☐

F Who can I ask about drills? ☐

G Will I need ID to buy this saw? ☐

H I need to hang a picture. ☐

I I'm looking for a hammer and nails. ☐

J I'm after some advice about plastering. ☐

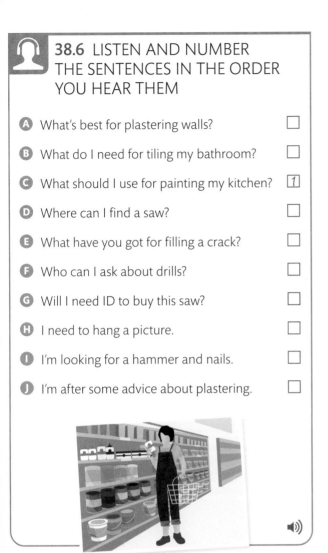

38.7 SAY THE SENTENCES OUT LOUD, REPLACING THE PICTURES WITH WORDS

1 I'm looking for a 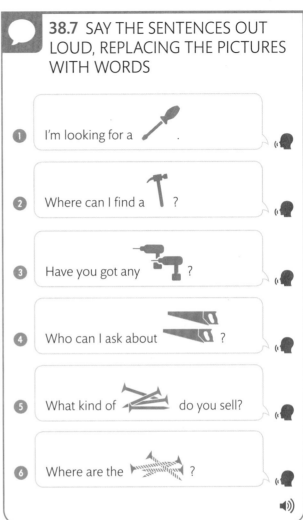 .

2 Where can I find a ?

3 Have you got any ?

4 Who can I ask about ?

5 What kind of do you sell?

6 Where are the ?

38.8 USE THE CHART TO CREATE NINE SENTENCES AND SAY THEM OUT LOUD

What do I need for plastering walls?

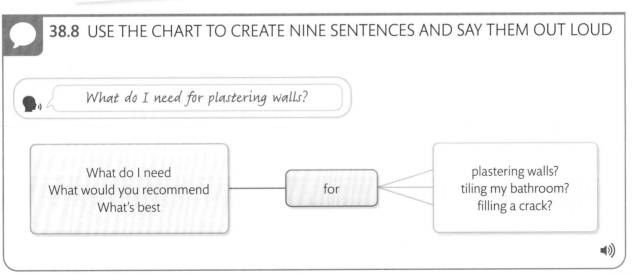

What do I need / What would you recommend / What's best	for	plastering walls? / tiling my bathroom? / filling a crack?

39 Buying clothes and shoes

39.1 AT THE CLOTHES SHOP

Have you got this shirt in a larger size?

Let me go and check.

Can I try these dresses on, please?

Yes, you can take up to four items in.

These trousers feel too big.

I'll go and get you the next size down.

39.2 AT THE SHOE SHOP

Have you got these trainers in a size 10?

I don't think so, but I'll just check for you.

Your website says you've got these sandals in stock.

Yes, they came in yesterday.

Are these boots in the sale?

SALE

Sorry, no. All the sale items are on this rack.

39.3 VOCABULARY CLOTHES AND SHOES

trousers

skirt

dress

jacket

coat

shorts

suit

jumper

shirt

T-shirt

sandals

trainers

boots

socks

39.4 LISTEN AND NUMBER THE PICTURES IN THE ORDER THEY ARE DESCRIBED

A [1]
B [ ]
C [ ]
D [ ]
E [ ]
F [ ]

39.5 LISTEN TO PERSON A AND RESPOND AS PERSON B

A **B**

1. Can I try these dresses on, please? — Yes, you can take up to four items in.

2. These trousers feel too big. — I'll go and get you the next size down.

3. Have you got these trainers in a size 10? — I don't think so, but I'll just check for you.

4. Have you got this shirt in a larger size? — Let me go and check.

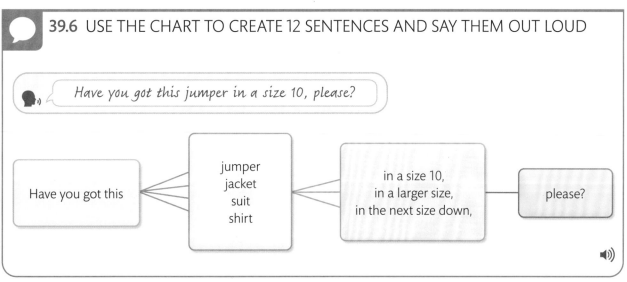

39.6 USE THE CHART TO CREATE 12 SENTENCES AND SAY THEM OUT LOUD

Have you got this jumper in a size 10, please?

| Have you got this | jumper jacket suit shirt | in a size 10, in a larger size, in the next size down, | please? |

40 Returning goods

40.1 EXPLAINING THE PROBLEM

Where can I return this bag? I bought the wrong colour.

Our returns desk is on the second floor.

I need to return these trousers.

Can I ask what the problem is?

They're too big.

RETURNS

40.2 MORE PHRASES

I bought the wrong size.

The lamp isn't working properly.

The shoes are too tight.

The dress doesn't fit properly.

The vase is broken.

40.3 REFUNDS AND EXCHANGES

I have to return this, but I lost my receipt.

Without a receipt, we can only offer an exchange, I'm afraid.

I'm returning this hat. I just don't like it!

Do you have a receipt?

No, it was a gift.

Don't worry, I'll give you a voucher.

I bought this online. Can I get a refund?

Yes, I just need your order number.

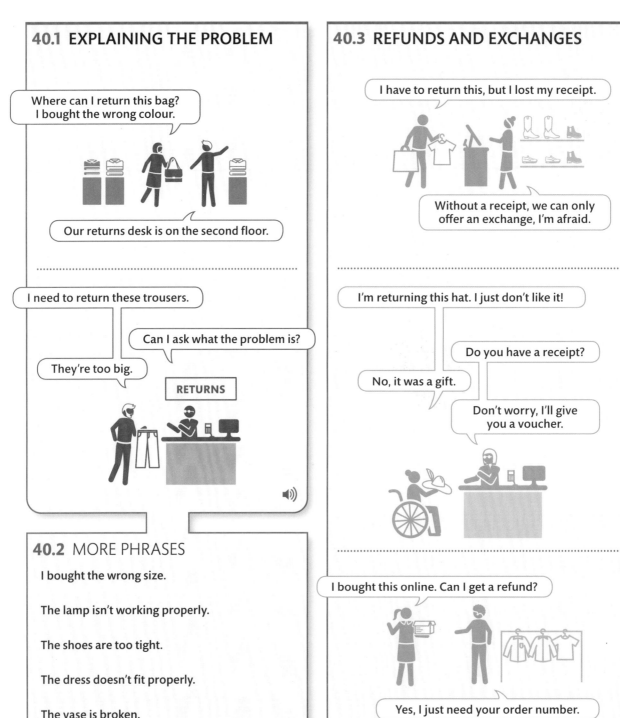

40.4 LISTEN TO PERSON A AND RESPOND AS PERSON B

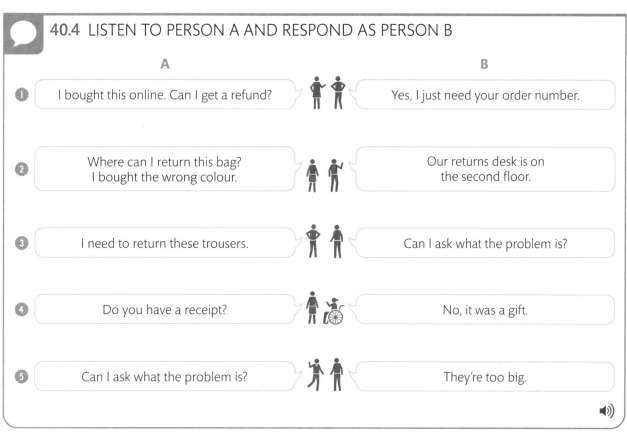

A

B

1. I bought this online. Can I get a refund? — Yes, I just need your order number.

2. Where can I return this bag? I bought the wrong colour. — Our returns desk is on the second floor.

3. I need to return these trousers. — Can I ask what the problem is?

4. Do you have a receipt? — No, it was a gift.

5. Can I ask what the problem is? — They're too big.

40.5 SAY THE SENTENCES OUT LOUD, REPLACING THE PICTURES WITH WORDS

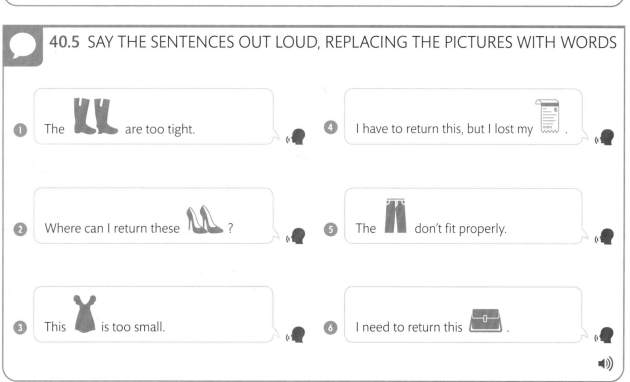

1. The ___ are too tight.

2. Where can I return these ___?

3. This ___ is too small.

4. I have to return this, but I lost my ___.

5. The ___ don't fit properly.

6. I need to return this ___.

41 Hair, beauty, and grooming

41.1 MAKING AN APPOINTMENT

Would you like to make an appointment?

Yes, please. Can you do Thursday at 3pm?

We're fully booked on Thursday, I'm afraid.

How about Friday morning?

Friday is fine. Is 9.30 okay?

41.2 MORE QUESTIONS

Would you like a cut and blow-dry?

Have you been to this salon before?

Who normally does your hair?

Can you come in on Monday?

Is Saturday afternoon any good?

What's the earliest you could fit me in?

Would you like to make another appointment?

41.3 AT THE BARBER'S

I just need a quick trim. Can you fit me in?

Could you wait 20 minutes? There's one person before you.

Not too much off the top, please.

Sure. No problem.

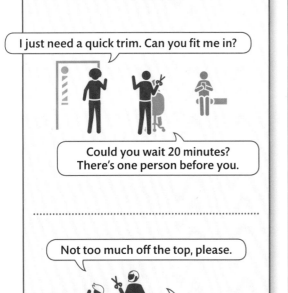

41.4 VOCABULARY HAIR AND BEAUTY

hairdresser

barber

beautician

beard trim

cut

blow-dry

highlights

fringe

facial

manicure

pedicure

waxing

41.5 LISTEN TO PERSON A AND RESPOND AS PERSON B

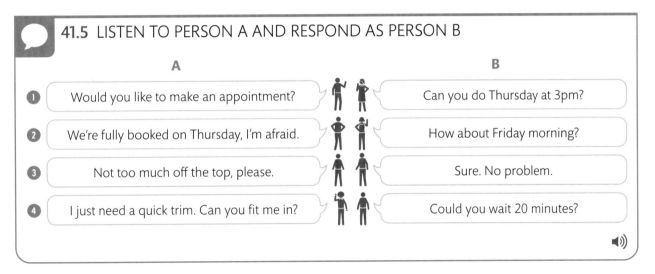

A	B
❶ Would you like to make an appointment?	Can you do Thursday at 3pm?
❷ We're fully booked on Thursday, I'm afraid.	How about Friday morning?
❸ Not too much off the top, please.	Sure. No problem.
❹ I just need a quick trim. Can you fit me in?	Could you wait 20 minutes?

41.6 MATCH THE SENTENCES AND SAY THEM OUT LOUD

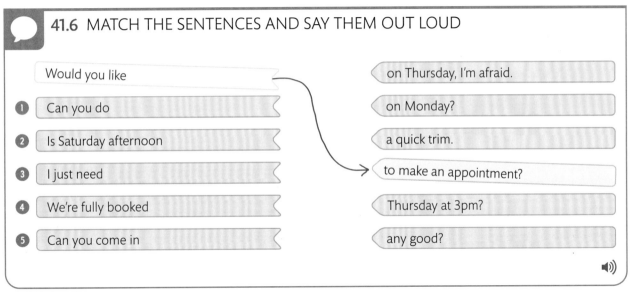

Would you like → to make an appointment?

❶ Can you do — on Thursday, I'm afraid.

❷ Is Saturday afternoon — on Monday?

❸ I just need — a quick trim.

❹ We're fully booked — Thursday at 3pm?

❺ Can you come in — any good?

41.7 USE THE CHART TO CREATE EIGHT SENTENCES AND SAY THEM OUT LOUD

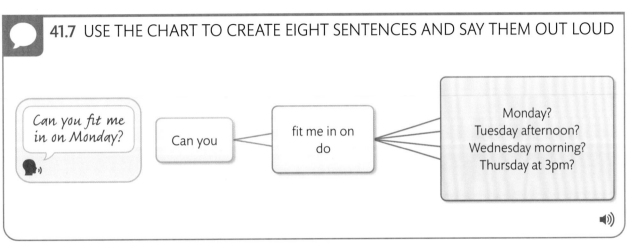

Can you fit me in on Monday?

Can you — fit me in on / do — Monday?
Tuesday afternoon?
Wednesday morning?
Thursday at 3pm?

41.8 CONSULTING THE STYLIST

So, what are we doing today?

Just my usual, I think.

I feel like a change, but I don't know what to go for.

Have a look through these styles, then we'll have a chat.

I was thinking of something like this...

I think a shorter style would really suit you.

41.9 MORE PHRASES

What colour would be best for me?

Could you cut it a bit shorter at the sides?

Leave it longer on top, please.

Could you cut the fringe a bit more?

I'll have some styling gel on it, please.

Do you think I should go for highlights?

41.10 BEAUTY AND GROOMING

I'd like a manicure and polish.

Okay. Have a look at these colours and take your pick.

I booked a back wax for 4pm.

Could I take your name, please?

So, you're having the aromatherapy facial today?

Yes, that's right.

41.11 LISTEN AND NUMBER THE SENTENCES IN THE ORDER YOU HEAR THEM

Ⓐ I'd like a manicure and polish. ☐

Ⓑ What colour would be best for me? ☑1

Ⓒ Do you think I should go for highlights? ☐

Ⓓ Could you cut it a bit shorter at the sides? ☐

Ⓔ Leave it longer on top, please. ☐

Ⓕ Could you cut the fringe a bit more? ☐

Ⓖ So, you're having the aromatherapy facial today? ☐

Ⓗ I feel like a change, but I don't know what to go for. ☐

Ⓘ I'll have some styling gel on it, please. ☐

41.12 SAY THE SENTENCES OUT LOUD, FILLING IN THE GAPS USING THE WORDS IN THE PANEL

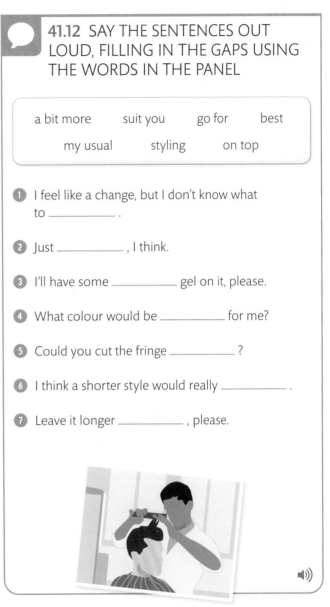

> a bit more   suit you   go for   best
> my usual   styling   on top

❶ I feel like a change, but I don't know what to _____ .

❷ Just _____ , I think.

❸ I'll have some _____ gel on it, please.

❹ What colour would be _____ for me?

❺ Could you cut the fringe _____ ?

❻ I think a shorter style would really _____ .

❼ Leave it longer _____ , please.

41.13 USE THE CHART TO CREATE NINE SENTENCES AND SAY THEM OUT LOUD

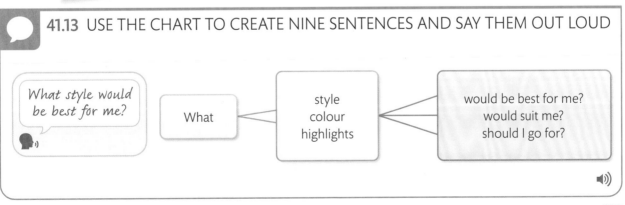

What style would be best for me?

What | style colour highlights | would be best for me? would suit me? should I go for?

42 Sending and receiving

42.1 AT THE POST OFFICE

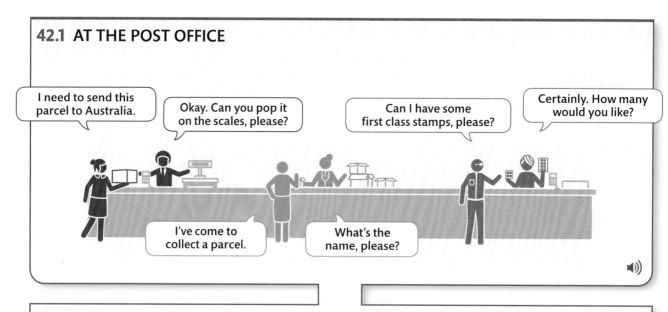

I need to send this parcel to Australia.

Okay. Can you pop it on the scales, please?

Can I have some first class stamps, please?

Certainly. How many would you like?

I've come to collect a parcel.

What's the name, please?

42.2 MORE PHRASES

How much is a second class stamp?

Can I send this letter to France?

How much does it cost to send this to Japan?

How soon will my parcel arrive?

Can I send this by special delivery?

What's the fastest way to send this parcel?

42.3 COURIER SERVICE

Can you sign for this, please?

Sure, I've been waiting for it to arrive!

Delivery for a Mr Jackson?

We're on the third floor. Thanks!

42.4 MORE PHRASES

I'd like to book a courier, please.

Can I arrange a parcel collection?

I need a parcel delivered urgently.

Do you do same-day delivery?

You've got the wrong address.

My parcel hasn't arrived.

42.5 LISTEN TO PERSON A AND RESPOND AS PERSON B

A		B
1 Can I have some first class stamps, please?		Certainly. How many would you like?
2 Can you sign for this, please?		Sure, I've been waiting for it to arrive!
3 I need to send this parcel to Australia.		Okay. Can you pop it on the scales, please?
4 Delivery for a Mr Jackson?		We're on the third floor. Thanks!

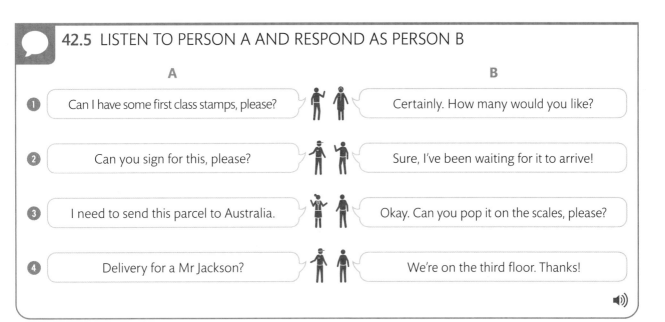

42.6 LISTEN AND NUMBER THE PICTURES IN THE ORDER THEY ARE DESCRIBED

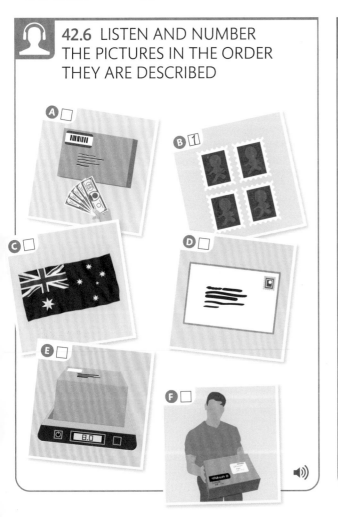

A ☐ B ☐ 1 C ☐ D ☐ E ☐ F ☐

42.7 SAY THE SENTENCES OUT LOUD, FILLING IN THE GAPS USING THE WORDS IN THE PANEL

cost   send   like   pop

waiting   collect   sign   arrive

1 How many would you _____ ?

2 Can you _____ it on the scales, please?

3 How much does it _____ to send this to Japan?

4 I've come to _____ a parcel.

5 Can you _____ for this, please?

6 How soon will my parcel _____ ?

7 Can I _____ this letter to France?

8 Sure, I've been _____ for it to arrive!

43 Money and finance

43.1 OPENING A BANK ACCOUNT

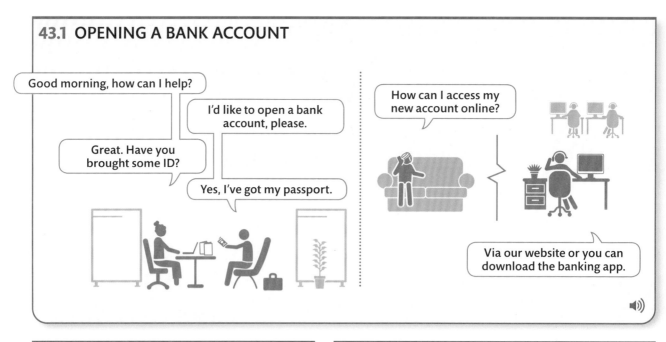

Good morning, how can I help?

I'd like to open a bank account, please.

Great. Have you brought some ID?

Yes, I've got my passport.

How can I access my new account online?

Via our website or you can download the banking app.

43.2 MAKING PAYMENTS AND WITHDRAWALS

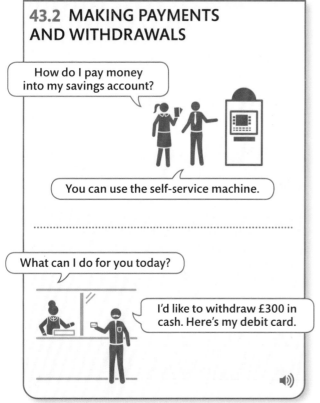

How do I pay money into my savings account?

You can use the self-service machine.

What can I do for you today?

I'd like to withdraw £300 in cash. Here's my debit card.

43.3 VOCABULARY AT THE BANK

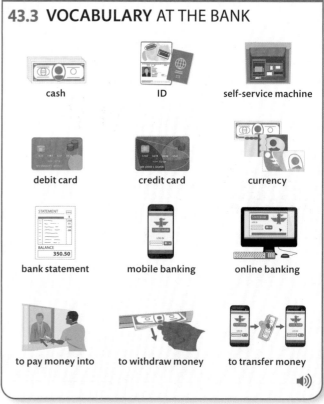

cash

ID

self-service machine

debit card

credit card

currency

bank statement

mobile banking

online banking

to pay money into

to withdraw money

to transfer money

43.4 LISTEN TO PERSON A AND RESPOND AS PERSON B

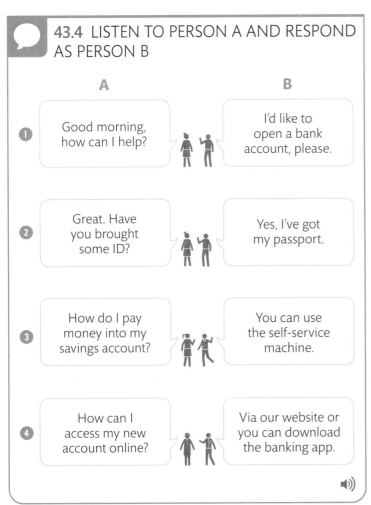

A

B

1. Good morning, how can I help? — I'd like to open a bank account, please.

2. Great. Have you brought some ID? — Yes, I've got my passport.

3. How do I pay money into my savings account? — You can use the self-service machine.

4. How can I access my new account online? — Via our website or you can download the banking app.

43.5 LISTEN AND CIRCLE THE ITEM YOU HEAR

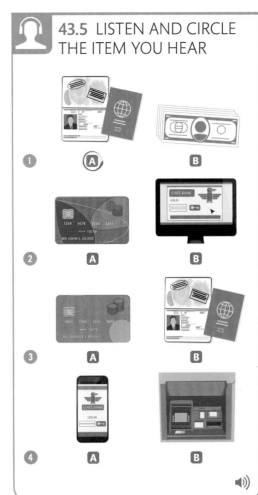

1. Ⓐ B

2. A B

3. A B

4. A B

43.6 USE THE CHART TO CREATE FIVE SENTENCES AND SAY THEM OUT LOUD

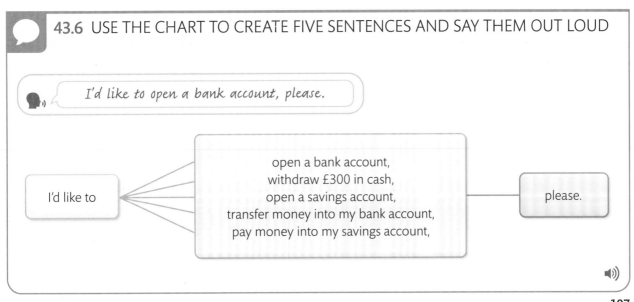

I'd like to open a bank account, please.

I'd like to →
- open a bank account,
- withdraw £300 in cash,
- open a savings account,
- transfer money into my bank account,
- pay money into my savings account,

please.

43.7 ORDERING CURRENCY

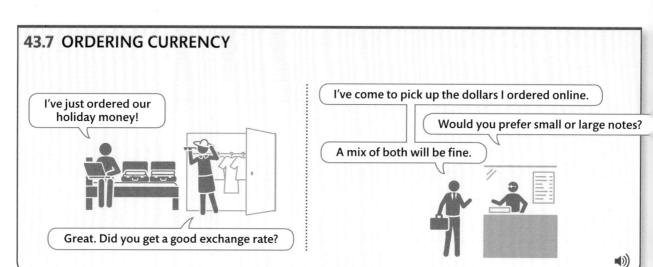

I've just ordered our holiday money!

Great. Did you get a good exchange rate?

I've come to pick up the dollars I ordered online.

Would you prefer small or large notes?

A mix of both will be fine.

43.8 CARD PROBLEMS

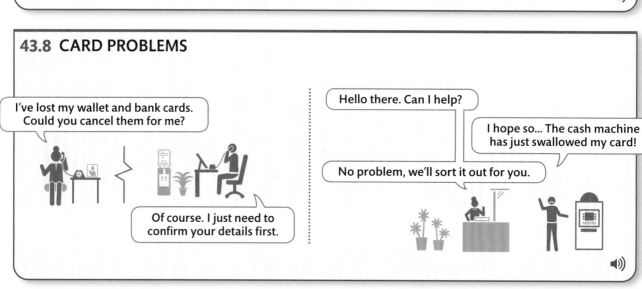

I've lost my wallet and bank cards. Could you cancel them for me?

Of course. I just need to confirm your details first.

Hello there. Can I help?

I hope so... The cash machine has just swallowed my card!

No problem, we'll sort it out for you.

43.9 WAYS TO PAY

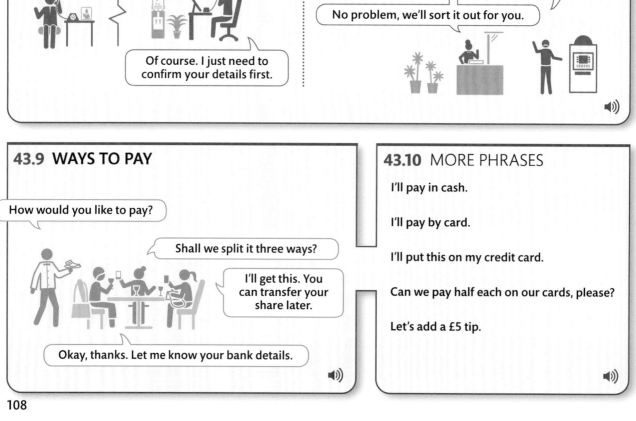

How would you like to pay?

Shall we split it three ways?

I'll get this. You can transfer your share later.

Okay, thanks. Let me know your bank details.

43.10 MORE PHRASES

I'll pay in cash.

I'll pay by card.

I'll put this on my credit card.

Can we pay half each on our cards, please?

Let's add a £5 tip.

43.11 LISTEN TO PERSON A AND RESPOND AS PERSON B

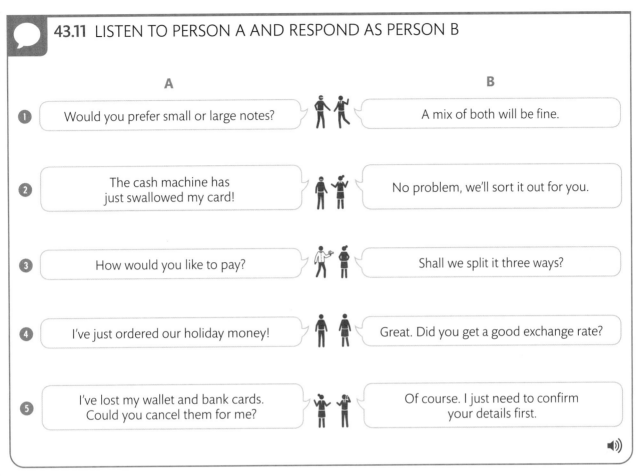

	A		B
1	Would you prefer small or large notes?		A mix of both will be fine.
2	The cash machine has just swallowed my card!		No problem, we'll sort it out for you.
3	How would you like to pay?		Shall we split it three ways?
4	I've just ordered our holiday money!		Great. Did you get a good exchange rate?
5	I've lost my wallet and bank cards. Could you cancel them for me?		Of course. I just need to confirm your details first.

43.12 MATCH THE SENTENCES AND SAY THEM OUT LOUD

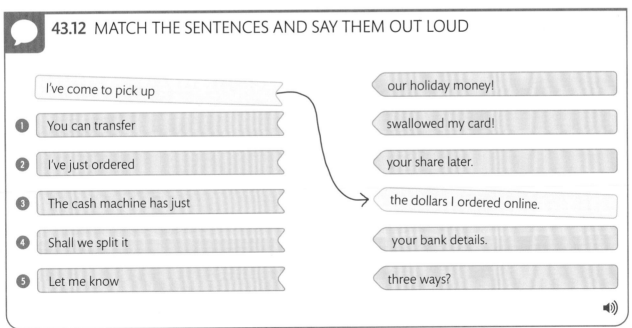

I've come to pick up — the dollars I ordered online.

1. You can transfer — your share later.
2. I've just ordered — our holiday money!
3. The cash machine has just — swallowed my card!
4. Shall we split it — three ways?
5. Let me know — your bank details.

44 At the library

44.1 JOINING THE LIBRARY

Hi there. How do I join the library?

I'll just need some ID and proof of your address.

Do you run computing courses here?

Yes, here's a list of all our classes.

44.2 USING THE LIBRARY

I'd like to take these books out.

If you've got your library card, you can use this scanner.

Have you got this as an audiobook?

Yes, we do. I'll show you how to download it.

Can we use a computer for our school project?

Of course. I'll book you one in the study space.

44.3 MORE PHRASES

I need to renew these books, please.

Where do I return these books?

Can you help me find a book, please?

Where is the children's section?

Could you recommend a good thriller?

Can I see your newspaper archive?

44.4 LISTEN TO PERSON A AND RESPOND AS PERSON B

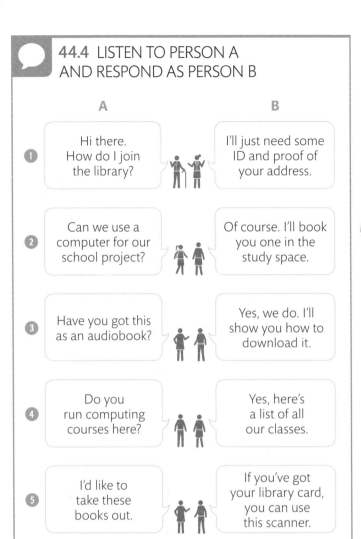

	A		B
1	Hi there. How do I join the library?		I'll just need some ID and proof of your address.
2	Can we use a computer for our school project?		Of course. I'll book you one in the study space.
3	Have you got this as an audiobook?		Yes, we do. I'll show you how to download it.
4	Do you run computing courses here?		Yes, here's a list of all our classes.
5	I'd like to take these books out.		If you've got your library card, you can use this scanner.

44.5 LISTEN AND NUMBER THE PICTURES IN THE ORDER THEY ARE DESCRIBED

A ①

B ☐

C ☐

D ☐ UNICORNS

E ☐

F ☐

44.6 SAY THE SENTENCES OUT LOUD, FILLING IN THE GAPS USING THE WORDS IN THE PANEL

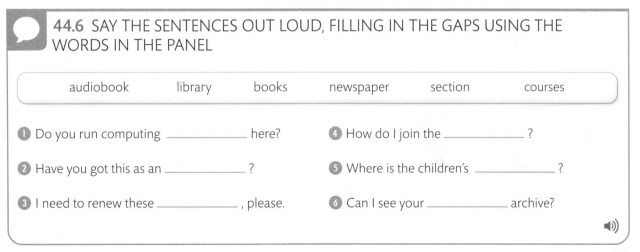

audiobook   library   books   newspaper   section   courses

1 Do you run computing _____ here?

2 Have you got this as an _____ ?

3 I need to renew these _____ , please.

4 How do I join the _____ ?

5 Where is the children's _____ ?

6 Can I see your _____ archive?

45 Work and study

45.1 JOBS / OCCUPATIONS

server

chef

teacher

cleaner

receptionist

lawyer

doctor

nurse

dentist

pharmacist

paramedic

childcare provider

courier

police officer

firefighter

security guard

pilot

flight attendant

mechanic

estate agent

librarian

accountant

vet

sales assistant

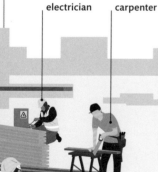
electrician
carpenter
engineer
architect
builder

app developer

farmer

hairdresser

plumber

artist

gardener

45.2 SCHOOL AND COLLEGE

school / college

classroom

lesson

students / pupils

homework

university

timetable

to take an exam / a test

to pass an exam / a test

to fail an exam / a test

lecture

dissertation

graduation

degree

diploma

45.3 WORLD OF WORK

employer

employee

freelancer

office worker

site worker

permanent job

temporary job

full-time job

part-time job

shift

overtime

flexitime

to go on maternity leave

to resign

to retire

wages

salary

hourly rate

payslip

benefits

pay rise

pay cut

bonus

annual leave

sick leave

46.1 CHOOSING A SCHOOL

We offer a wide range of subjects.

Is music part of the curriculum?

The children have maths every day.

How often do they have science lessons?

46.2 MORE QUESTIONS

How many children are in each class?

How much homework is there?

What clubs do you offer?

Do you have a school uniform?

Is there an after-school club?

46.3 STARTING SCHOOL

You must be our new student. Welcome!

Yes, this is Tom. He's a bit nervous for his first day!

There's no need to worry, Tom. Let's go and meet your new class.

46.4 PARENTS' EVENING

Zia is settling in very well.

Oh, good. How is she getting on with English?

She's making really good progress.

46.5 VOCABULARY SCHOOL SUBJECTS

 English

 maths

 science

 computing

 history

 geography

 languages

 physical education (PE)

 art

 music

 drama

 religious studies

46.6 LISTEN TO PERSON A AND RESPOND AS PERSON B

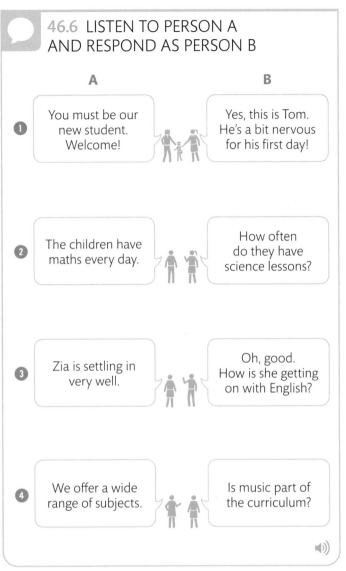

A / **B**

1. You must be our new student. Welcome! / Yes, this is Tom. He's a bit nervous for his first day!

2. The children have maths every day. / How often do they have science lessons?

3. Zia is settling in very well. / Oh, good. How is she getting on with English?

4. We offer a wide range of subjects. / Is music part of the curriculum?

46.7 LISTEN AND CIRCLE THE ITEM YOU HEAR

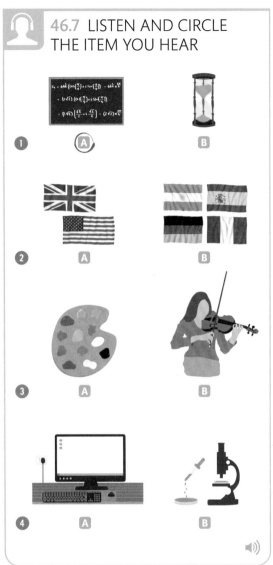

1. Ⓐ B
2. A B
3. A B
4. A B

46.8 USE THE CHART TO CREATE FIVE SENTENCES AND SAY THEM OUT LOUD

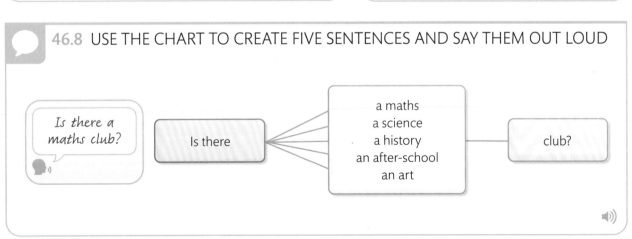

Is there a maths club?

Is there → a maths / a science / a history / an after-school / an art → club?

47 Further and higher education

47.1 CHOOSING A COURSE

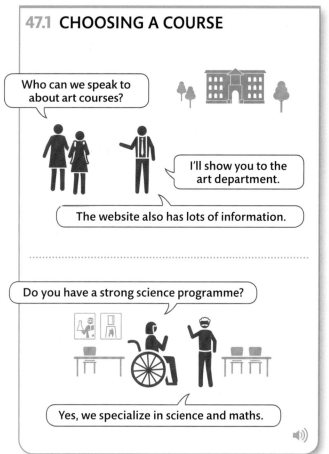

Who can we speak to about art courses?

I'll show you to the art department.

The website also has lots of information.

Do you have a strong science programme?

Yes, we specialize in science and maths.

47.2 VOCATIONAL COURSES

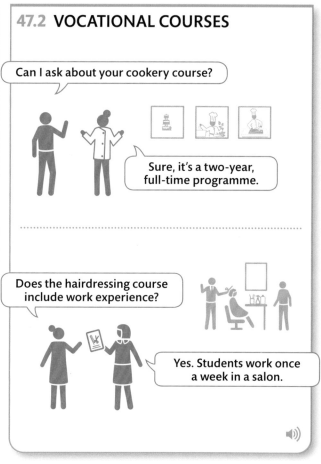

Can I ask about your cookery course?

Sure, it's a two-year, full-time programme.

Does the hairdressing course include work experience?

Yes. Students work once a week in a salon.

47.3 MORE QUESTIONS TO ASK

What qualifications do I need?

What are your entry requirements?

What qualification will I get?

How long does the course last?

How do I apply?

Is there a chance to study abroad?

47.4 EVENING CLASSES

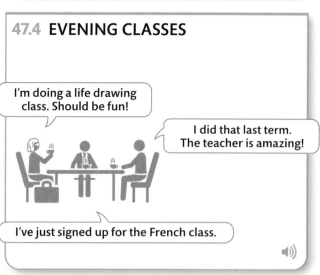

I'm doing a life drawing class. Should be fun!

I did that last term. The teacher is amazing!

I've just signed up for the French class.

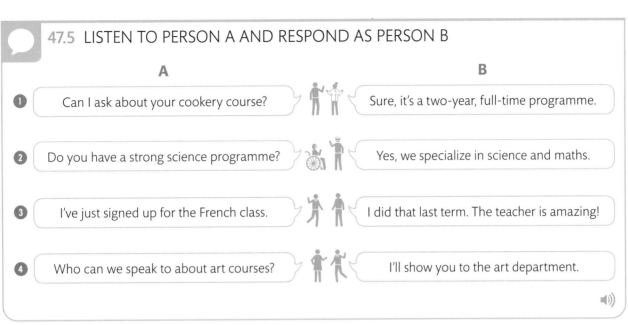

47.5 LISTEN TO PERSON A AND RESPOND AS PERSON B

A | **B**

1. Can I ask about your cookery course? — Sure, it's a two-year, full-time programme.

2. Do you have a strong science programme? — Yes, we specialize in science and maths.

3. I've just signed up for the French class. — I did that last term. The teacher is amazing!

4. Who can we speak to about art courses? — I'll show you to the art department.

47.6 LISTEN AND NUMBER THE SENTENCES IN THE ORDER YOU HEAR THEM

A Can I ask about your cookery course? ☐

B Does the hairdressing course include work experience? ☐1

C Who can we speak to about art courses? ☐

D Yes. Students work once a week in a salon. ☐

E I'll show you to the art department. ☐

F I'm doing a life drawing class. Should be fun! ☐

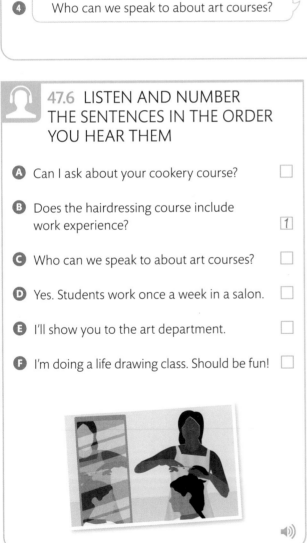

47.7 SAY THE SENTENCES OUT LOUD, FILLING IN THE GAPS USING THE WORDS IN THE PANEL

full-time	qualifications	website
salon	teacher	class
requirements	abroad	

1 What are your entry _____ ?

2 Sure, it's a two-year, _____ programme.

3 I've just signed up for the French _____ .

4 The _____ is amazing!

5 The _____ also has lots of information.

6 What _____ do I need?

7 Is there a chance to study _____ ?

8 Students work once a week in a _____ .

47.8 VOCABULARY DEPARTMENTS AND SUBJECTS

humanities

social sciences

chemistry

physics

biology

medicine

law

engineering

art and design

business

economics

politics

47.9 FIRST DAY AT COLLEGE

Excuse me, I'm new here. Do you know where I can leave my bike?

Yes, the bike store is round the corner. Enjoy your first day!

Hi, I'm Amy. I'm here for the business lecture.

Me too. I'm Lucas.

Hello, I'm your lecturer, Professor Li. Take a seat.

47.10 FINDING YOUR WAY AROUND

Can you tell me where the biology department is?

I'm going there, too. I'll show you.

Any idea where the art school is?

No, sorry. But I do know where the café is. Maybe you can ask in there?

47.11 LISTEN TO PERSON A AND RESPOND AS PERSON B

A | **B**

1. Do you know where I can leave my bike? | Yes, the bike store is round the corner.

2. Hi, I'm Amy. I'm here for the business lecture. | Hello, I'm your lecturer, Professor Li.

3. Can you tell me where the biology department is? | I'm going there, too. I'll show you.

4. Any idea where the art school is? | No, sorry. But I do know where the café is.

47.12 LISTEN AND NUMBER THE PICTURES IN THE ORDER THEY ARE DESCRIBED

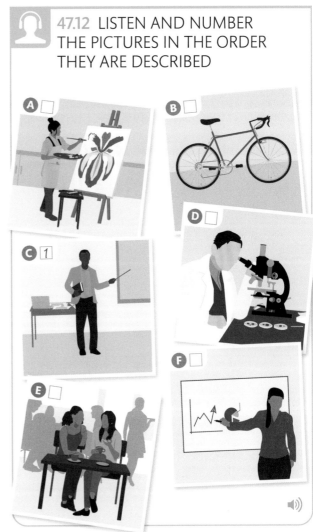

A ☐   B ☐

C 1   D ☐

E ☐   F ☐

47.13 USE THE CHART TO CREATE 12 SENTENCES AND SAY THEM OUT LOUD

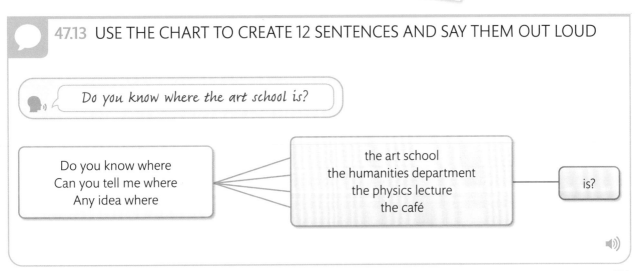

Do you know where the art school is?

Do you know where	the art school	
Can you tell me where	the humanities department	is?
Any idea where	the physics lecture	
	the café	

47.14 SETTLING IN

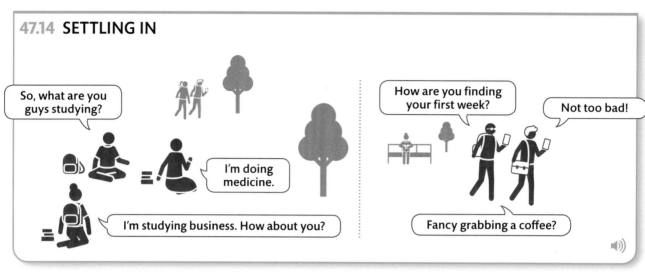

So, what are you guys studying?

I'm doing medicine.

I'm studying business. How about you?

How are you finding your first week?

Not too bad!

Fancy grabbing a coffee?

47.15 STUDENT SUPPORT

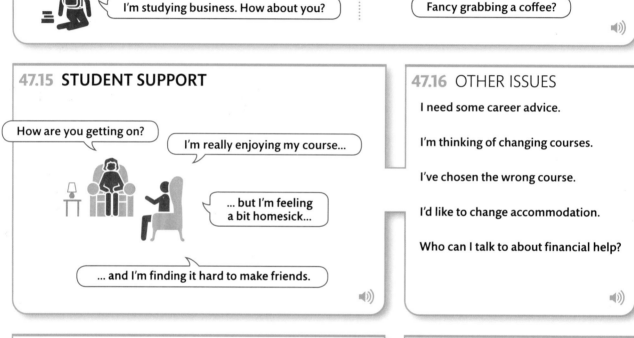

How are you getting on?

I'm really enjoying my course...

... but I'm feeling a bit homesick...

... and I'm finding it hard to make friends.

47.16 OTHER ISSUES

I need some career advice.

I'm thinking of changing courses.

I've chosen the wrong course.

I'd like to change accommodation.

Who can I talk to about financial help?

47.17 JOINING CLUBS

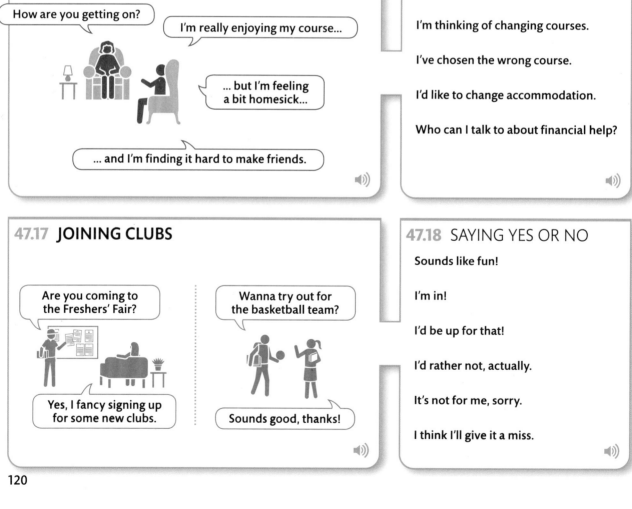

Are you coming to the Freshers' Fair?

Yes, I fancy signing up for some new clubs.

Wanna try out for the basketball team?

Sounds good, thanks!

47.18 SAYING YES OR NO

Sounds like fun!

I'm in!

I'd be up for that!

I'd rather not, actually.

It's not for me, sorry.

I think I'll give it a miss.

47.19 LISTEN AND CIRCLE THE ITEM YOU HEAR

1. (A) / B
2. A / B
3. A / B
4. A / B

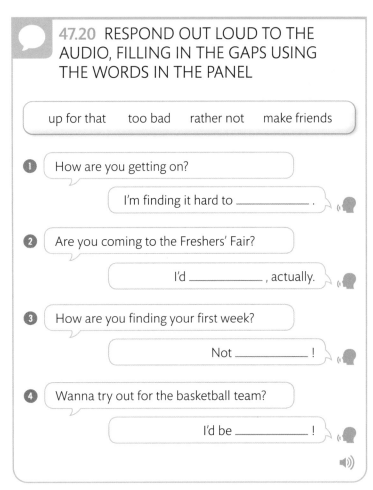

47.20 RESPOND OUT LOUD TO THE AUDIO, FILLING IN THE GAPS USING THE WORDS IN THE PANEL

up for that   too bad   rather not   make friends

1. How are you getting on?

   I'm finding it hard to _____ .

2. Are you coming to the Freshers' Fair?

   I'd _____ , actually.

3. How are you finding your first week?

   Not _____ !

4. Wanna try out for the basketball team?

   I'd be _____ !

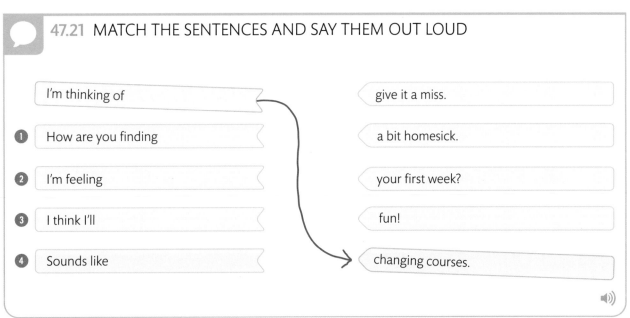

47.21 MATCH THE SENTENCES AND SAY THEM OUT LOUD

| I'm thinking of | → | changing courses. |

- give it a miss.
- a bit homesick.

1. How are you finding — your first week?
2. I'm feeling
3. I think I'll
4. Sounds like — fun!

48 Looking for work

48.1 JOB SEARCHING

This job looks interesting...

... flexible hours...

... no experience needed...

... sounds ideal!

Have you used this job search website?

Yes, I found my current job on there.

Is the job in the window still vacant?

BAR STAFF WANTED

Yes, could you email us your CV?

48.2 AT THE EMPLOYMENT AGENCY

How can I help?

I'm looking for a part-time sales job.

Okay, let me take some details about you.

Have you worked in a restaurant before?

I worked as a server last summer.

48.3 QUESTIONS YOU MAY HEAR

What skills have you got?

What hours can you work?

What experience have you got?

What salary are you looking for?

Why did you leave your last job?

48.4 LISTEN TO PERSON A AND RESPOND AS PERSON B

A		B
① How can I help?		I'm looking for a part-time sales job.
② Is the job in the window still vacant?		Yes, could you email us your CV?
③ Have you used this job search website?		Yes, I found my current job on there.
④ Have you worked in a restaurant before?		I worked as a server last summer.

48.5 LISTEN AND NUMBER THE SENTENCES IN THE ORDER YOU HEAR THEM

Ⓐ What hours can you work? ☐

Ⓑ What skills have you got? ☐

Ⓒ What salary are you looking for? ☐

Ⓓ What experience have you got? ☐

Ⓔ Have you worked in a restaurant before? ☐

Ⓕ How can I help? [1]

Ⓖ Is the job in the window still vacant? ☐

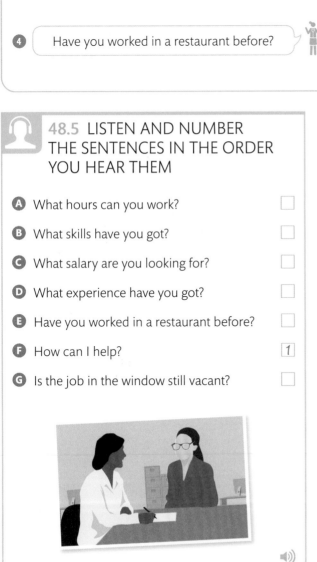

48.6 SAY THE SENTENCES OUT LOUD, FILLING IN THE GAPS USING THE WORDS IN THE PANEL

skills	website	part-time
details	window	job
hours	CV	

① Okay, let me take some _____ about you.

② This _____ looks interesting...

③ I'm looking for a _____ sales job.

④ What _____ can you work?

⑤ Have you used this job search _____ ?

⑥ Yes, could you email us your _____ ?

⑦ What _____ have you got?

⑧ Is the job in the _____ still vacant?

49 Applying for a job

49.1 PREPARING A CV

I really want to apply for this job. I must update my CV!

There are loads of examples online to help you.

It says the deadline for applications is tomorrow.

Really? I'd better email my CV tonight, then.

My CV is all checked and ready to go...

Don't forget to send your covering letter, too!

49.2 APPLICATION FORMS

Have you finished your application yet?

I just need to fill in my personal details and it'll be ready.

This application form is taking ages!

Why don't you save it and take a break?

49.3 VOCABULARY JOB APPLICATIONS

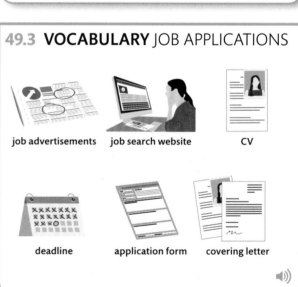

job advertisements   job search website   CV

deadline   application form   covering letter

49.4 LISTEN TO PERSON A AND RESPOND AS PERSON B

A   **B**

1 I must update my CV!   There are loads of examples online to help you.

2 It says the deadline for applications is tomorrow.   Really? I'd better email my CV tonight, then.

3 Have you finished your application yet?   I just need to fill in my personal details and it'll be ready.

4 This application form is taking ages!   Why don't you save it and take a break?

49.5 LISTEN AND CIRCLE THE ITEM YOU HEAR

49.6 MATCH THE SENTENCES AND SAY THEM OUT LOUD

I must update → my CV!

1 I really want to apply for — this job.

2 I just need to fill in — my personal details and it'll be ready.

3 Don't forget to send — your covering letter, too!

4 Have you finished — your application yet?

your application yet?

50 Job interviews

50.1 INTERVIEWERS' QUESTIONS

Why are you right for this position?

I've got the qualifications and experience you're looking for.

What can you bring to our company?

Enthusiasm, energy, and lots of ideas.

Why did you apply for this job?

I'm really keen to use my planning skills.

50.2 MORE QUESTIONS YOU MAY HEAR

What experience do you have in...?

What are your strengths?

What do you enjoy doing outside work?

What are your goals for the future?

Why do you want to leave your current job?

What salary are you expecting?

What's the notice period in your current job?

How soon could you start?

50.3 TALKING ABOUT YOURSELF

Tell me about yourself.

I'm reliable and organized.

I work well in a team.

I'm good with customers.

I'm used to working under pressure.

50.4 MORE PHRASES

I can adapt to new situations.

I'm a quick learner.

I'm self-motivated.

I have an excellent track record.

I enjoy solving problems.

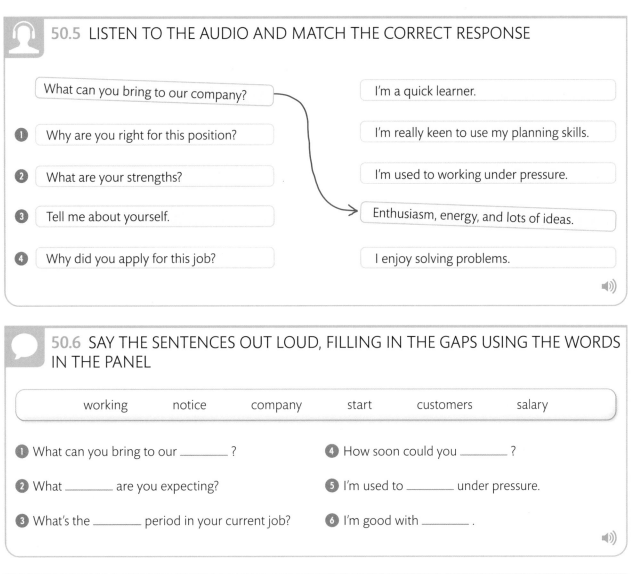

50.5 LISTEN TO THE AUDIO AND MATCH THE CORRECT RESPONSE

What can you bring to our company? → Enthusiasm, energy, and lots of ideas.

I'm a quick learner.

❶ Why are you right for this position?

I'm really keen to use my planning skills.

❷ What are your strengths?

I'm used to working under pressure.

❸ Tell me about yourself.

I enjoy solving problems.

❹ Why did you apply for this job?

50.6 SAY THE SENTENCES OUT LOUD, FILLING IN THE GAPS USING THE WORDS IN THE PANEL

| working | notice | company | start | customers | salary |

❶ What can you bring to our _____ ?

❷ What _____ are you expecting?

❸ What's the _____ period in your current job?

❹ How soon could you _____ ?

❺ I'm used to _____ under pressure.

❻ I'm good with _____ .

50.7 USE THE CHART TO CREATE FIVE SENTENCES AND SAY THEM OUT LOUD

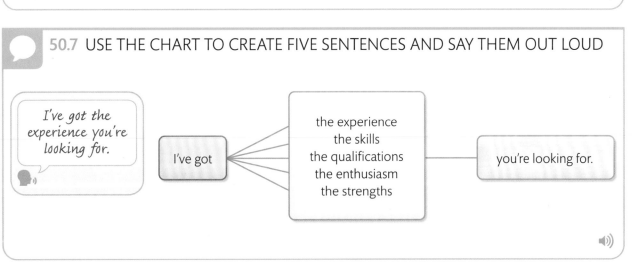

I've got the experience you're looking for.

I've got | the experience / the skills / the qualifications / the enthusiasm / the strengths | you're looking for.

51 Starting a new job

51.1 SETTING UP

Hello, I'm Christina. It's my first day.

Welcome! Here's your pass. I'll let the manager know you're here.

I've set up your email account. Can you type in a password?

Okay. How long does it have to be?

51.2 MORE PHRASES

Your supervisor will show you where everything is.

Let's find you a locker.

Anything you need, just ask.

You'll need to clock out at the end of your shift.

Your first break is at 12.30.

51.3 MEETING COLLEAGUES

How's it going so far?

There's lots to remember, but I'm getting there!

Let me know if you get stuck.

51.4 MORE PHRASES

It's great to have you on the team.

How's your morning been?

Have you got everything you need?

Have you met everybody now?

Shall we grab some lunch?

51.5 HEALTH & SAFETY

You need to read these safety rules carefully.

And always wear your hard hat!

51.6 LISTEN TO PERSON A AND RESPOND AS PERSON B

A | **B**

1. Hello, I'm Christina. It's my first day. | Here's your pass. I'll let the manager know you're here.

2. How's it going so far? | There's lots to remember, but I'm getting there!

3. Can you type in a password? | Okay. How long does it have to be?

4. You need to read these safety rules carefully. | And always wear your hard hat!

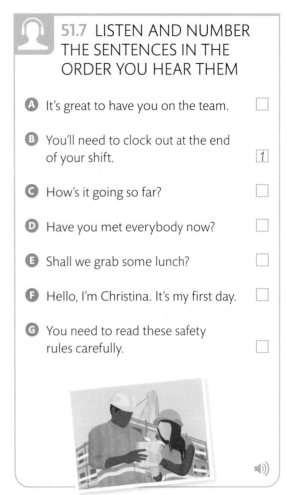

51.7 LISTEN AND NUMBER THE SENTENCES IN THE ORDER YOU HEAR THEM

A) It's great to have you on the team. ☐

B) You'll need to clock out at the end of your shift. ☐ 1

C) How's it going so far? ☐

D) Have you met everybody now? ☐

E) Shall we grab some lunch? ☐

F) Hello, I'm Christina. It's my first day. ☐

G) You need to read these safety rules carefully. ☐

51.8 SAY THE SENTENCES OUT LOUD, FILLING IN THE GAPS USING THE WORDS IN THE PANEL

break   everything   hard hat   password

email   lunch   morning   team

1. Your first _____ is at 12.30.

2. And always wear your _____ !

3. It's great to have you on the _____ .

4. I've set up your _____ account.

5. Shall we grab some _____ ?

6. How's your _____ been?

7. Have you got _____ you need?

8. Can you type in a _____ ?

52 In the workplace

52.1 WORKPLACE ROUTINES

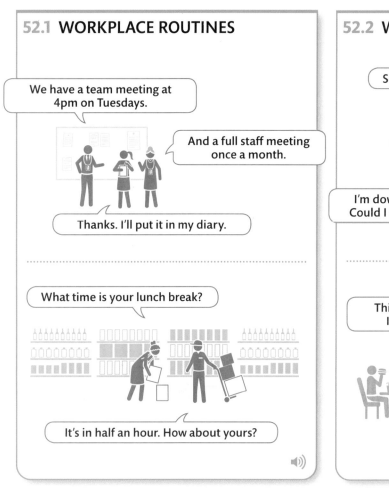

We have a team meeting at 4pm on Tuesdays.

And a full staff meeting once a month.

Thanks. I'll put it in my diary.

What time is your lunch break?

It's in half an hour. How about yours?

52.2 WORKPLACE ISSUES

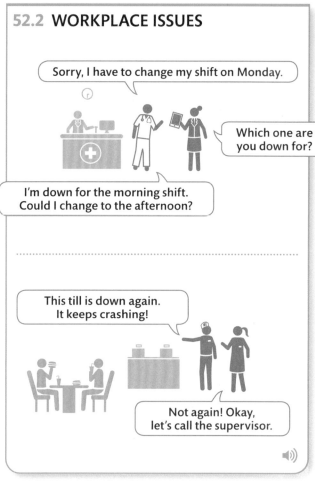

Sorry, I have to change my shift on Monday.

Which one are you down for?

I'm down for the morning shift. Could I change to the afternoon?

This till is down again. It keeps crashing!

Not again! Okay, let's call the supervisor.

52.3 VOCABULARY AT WORK

meeting

lunch break

tea break

morning shift

afternoon shift

evening shift

manager

supervisor

colleague

team

to clock in / out

locker

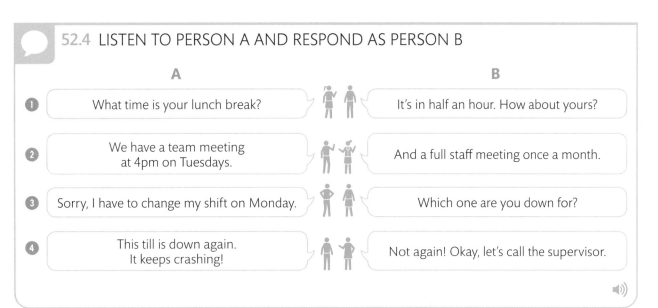

52.4 LISTEN TO PERSON A AND RESPOND AS PERSON B

A

B

1. What time is your lunch break? / It's in half an hour. How about yours?

2. We have a team meeting at 4pm on Tuesdays. / And a full staff meeting once a month.

3. Sorry, I have to change my shift on Monday. / Which one are you down for?

4. This till is down again. It keeps crashing! / Not again! Okay, let's call the supervisor.

52.5 LISTEN AND CIRCLE THE ITEM YOU HEAR

1. Ⓐ Ⓑ

2. Ⓐ Ⓑ

3. Ⓐ Ⓑ

4. Ⓐ Ⓑ

52.6 RESPOND OUT LOUD TO THE AUDIO, FILLING IN THE GAPS USING THE WORDS IN THE PANEL

down for   let's call   How about   put it in

1. What time is your lunch break?

   It's in half an hour. _____ yours?

2. This till is down again. It keeps crashing!

   Not again! Okay, _____ the supervisor.

3. Which one are you down for?

   I'm _____ the morning shift.

4. We have a team meeting at 4pm on Tuesdays.

   Thanks. I'll _____ my diary.

53 Giving a presentation

53.1 GETTING STARTED

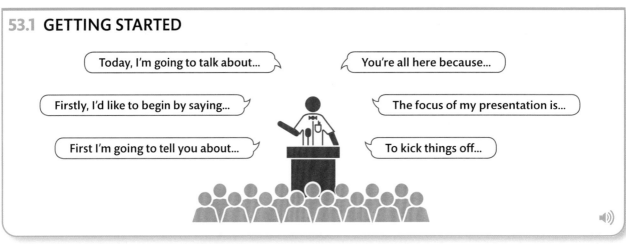

Today, I'm going to talk about...

You're all here because...

Firstly, I'd like to begin by saying...

The focus of my presentation is...

First I'm going to tell you about...

To kick things off...

53.2 CHANGING THE SUBJECT

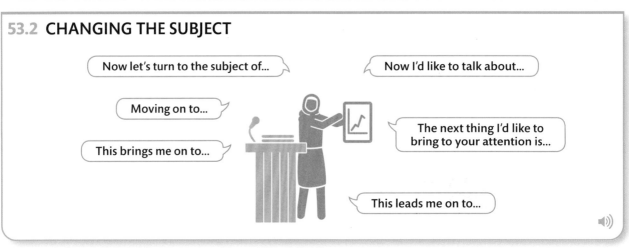

Now let's turn to the subject of...

Now I'd like to talk about...

Moving on to...

The next thing I'd like to bring to your attention is...

This brings me on to...

This leads me on to...

53.3 FINISHING UP

Lastly, I'd like to finish by saying...

I think I've covered everything. Any questions?

Finally, I want to let you know that...

Does anyone have anything to add?

So, to sum up, I'd say...

53.4 LISTEN AND NUMBER THE SENTENCES IN THE ORDER YOU HEAR THEM

A To kick things off... ☐

B So, to sum up, I'd say... ☐1

C Moving on to... ☐

D First, I'm going to tell you about... ☐

E Lastly, I'd like to finish by saying... ☐

F This leads me on to... ☐

G Firstly, I'd like to begin by saying... ☐

H Does anyone have anything to add? ☐

53.5 MATCH THE SENTENCES AND SAY THEM OUT LOUD

I think I've covered everything.

1 Now let's turn to

2 The focus of

3 Lastly,

4 Does anyone have

5 Now I'd like to

6 Firstly,

my presentation is...

I'd like to begin by saying...

Any questions?

anything to add?

talk about...

the subject of...

I'd like to finish by saying...

53.6 USE THE CHART TO CREATE 10 SENTENCES AND SAY THEM OUT LOUD

Today, I'd like to talk about...

| Today, Firstly, Now Lastly, Finally, | I'd like to I'm going to | talk about... |

54 Work meetings

54.1 SETTING THE AGENDA

I think we're all here, so let's get started.

What's on today's agenda?

We're starting with how to improve our customer service.

Listen up, everyone! There's a lot to get through.

First up is deciding next week's menus...

... then we'll move on to the rotas.

54.2 TAKING TURNS TO TALK

So that's the situation. Let's hear your thoughts.

If I can just add... It will be a slow process.

Can I go first? For me, these changes are important.

Let's hear from James on this point.

Just to clarify... Which changes exactly?

Could I just jump in? I totally agree.

54.3 SHARING OPINIONS

Let's go round the table and see where we all stand.

I'm 100% on board with this.

If you ask me, it's a non-starter.

54.4 MORE PHRASES

Why don't we try...?

The way I see it is...

How about if we...?

I see where you're coming from, so...

I'm wondering if we could...?

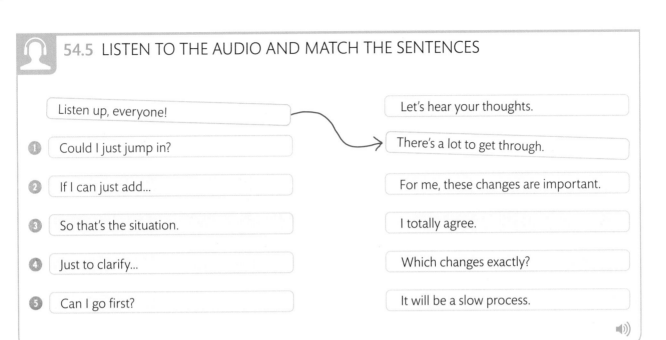

54.5 LISTEN TO THE AUDIO AND MATCH THE SENTENCES

Listen up, everyone!

Let's hear your thoughts.

1 Could I just jump in?

There's a lot to get through.

2 If I can just add...

For me, these changes are important.

3 So that's the situation.

I totally agree.

4 Just to clarify...

Which changes exactly?

5 Can I go first?

It will be a slow process.

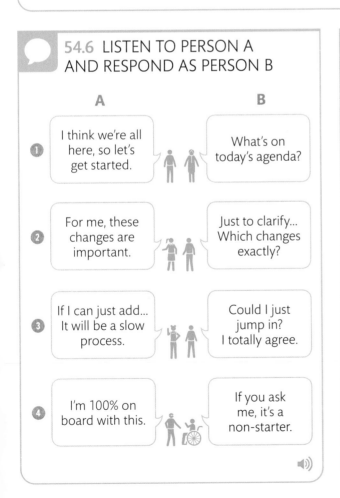

54.6 LISTEN TO PERSON A AND RESPOND AS PERSON B

A | B

1 I think we're all here, so let's get started. | What's on today's agenda?

2 For me, these changes are important. | Just to clarify... Which changes exactly?

3 If I can just add... It will be a slow process. | Could I just jump in? I totally agree.

4 I'm 100% on board with this. | If you ask me, it's a non-starter.

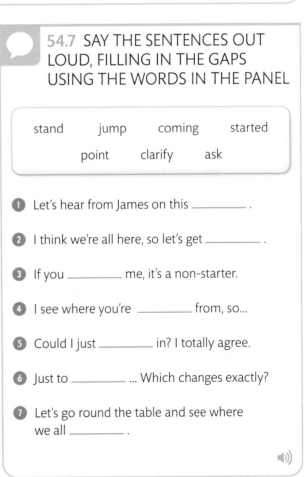

54.7 SAY THE SENTENCES OUT LOUD, FILLING IN THE GAPS USING THE WORDS IN THE PANEL

stand   jump   coming   started
point   clarify   ask

1 Let's hear from James on this _____ .

2 I think we're all here, so let's get _____ .

3 If you _____ me, it's a non-starter.

4 I see where you're _____ from, so...

5 Could I just _____ in? I totally agree.

6 Just to _____ ... Which changes exactly?

7 Let's go round the table and see where we all _____ .

54.8 ENDING THE MEETING

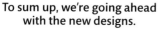

"To sum up, we're going ahead with the new designs."

"Any questions before we wrap up?"

"To recap, we've agreed to change the timetable."

"I'll email the action points to you all later."

"Great. Thanks everyone for your input!"

54.9 NETWORKING

"I understand you work for AbiCo."

"That's right. Sorry, I didn't catch your name."

"It was great meeting you."

"You, too. Let's stay in touch. Here's my card."

"Thanks. I'll let you know if something suitable comes up."

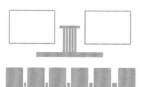

"Your project sounds really interesting."

"I've enjoyed our discussion."

"I'd love to keep the conversation going."

"Me too. Let's follow it up in the office."

54.10 LISTEN TO PERSON A AND RESPOND AS PERSON B

A   **B**

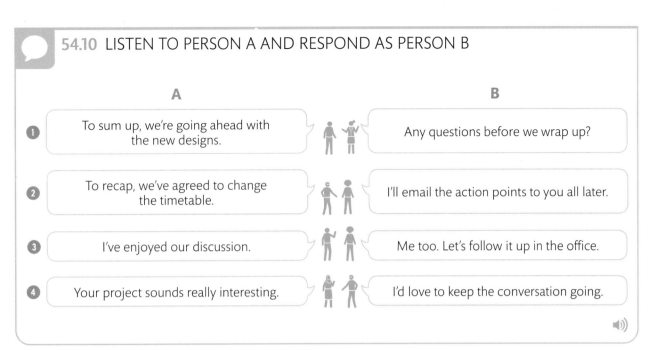

1. To sum up, we're going ahead with the new designs. → Any questions before we wrap up?

2. To recap, we've agreed to change the timetable. → I'll email the action points to you all later.

3. I've enjoyed our discussion. → Me too. Let's follow it up in the office.

4. Your project sounds really interesting. → I'd love to keep the conversation going.

54.11 LISTEN AND NUMBER THE SENTENCES IN THE ORDER YOU HEAR THEM

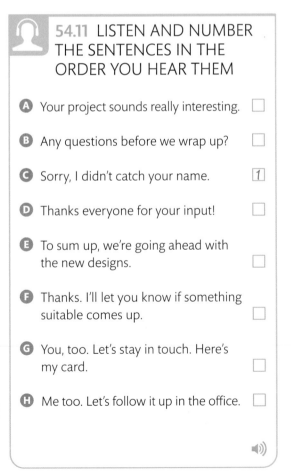

A. Your project sounds really interesting. ☐

B. Any questions before we wrap up? ☐

C. Sorry, I didn't catch your name. ☐ 1

D. Thanks everyone for your input! ☐

E. To sum up, we're going ahead with the new designs. ☐

F. Thanks. I'll let you know if something suitable comes up. ☐

G. You, too. Let's stay in touch. Here's my card. ☐

H. Me too. Let's follow it up in the office. ☐

54.12 RESPOND OUT LOUD TO THE AUDIO, FILLING IN THE GAPS USING THE WORDS IN THE PANEL

your name   in touch   follow it up

1. It was great meeting you.

   You, too. Let's stay _____ .

2. I understand you work for AbiCo.

   That's right. Sorry, I didn't catch _____ .

3. I've enjoyed our discussion.

   Me too. Let's _____ in the office.

137

55 Online meetings

55.1 GETTING STARTED

Let's get going, shall we?

I'll share the presentation on my screen.

Can you hear me?

I think you're on mute.

That's everyone now.

Right, I'll run through the key points.

55.2 MORE PHRASES

Would you like to speak first?

Could you repeat that, please?

Can you enlarge it on your screen?

Sorry for interrupting, please carry on.

55.3 CONNECTION PROBLEMS

I think we've lost Sam.

My connection keeps dropping out.

Sorry everyone, my Wi-Fi's slow.

Sorry, my screen has frozen.

We can hear you, but we can't see you.

Try leaving the meeting and joining again.

55.4 THE NEXT MEETING

Shall we put in another meeting?

Good idea. I'll send you an invite.

55.5 LISTEN TO PERSON A AND RESPOND AS PERSON B

A   **B**

1. Let's get going, shall we? — I'll share the presentation on my screen.
2. Can you hear me? — I think you're on mute.
3. I think we've lost Sam. — My connection keeps dropping out.
4. Sorry, my screen has frozen. — Try leaving the meeting and joining again.

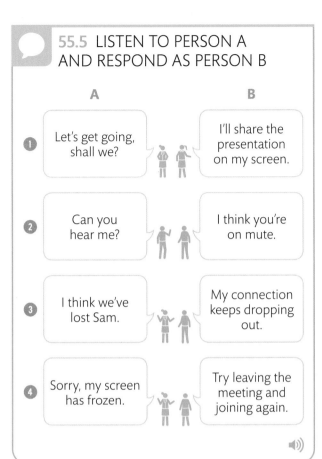

55.6 LISTEN AND NUMBER THE SENTENCES IN THE ORDER THAT YOU HEAR THEM

- **A** Let's get going, shall we? ☐
- **B** I think you're on mute. ☐
- **C** Sorry, my screen has frozen. ☐
- **D** Try leaving the meeting and joining again. [1]
- **E** Can you hear me? ☐
- **F** I'll share the presentation on my screen. ☐
- **G** My connection keeps dropping out. ☐

55.7 MATCH THE SENTENCES AND SAY THEM OUT LOUD

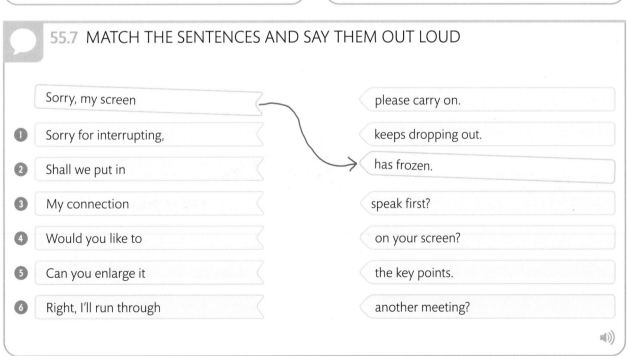

Sorry, my screen — has frozen.

1. Sorry for interrupting, — please carry on.
2. Shall we put in — keeps dropping out.
3. My connection — speak first?
4. Would you like to — on your screen?
5. Can you enlarge it — the key points.
6. Right, I'll run through — another meeting?

56 Home

Home

56.1 HOMES AND NEIGHBOURHOODS

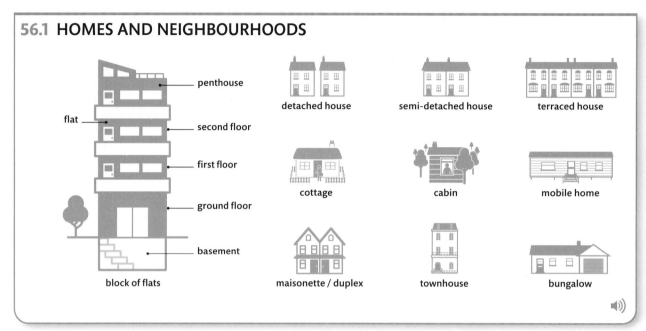

penthouse

flat

second floor

first floor

ground floor

basement

block of flats

detached house

semi-detached house

terraced house

cottage

cabin

mobile home

maisonette / duplex

townhouse

bungalow

56.2 ROOMS AND HOME AREAS

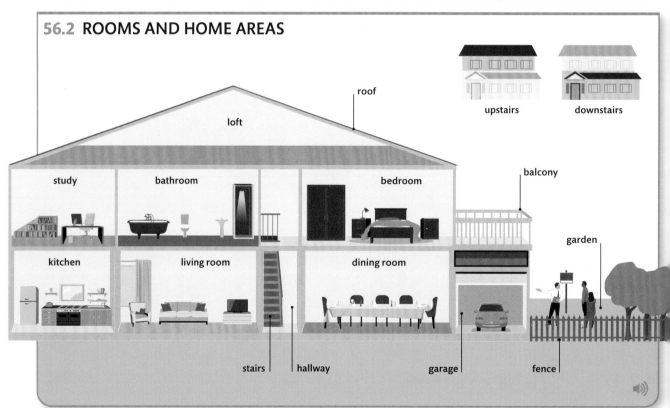

roof

loft

upstairs

downstairs

balcony

study

bathroom

bedroom

garden

kitchen

living room

dining room

stairs

hallway

garage

fence

56.3 HOME IMPROVEMENTS

to paint a door

to grout tiles

to strip the walls

to fill a crack

to rewire the house

to fix a fence

to put up shelves

to fit a carpet

to make curtains

to build an extension

56.4 APPLIANCES AND FURNITURE

fridge-freezer

oven

washing machine

dishwasher

sink

bath

shower

toilet

wash basin

mirror

bed

cot

wardrobe

bedside table

chest of drawers

sofa

armchair

coffee table

ottoman

toy box

shelf

bookcase

dining table

dining chair

television / TV

sideboard

57 Finding a new home

57.1 HOUSE-HUNTING

What sort of property are you looking for?

A one-bedroom place in the city centre.

57.2 SAYING WHAT YOU WANT

I'm looking for a flat on the ground floor.

We'd like a house with a garden.

I want a property close to the station.

We'd prefer somewhere near a school.

We need at least two bedrooms.

57.3 VIEWING A PROPERTY

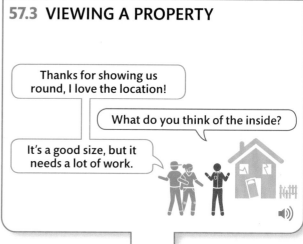

Thanks for showing us round, I love the location!

What do you think of the inside?

It's a good size, but it needs a lot of work.

57.4 GIVING FEEDBACK

I think it's too small for us.

It's on a busy road.

I quite like the layout.

We'd need to put in a new kitchen.

We like it, but the price is too high.

57.5 PUTTING IN AN OFFER

How do you feel after seeing it again?

We love it even more!

Would you like to put in an offer?

Yes, for £5,000 under the asking price.

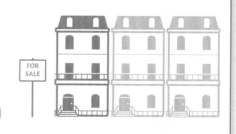

FOR SALE

57.6 LISTEN TO PERSON A AND RESPOND AS PERSON B

A		B
❶ What sort of property are you looking for?		A one-bedroom place in the city centre.
❷ What do you think of the inside?		It's a good size, but it needs a lot of work.
❸ How do you feel after seeing it again?		We love it even more!
❹ Would you like to put in an offer?		Yes, for £5,000 under the asking price.

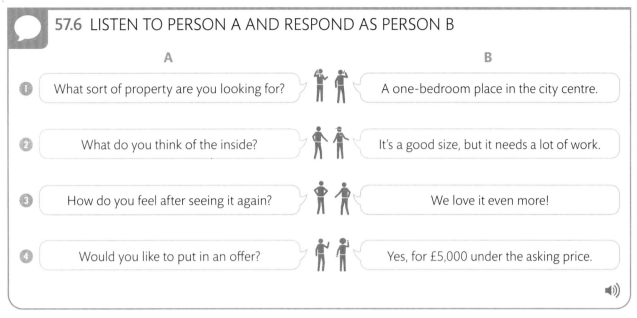

57.7 MATCH THE SENTENCES AND SAY THEM OUT LOUD

It's on → a busy road.

❶ We'd need to — put in a new kitchen.

❷ I want a property — the layout.

❸ I quite like — it's too small for us.

❹ I think — close to the station.

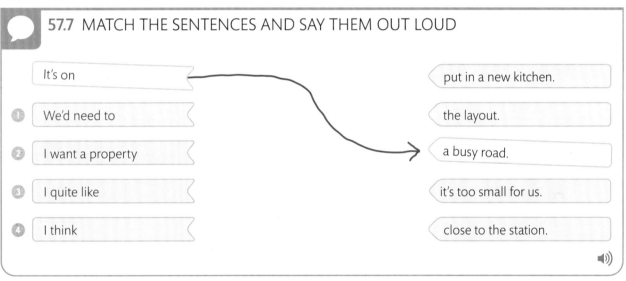

57.8 USE THE CHART TO CREATE NINE SENTENCES AND SAY THEM OUT LOUD

We'd like a house with a garden.

| We'd like | a house
a flat
a property | with a garden.
close to the station.
near a school. |

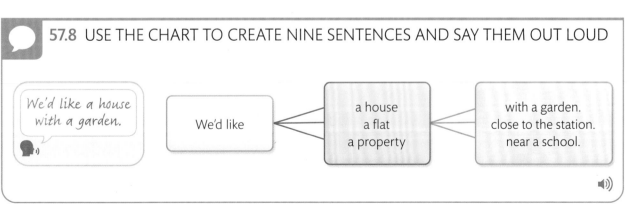

57.9 RENTING A HOME

How long does the tenancy run for?

One year, with an option to renew.

How soon could we move in?

As soon as you've signed the tenancy agreement!

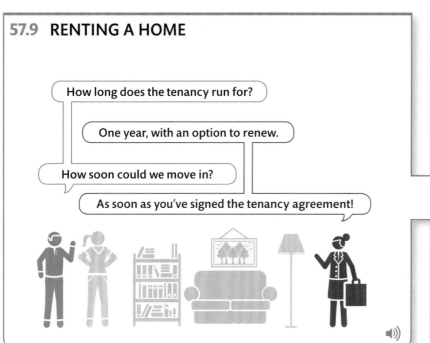

57.10 MORE QUESTIONS

How much is the rent?

Do I pay the rent monthly?

Can I rent it unfurnished?

Do you need a deposit?

Are utility bills included?

Are pets allowed?

Can I have a flatmate?

What references do you need?

57.11 DURING THE TENANCY

Can I put this picture up?

Yes, as long as it doesn't leave marks on the wall.

The washing machine is leaking.

I'll get an engineer to come and look at it.

57.12 VOCABULARY RENTING PROPERTY

landlord / landlady

tenant

flatmate

rent

deposit

tenancy agreement

furnished

unfurnished

utility bills

57.13 LISTEN AND NUMBER THE SENTENCES IN THE ORDER YOU HEAR THEM

A How soon could we move in? ☐

B One year, with an option to renew. 1

C Can I rent it unfurnished? ☐

D The washing machine is leaking. ☐

E Can I have a flatmate? ☐

F How much is the rent? ☐

🔊

57.14 SAY THE SENTENCES OUT LOUD, REPLACING THE PICTURES WITH WORDS

1 How much is the [picture] ?

2 Are [picture] included?

3 Can I put this [picture] up?

4 The [picture] is leaking.

5 Are [picture] allowed?

6 As soon as you've signed the [picture] !

🔊

57.15 SAY THE SENTENCES OUT LOUD, FILLING IN THE GAPS USING THE WORDS IN THE PANEL

bills	unfurnished	pay	renew	deposit	references

1 Can I rent it _____ ?

2 One year, with an option to _____ .

3 Are utility _____ included?

4 Do you need a _____ ?

5 Do I _____ the rent monthly?

6 What _____ do you need?

🔊

145

58 Moving house

58.1 PACKING UP

I'm moving house! Do you have any spare boxes?

There are lots in the back. Help yourself!

Is everything packed and ready?

Yes, we're done. Let's load the van!

58.2 MOVING DAY

I'm here to pick up the keys to my flat.

Here you are. Hope the move goes well!

Where do you want us to start?

Can you take the boxes in the kitchen first?

That's the unpacking done!

Nice work! Now, you sit down and have a cup of tea.

58.3 VOCABULARY RELOCATION

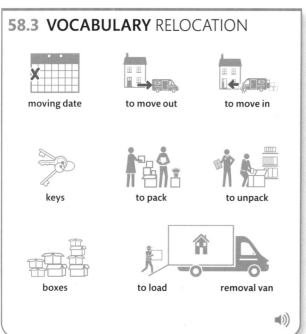

moving date

to move out

to move in

keys

to pack

to unpack

boxes

to load

removal van

58.4 MORE PHRASES

I've told everyone our moving date.

We have to move out by the weekend.

I've packed up the bedroom.

Let's load the removal van!

We can unpack in the morning.

58.5 LISTEN AND NUMBER THE PICTURES IN THE ORDER THEY ARE DESCRIBED

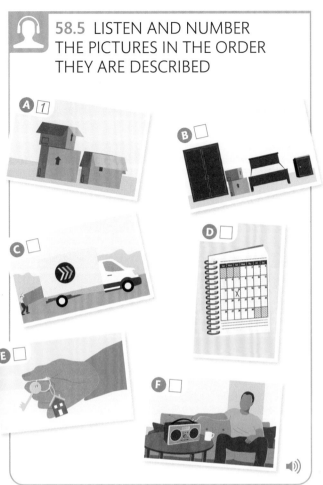

A 1
B ☐
C ☐
D ☐
E ☐
F ☐

58.6 SAY THE SENTENCES OUT LOUD, FILLING IN THE GAPS USING THE WORDS IN THE PANEL

| unpack | ready | the move | packed |
| weekend | load | boxes | moving |

1 Is everything packed and _____ ?

2 Hope _____ goes well!

3 Do you have any spare _____ ?

4 I've told everyone our _____ date.

5 We have to move out by the _____ .

6 I've _____ up the bedroom.

7 Let's _____ the removal van!

8 We can _____ in the morning.

58.7 MATCH THE SENTENCES AND SAY THEM OUT LOUD

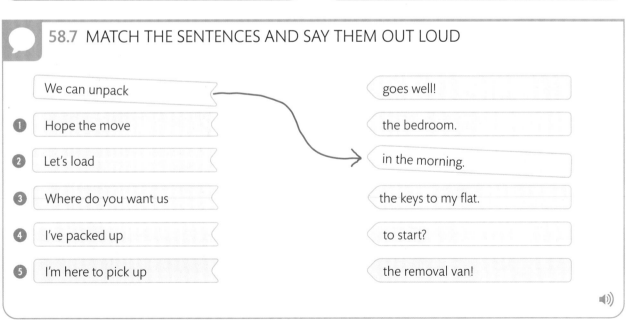

We can unpack → in the morning.

1 Hope the move — goes well!

2 Let's load — the bedroom.

3 Where do you want us — the keys to my flat.

4 I've packed up — to start?

5 I'm here to pick up — the removal van!

59 Meeting the neighbours

59.1 INTRODUCING YOURSELF

Hi! I've just moved in next door.

Yes, I saw you arrive. Welcome to the neighbourhood!

Hello, I live downstairs. I've brought you a housewarming gift.

That's so kind of you!

59.2 MORE PHRASES

It's so nice to meet you.

We've moved here from Beijing.

I'm your new neighbour.

I wanted to introduce myself.

I just came over to say hello.

59.3 SOCIALIZING

We're having a housewarming party on Saturday – would you like to join us?

I'd love to, thank you!

59.4 MORE PHRASES

Would you like to pop over for drinks later?

Are you free for lunch on Sunday?

Can you come over for coffee tomorrow?

I'd love you to come to my barbecue next week.

59.5 SHARING INFORMATION

Would you like to join our local group chat?

Yes, please! I'd love to get to know the neighbours.

Street Chat

Does anyone know a good plumber?

I do! I'll find their number and send it to you.

I know one, too!

59.6 LISTEN TO PERSON A AND RESPOND AS PERSON B

A	B
1 Hi! I've just moved in next door.	Yes, I saw you arrive. Welcome to the neighbourhood!
2 Hello, I live downstairs. I've brought you a housewarming gift.	That's so kind of you!
3 We're having a housewarming party on Saturday – would you like to join us?	I'd love to, thank you!
4 Would you like to join our local group chat?	Yes, please! I'd love to get to know the neighbours.
5 Does anyone know a good plumber?	I do! I'll find their number and send it to you.

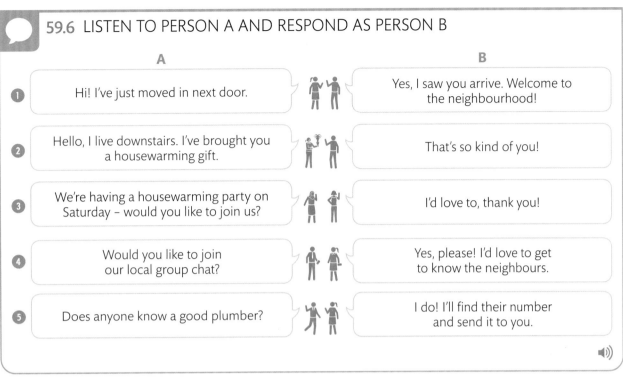

59.7 LISTEN AND NUMBER THE SENTENCES IN THE ORDER YOU HEAR THEM

A It's so nice to meet you. ☐

B Can you come over for coffee tomorrow? ☐

C I'm your new neighbour. ☐

D I'd love you to come to my barbecue next week. ☐

E I just came over to say hello. ☐

F Are you free for lunch on Sunday? ☐

G We've moved here from Beijing. 1

H Would you like to pop over for drinks later? ☐

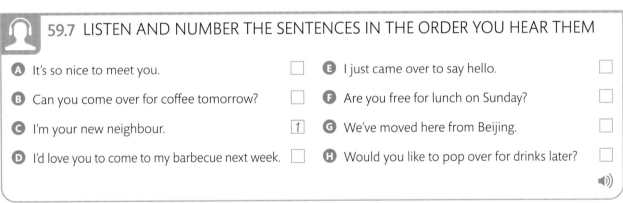

59.8 USE THE CHART TO CREATE NINE SENTENCES AND SAY THEM OUT LOUD

Are you free for drinks later?

Are you free for → drinks / lunch / coffee → later? / tomorrow? / on Sunday?

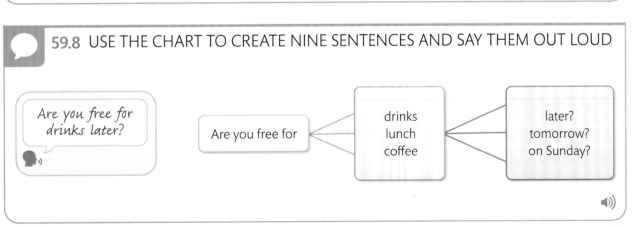

60 Household chores

60.1 SHARING TASKS

Hey, what are you up to?

I'm making a rota for the chores.

Your turn to do the washing-up, then!

Whose turn is it to empty the dishwasher?

I did it last time, so it's yours!

Have you finished doing the laundry yet?

Nearly! Can you help me put it away?

GOOD TO KNOW

In English, it's easy to confuse the verbs **to make** and **to do**! **To do** is associated with work and often used for chores. The main exception is **to make the bed**.

60.2 SPRING CLEANING

There we go. The house looks much tidier now!

Phew! That was a proper spring clean!

I've cleaned the worktops and the oven.

Great job! The kitchen was in a right state.

60.3 VOCABULARY HOUSEWORK

to do the laundry

to do the washing-up

to do the vacuuming

to empty the dishwasher

to clean the bath

to sweep the floor

to put the rubbish out

to tidy up

to make the bed

60.4 LISTEN TO PERSON A AND RESPOND AS PERSON B

A

B

1. Hey, what are you up to? → I'm making a rota for the chores.

2. Have you finished doing the laundry yet? → Nearly! Can you help me put it away?

3. I've cleaned the worktops and the oven. → Great job! The kitchen was in a right state.

4. There we go. The house looks much tidier now! → Phew! That was a proper spring clean!

60.5 LISTEN AND CIRCLE THE ITEM YOU HEAR

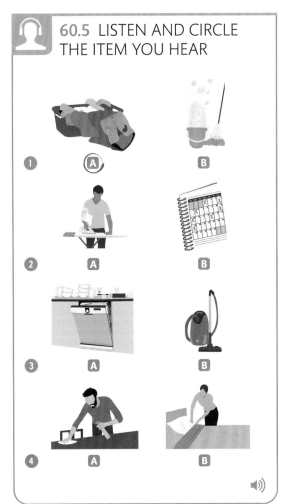

1. A B
2. A B
3. A B
4. A B

60.6 MATCH THE SENTENCES AND SAY THEM OUT LOUD

Have you finished doing → the laundry yet?

1. Whose turn is it to empty — the dishwasher?

2. I've cleaned the worktops — and the oven.

3. Great job! The kitchen — was in a right state.

4. Phew! That was — a proper spring clean!

61 Home improvements

61.1 DIY DECORATING

How are you getting on?

The tiles are all up. Just the grouting to go and I'm done!

I've finished stripping the walls.

Great! Let's hang this new wallpaper, then.

It's looking good!

Thank you, one more coat of paint should do it, I reckon.

61.2 HIRING A PROFESSIONAL

ABC Decorators, how can I help?

Hi, we need someone to put up some shelves.

Sure, we can do that for you.

Are you able to come round and give us a quote?

I could come over on Thursday.

61.3 MORE PHRASES

Could you put up this wardrobe?

Can you give us a quote for fixing our fence?

We need someone to paint our kitchen walls.

I'd like a quote for fitting a carpet.

Is that your best quote?

Will you supply the materials?

61.4 LISTEN TO PERSON A AND RESPOND AS PERSON B

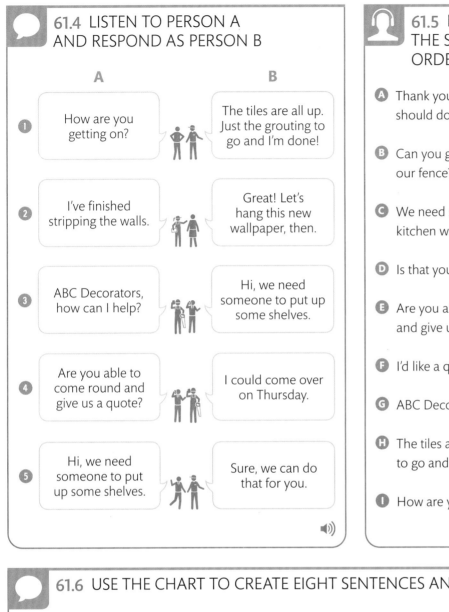

A

1 How are you getting on?

2 I've finished stripping the walls.

3 ABC Decorators, how can I help?

4 Are you able to come round and give us a quote?

5 Hi, we need someone to put up some shelves.

B

The tiles are all up. Just the grouting to go and I'm done!

Great! Let's hang this new wallpaper, then.

Hi, we need someone to put up some shelves.

I could come over on Thursday.

Sure, we can do that for you.

61.5 LISTEN AND NUMBER THE SENTENCES IN THE ORDER YOU HEAR THEM

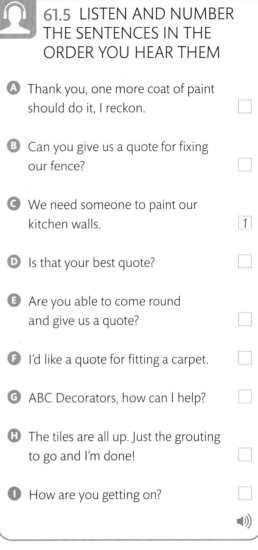

A Thank you, one more coat of paint should do it, I reckon. ☐

B Can you give us a quote for fixing our fence? ☐

C We need someone to paint our kitchen walls. ☐ *1*

D Is that your best quote? ☐

E Are you able to come round and give us a quote? ☐

F I'd like a quote for fitting a carpet. ☐

G ABC Decorators, how can I help? ☐

H The tiles are all up. Just the grouting to go and I'm done! ☐

I How are you getting on? ☐

61.6 USE THE CHART TO CREATE EIGHT SENTENCES AND SAY THEM OUT LOUD

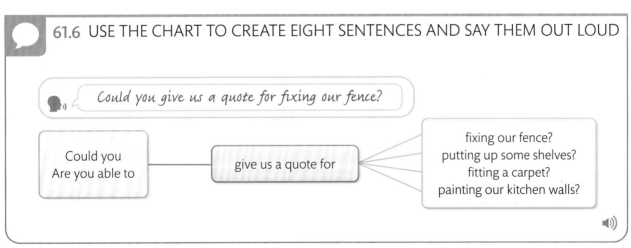

Could you give us a quote for fixing our fence?

| Could you / Are you able to | give us a quote for | fixing our fence? / putting up some shelves? / fitting a carpet? / painting our kitchen walls? |

62 Pets

62.1 ADOPTING A RESCUE ANIMAL

"Hi, I'd like to adopt a cat."

"I'm looking to home one of your dogs."

"Does she like other cats?"

"Is anyone home during the day?"

"Are you after a particular breed?"

"Is she good with children?"

"Yes, I work from home."

62.2 SEEING THE VET

"What seems to be the problem?"

"I think he's got a broken leg."

"She's lost weight and gone off her food."

"Yes, we'll need to do an X-ray."

62.3 MORE PROBLEMS

My dog has hurt his paw.

My cat keeps being sick.

My rabbit is losing her fur.

My puppy is very quiet.

She's always thirsty.

62.4 VOCABULARY PET CARE

vaccination

flea treatment

eye drops

grooming

microchip

pet passport

62.5 LOOKING AFTER YOUR PET

"So, we have to get him microchipped..."

"... give him his flea treatment..."

"... get him a passport..."

"... and book his vaccinations!"

62.6 LISTEN TO PERSON A AND RESPOND AS PERSON B

A	B
1 I'm looking to home one of your dogs.	Are you after a particular breed?
2 Is anyone home during the day?	Yes, I work from home.
3 What seems to be the problem?	She's lost weight and gone off her food.
4 I think he's got a broken leg.	Yes, we'll need to do an X-ray.

62.7 LISTEN AND NUMBER THE PICTURES IN THE ORDER THEY ARE DESCRIBED

Ⓐ 1   Ⓑ ☐

Ⓒ ☐   Ⓓ ☐

Ⓔ ☐   Ⓕ ☐

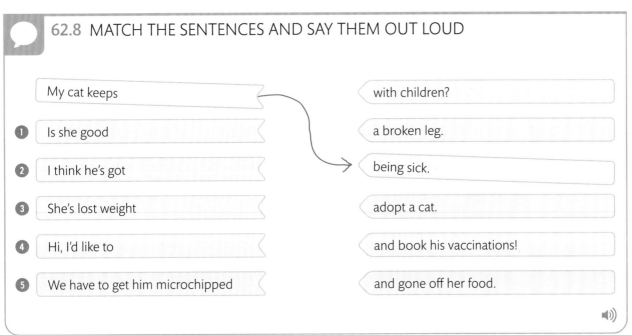

62.8 MATCH THE SENTENCES AND SAY THEM OUT LOUD

My cat keeps	with children?
1 Is she good	a broken leg.
2 I think he's got	being sick.
3 She's lost weight	adopt a cat.
4 Hi, I'd like to	and book his vaccinations!
5 We have to get him microchipped	and gone off her food.

63 Home emergencies

63.1 POWER PROBLEMS

What's happening?

The power has gone off. I'll check the fuse box.

A switch has flipped. Let's see if I can get it working...

Try turning the lights on now...

The power is back on!

63.2 PROFESSIONAL HELP

My dishwasher's leaking...

I can be there in an hour. My callout charge is £80.

Right, so what seems to be the problem?

The tap has been dripping for days.

My shower keeps going cold!

When was the boiler last serviced?

63.3 MORE PHRASES

I have a leaking roof.

My toilet is overflowing.

There's no hot water.

The heating won't come on.

The window is broken.

63.4 VOCABULARY HOUSEHOLD PROBLEMS

broken window

burst pipe

broken-down boiler

overflowing toilet

leaking roof

blocked sink

dripping tap

power cut

63.5 LISTEN TO PERSON A AND RESPOND AS PERSON B

A	B
1 What's happening?	The power has gone off.
2 Try turning the lights on now...	The power is back on!
3 Right, so what seems to be the problem?	The tap has been dripping for days.
4 My shower keeps going cold!	When was the boiler last serviced?

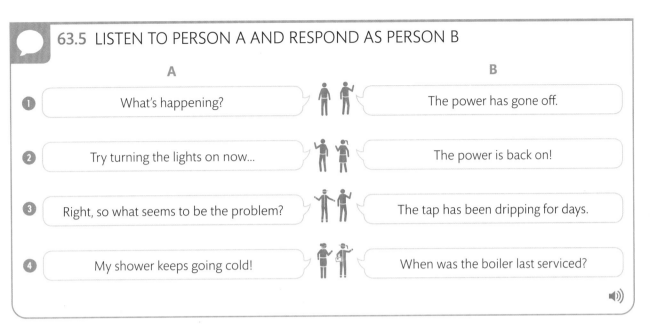

63.6 LISTEN AND NUMBER THE SENTENCES IN THE ORDER YOU HEAR THEM

A My toilet is overflowing. ☐

B When was the boiler last serviced? ☐

C Try turning the lights on now... ☐

D The window is broken. ☐ 1

E The power is back on! ☐

F I have a leaking roof. ☐

G There's no hot water. ☐

H A switch has flipped. ☐

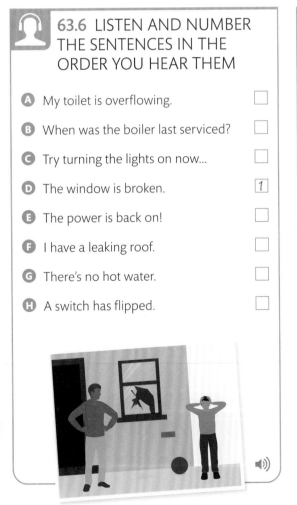

63.7 RESPOND OUT LOUD TO THE AUDIO, FILLING IN THE GAPS USING THE WORDS IN THE PANEL

back on	serviced	dripping	gone off

1 What's happening?

The power has _____ .

2 Try turning the lights on now...

The power is _____ !

3 Right, so what seems to be the problem?

The tap has been _____ for days.

4 My shower keeps going cold!

When was the boiler last _____ ?

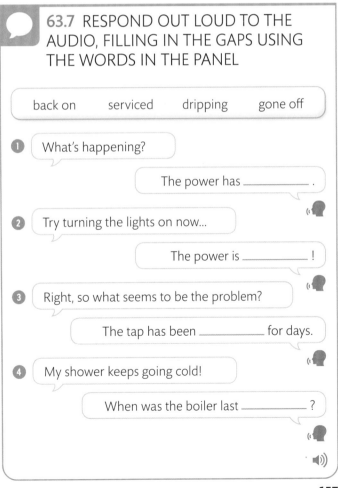

64 Home entertainment

64.1 WATCHING TV

What shall we watch tonight?

We could try this new detective series.

That was great – shall we check out the next episode?

It's not streaming yet. How about some sport?

Have you got the remote? I can't hear anything.

Yes, here it is. I'll turn it up.

64.2 GAMING

I'm so gonna win this!

Damn! You got me again!

Your screen time's up now.

But I really want to finish this game! Just five more minutes...

Shall we play the next level?

I'm just grabbing a bite to eat – be right back!

64.3 MORE PHRASES

Can you turn on the subtitles?

Have you got another controller?

My tablet has frozen!

Is the console plugged in?

64.4 VOCABULARY HOME ENTERTAINMENT

smart TV

remote

subtitles

headphones

console

smart speakers

controller

tablet

64.5 LISTEN TO PERSON A AND RESPOND AS PERSON B

A   **B**

1. What shall we watch tonight? — We could try this new detective series.

2. Have you got the remote? I can't hear anything. — Yes, here it is. I'll turn it up.

3. I'm so gonna win this! — Damn! You got me again!

4. Shall we play the next level? — I'm just grabbing a bite to eat – be right back!

64.6 LISTEN AND NUMBER THE PICTURES IN THE ORDER THEY ARE DESCRIBED

A ☐

B 1

"Hey, Bruno! Come back here right now, you bad dog!"

C ☐

D ☐

E ☐

F ☐

G ☐

H ☐

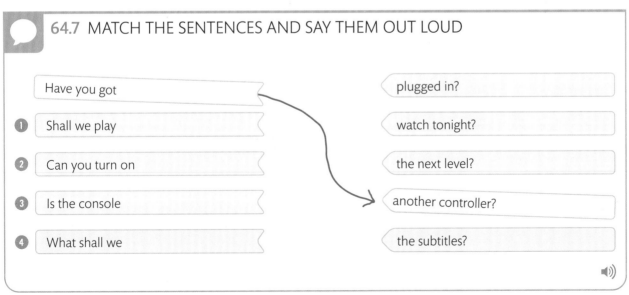

64.7 MATCH THE SENTENCES AND SAY THEM OUT LOUD

Have you got — another controller?

1. Shall we play — the next level?

2. Can you turn on — the subtitles?

3. Is the console — plugged in?

4. What shall we — watch tonight?

65 Getting around

65.1 TRANSPORT

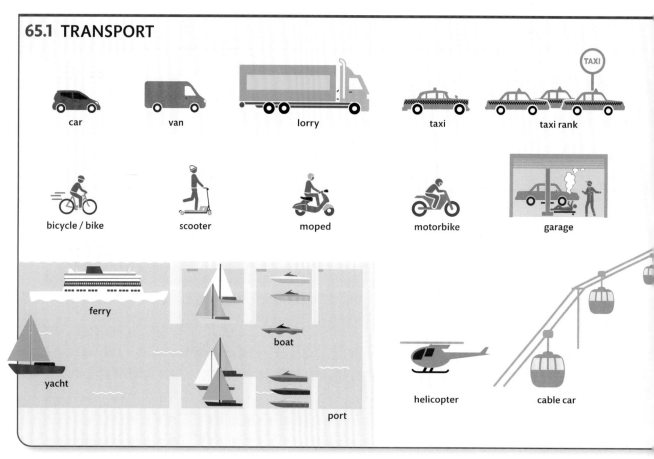

car

van

lorry

taxi

taxi rank

bicycle / bike

scooter

moped

motorbike

garage

ferry

boat

yacht

port

helicopter

cable car

65.2 VERBS

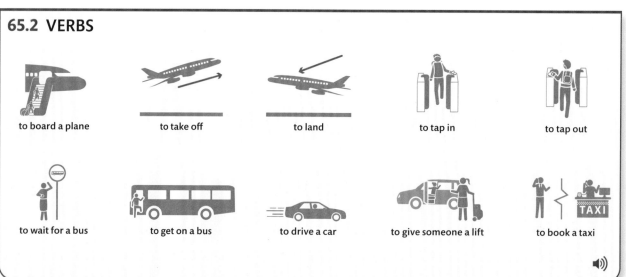

to board a plane

to take off

to land

to tap in

to tap out

to wait for a bus

to get on a bus

to drive a car

to give someone a lift

to book a taxi

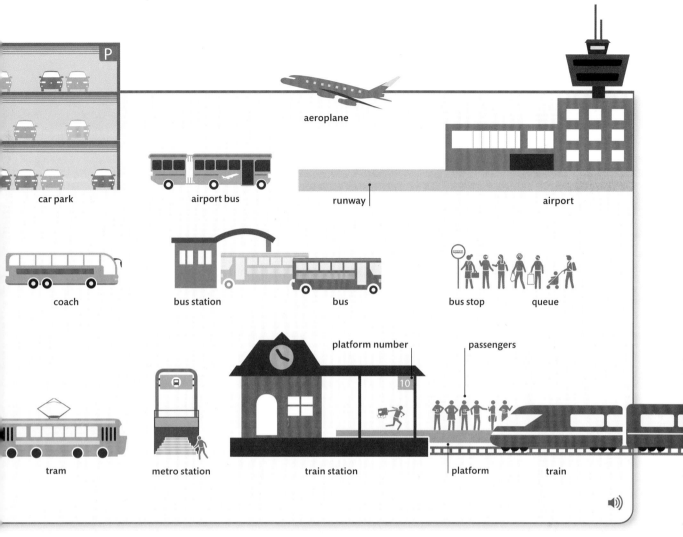

car park

airport bus

aeroplane

runway

airport

coach

bus station

bus

bus stop

queue

tram

metro station

train station

platform number

platform

passengers

train

65.3 TRAVEL ESSENTIALS

single ticket

return ticket

e-ticket

railcard

driving licence

departure board

destinations

departure times

DUE	DESTINATION	PLAT	INFORMATION	
7:20	Exeter	1	On Time	
7:28	Brighton	3	Expected 7:45	delayed
7:45	Oxford	9	On Time	
7:53	Cardiff	4	On Time	
8:05	Dundee	7	On Time	
8:18	Swindon	4	Cancelled	cancelled
8:48	Bristol	8	Expected 9:05	
9:00	Reading	6	On Time	
9:12	London	5	On Time	
9:34	Weston-Super-Mare	3	On Time	

66 Buses and coaches

66.1 GETTING THE BUS

Does this bus go to the town centre?

Yes, via the train station.

Can I have a single to the museum, please?

That'll be £3.

Thanks. I'll pay by contactless.

Are we nearly at the library?

We're almost there – it's the next stop.

66.2 MORE QUESTIONS

Where is the nearest bus stop?

Is this the right stop for the airport bus?

How much is the fare?

Are you stopping at the shopping centre?

What time is the next bus?

What time is the last bus from this stop?

66.3 COACH JOURNEYS

Could I see your ticket, please?

Here you go.

Lovely. We arrive in Cardiff at 16.45.

Hello, are there toilets on the coach?

And is there Wi-Fi on board?

Yes, they're right at the back.

Yup, just log on to our network.

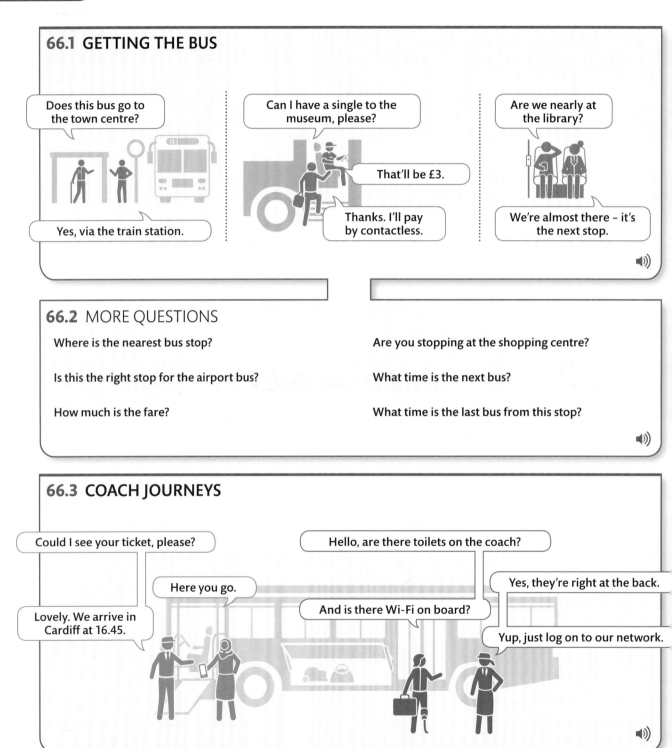

66.4 LISTEN TO PERSON A AND RESPOND AS PERSON B

	A		B
①	Could I see your ticket, please?		Here you go.
②	Does this bus go to the town centre?		Yes, via the train station.
③	That'll be £3.		Thanks. I'll pay by contactless.
④	Are we nearly at the library?		We're almost there – it's the next stop.

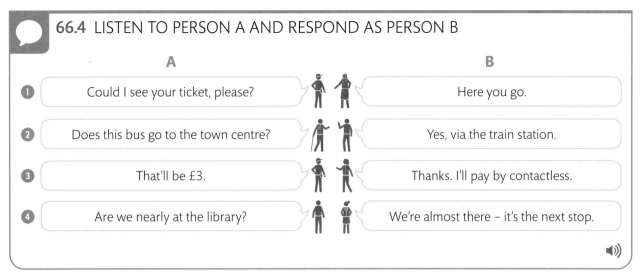

66.5 LISTEN TO THE AUDIO AND MATCH THE CORRECT RESPONSE

Can I have a single to the museum, please?

Yup, just log on to our network.

① Are we nearly at the library?

Yes, via the train station.

② Does this bus go to the town centre?

We're almost there – it's the next stop.

③ Hello, are there toilets on the coach?

That'll be £3.

④ Is there Wi-Fi on board?

Yes, they're right at the back.

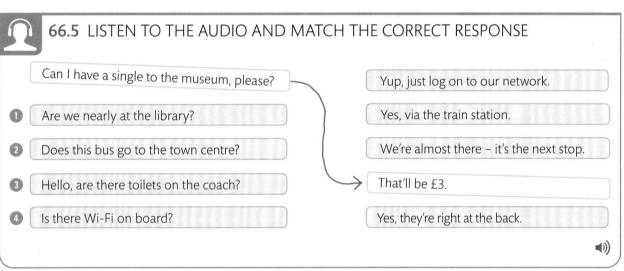

66.6 USE THE CHART TO CREATE NINE SENTENCES AND SAY THEM OUT LOUD

Excuse me, does this bus go to the library?

Excuse me,	does this bus go to are we nearly at is this the right stop for	the library? the town centre? the shopping centre?

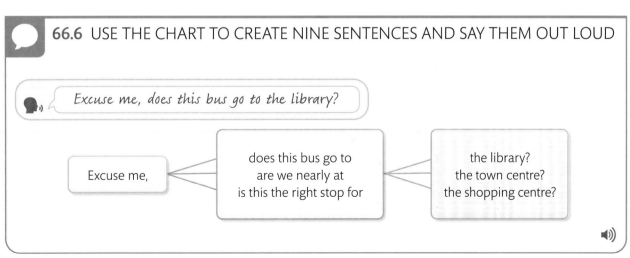

67 Train and metro travel

67.1 BUYING TICKETS

Hello, how can I help?

A single to Leeds, please.

Hello, can we book two return tickets to Leeds, please?

Absolutely. Are you travelling today?

67.2 MORE PHRASES

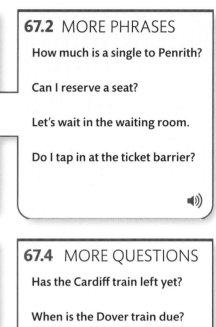

How much is a single to Penrith?

Can I reserve a seat?

Let's wait in the waiting room.

Do I tap in at the ticket barrier?

67.3 ASKING FOR INFORMATION

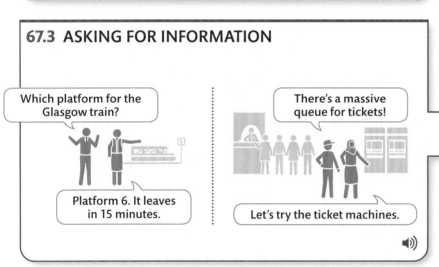

Which platform for the Glasgow train?

Platform 6. It leaves in 15 minutes.

There's a massive queue for tickets!

Let's try the ticket machines.

67.4 MORE QUESTIONS

Has the Cardiff train left yet?

When is the Dover train due?

Does this train stop at Birmingham?

What time is the next train to Newcastle?

67.5 VOCABULARY TRAIN TRAVEL

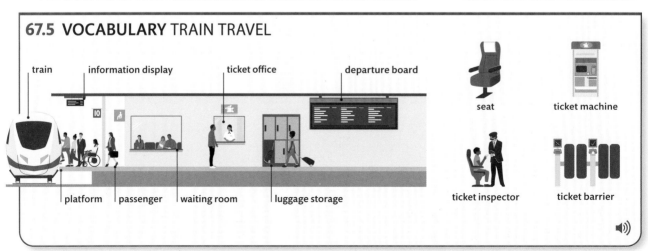

train

information display

ticket office

departure board

seat

ticket machine

platform   passenger   waiting room   luggage storage

ticket inspector

ticket barrier

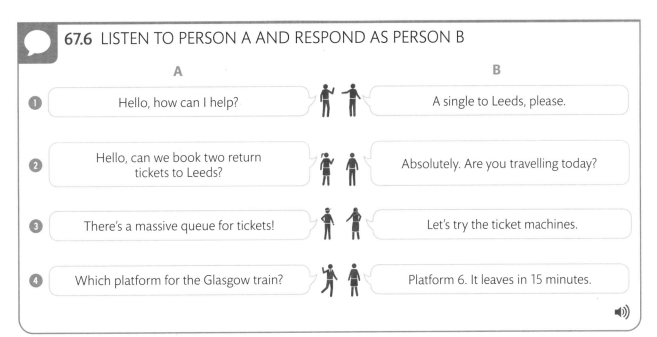

67.6 LISTEN TO PERSON A AND RESPOND AS PERSON B

A	B
1 Hello, how can I help?	A single to Leeds, please.
2 Hello, can we book two return tickets to Leeds?	Absolutely. Are you travelling today?
3 There's a massive queue for tickets!	Let's try the ticket machines.
4 Which platform for the Glasgow train?	Platform 6. It leaves in 15 minutes.

67.7 LISTEN AND NUMBER THE PICTURES IN THE ORDER THEY ARE DESCRIBED

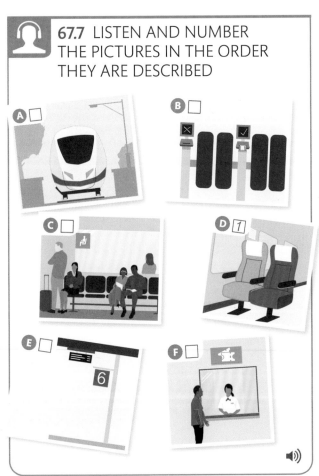

67.8 SAY THE SENTENCES OUT LOUD, FILLING IN THE GAPS USING THE WORDS IN THE PANEL

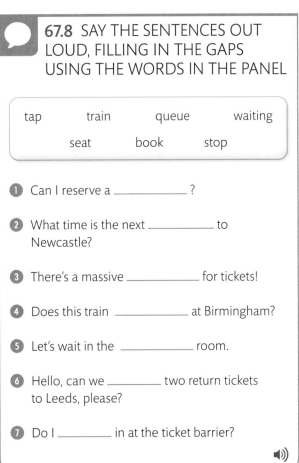

tap	train	queue	waiting
seat	book	stop	

1. Can I reserve a _____ ?

2. What time is the next _____ to Newcastle?

3. There's a massive _____ for tickets!

4. Does this train _____ at Birmingham?

5. Let's wait in the _____ room.

6. Hello, can we _____ two return tickets to Leeds, please?

7. Do I _____ in at the ticket barrier?

165

67.9 PROBLEMS AND WARNINGS

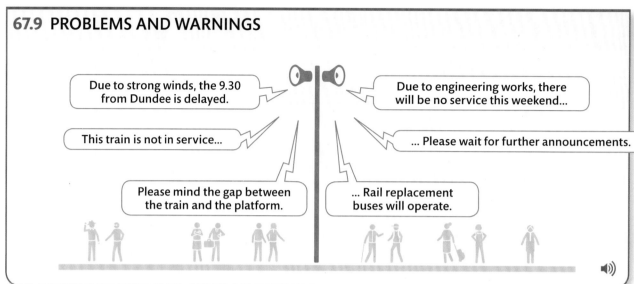

67.10 ON THE TRAIN

67.11 ON THE METRO

67.12 LISTEN TO PERSON A AND RESPOND AS PERSON B

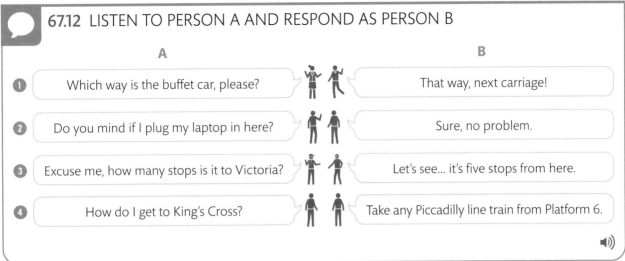

	A		B
1	Which way is the buffet car, please?		That way, next carriage!
2	Do you mind if I plug my laptop in here?		Sure, no problem.
3	Excuse me, how many stops is it to Victoria?		Let's see... it's five stops from here.
4	How do I get to King's Cross?		Take any Piccadilly line train from Platform 6.

67.13 LISTEN AND NUMBER THE SENTENCES IN THE ORDER YOU HEAR THEM

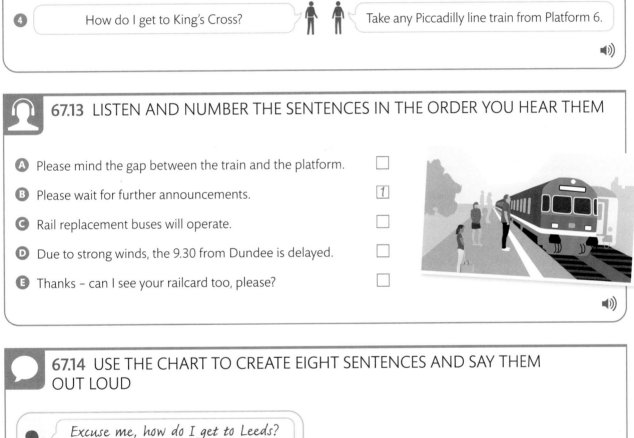

A Please mind the gap between the train and the platform. ☐

B Please wait for further announcements. ☐ 1

C Rail replacement buses will operate. ☐

D Due to strong winds, the 9.30 from Dundee is delayed. ☐

E Thanks – can I see your railcard too, please? ☐

67.14 USE THE CHART TO CREATE EIGHT SENTENCES AND SAY THEM OUT LOUD

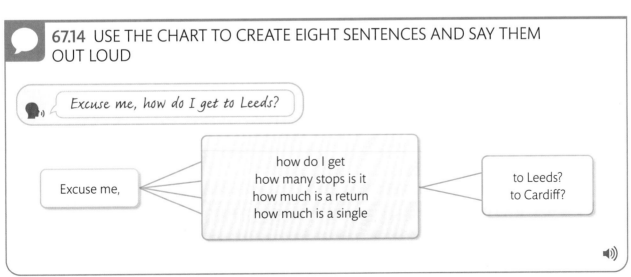

Excuse me, how do I get to Leeds?

Excuse me,	how do I get	to Leeds?
	how many stops is it	to Cardiff?
	how much is a return	
	how much is a single	

68 At the airport

68.1 DEPARTURES

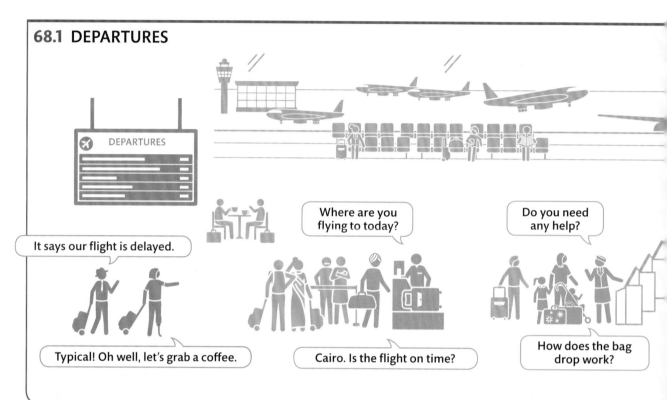

It says our flight is delayed.

Typical! Oh well, let's grab a coffee.

Where are you flying to today?

Cairo. Is the flight on time?

Do you need any help?

How does the bag drop work?

68.3 LISTEN TO PERSON A AND RESPOND AS PERSON B

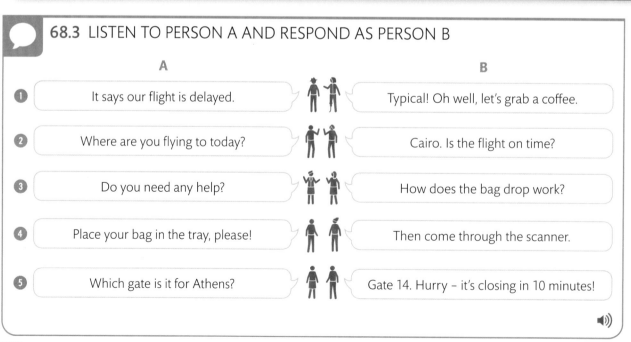

A		B
① It says our flight is delayed.		Typical! Oh well, let's grab a coffee.
② Where are you flying to today?		Cairo. Is the flight on time?
③ Do you need any help?		How does the bag drop work?
④ Place your bag in the tray, please!		Then come through the scanner.
⑤ Which gate is it for Athens?		Gate 14. Hurry – it's closing in 10 minutes!

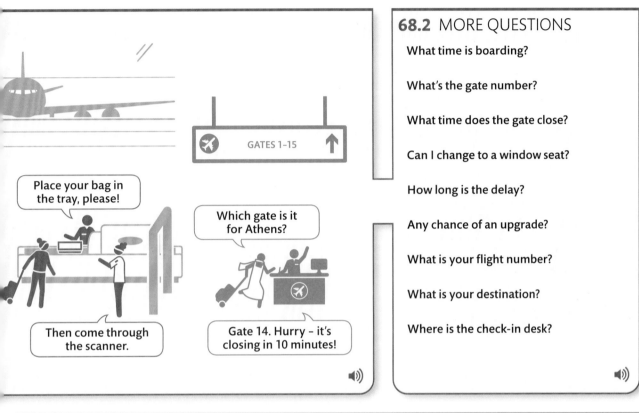

Place your bag in the tray, please!

Then come through the scanner.

GATES 1–15

Which gate is it for Athens?

Gate 14. Hurry – it's closing in 10 minutes!

68.2 MORE QUESTIONS

What time is boarding?

What's the gate number?

What time does the gate close?

Can I change to a window seat?

How long is the delay?

Any chance of an upgrade?

What is your flight number?

What is your destination?

Where is the check-in desk?

68.4 SAY THE SENTENCES OUT LOUD, FILLING IN THE GAPS USING THE WORDS IN THE PANEL

delay	tray	seat	time
upgrade	number	gate	check-in

1 What _____ is boarding?

2 Can I change to a window _____ ?

3 What's the gate _____ ?

4 How long is the _____ ?

5 Any chance of an _____ ?

6 What time does the _____ close?

7 Place your bag in the _____ , please!

8 Where is the _____ desk?

68.5 BOARDING AND TAKING OFF

Welcome! Can I see your boarding pass?

Hello! Here you go.

I'll put our stuff in the overhead locker.

Thanks. I'll keep my bag under the seat.

Ladies and gentlemen, welcome to Flight 86A for Beijing.

We are ready for departure.

68.6 DURING THE FLIGHT

We'll shortly be passing through the cabin with snacks and drinks.

This is your captain speaking. We are experiencing some turbulence.

Please return to your seat and fasten your seat belt.

68.7 LANDING

Your tray tables should be securely fastened.

Make sure your seat is in the upright position.

Please switch your digital devices to "airplane" mode.

We will arrive in Beijing at 9.20 local time.

68.8 VOCABULARY IN THE CABIN

overhead locker

reading light

window

row

row number

life jacket

tray table

seat belt

window seat

aisle seat

68.9 LISTEN AND NUMBER THE PICTURES IN THE ORDER THEY ARE DESCRIBED

A ☐
B ☐ 1
C ☐
D ☐
E ☐
F ☐

68.10 LISTEN AND NUMBER THE SENTENCES IN THE ORDER YOU HEAR THEM

A I'll put our stuff in the overhead locker. ☐

B We are experiencing some turbulence. ☐

C Ladies and gentlemen, welcome to Flight 86A for Beijing. ☐

D Make sure your seat is in the upright position. ☐ 1

E We will arrive in Beijing at 9.20 local time. ☐

F We are ready for departure. ☐

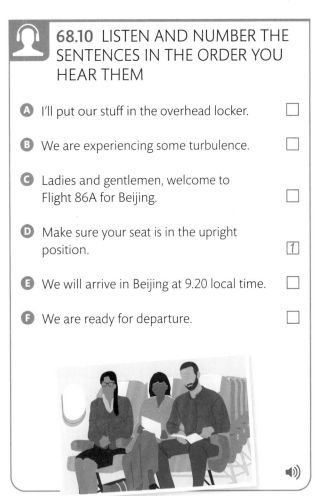

68.11 MATCH THE SENTENCES AND SAY THEM OUT LOUD

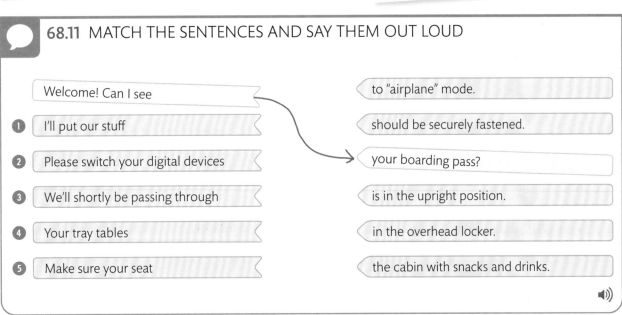

Welcome! Can I see ——→ your boarding pass?

to "airplane" mode.

should be securely fastened.

1 I'll put our stuff

2 Please switch your digital devices

3 We'll shortly be passing through

4 Your tray tables

5 Make sure your seat

is in the upright position.

in the overhead locker.

the cabin with snacks and drinks.

68.12 ARRIVALS

What is the purpose of your trip?

I'm visiting friends.

Which baggage reclaim belt do we need to go to?

It's Belt 3. I'll grab a trolley.

I can't see our suitcases anywhere!

Let's go and check at the baggage desk.

68.13 HIRING A CAR

Hi! I'm here to pick up a hire car. Here's my booking confirmation.

Great! Can I see your driving licence, please?

Is the car ready for us?

6

Yes, it's in Bay 6. Enjoy your trip!

68.14 LISTEN AND CIRCLE THE ITEM YOU HEAR

1 A B

2 A B

3 A B

4 A B

Can I see your customs declaration form?

CUSTOMS

Here it is!

Hi, can I help?

Yes, I need to change some Euros. What's your rate?

Where do we meet our taxi?

The driver should be waiting for us.

68.15 LISTEN TO PERSON A AND RESPOND AS PERSON B

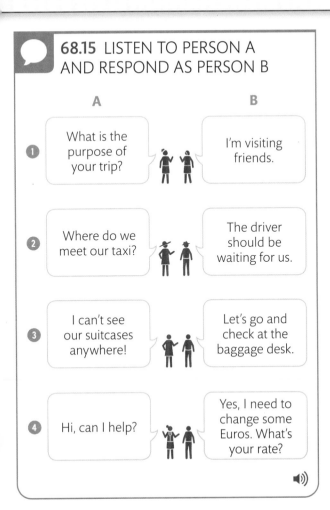

A

1. What is the purpose of your trip?
2. Where do we meet our taxi?
3. I can't see our suitcases anywhere!
4. Hi, can I help?

B

1. I'm visiting friends.
2. The driver should be waiting for us.
3. Let's go and check at the baggage desk.
4. Yes, I need to change some Euros. What's your rate?

68.16 SAY THE SENTENCES OUT LOUD, REPLACING THE PICTURES WITH WORDS

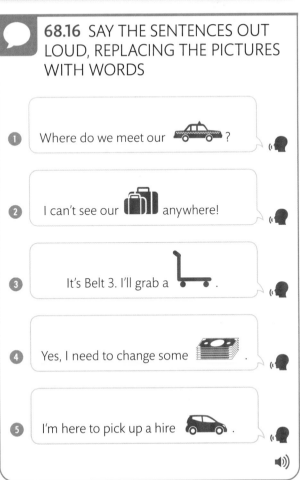

1. Where do we meet our [taxi] ?
2. I can't see our [suitcases] anywhere!
3. It's Belt 3. I'll grab a [cart] .
4. Yes, I need to change some [money] .
5. I'm here to pick up a hire [car] .

69 Cycling

69.1 BUYING A BIKE

I need a bike to get to and from work.

What do you want to use the e-bike for?

Okay, let's look at some commuter bikes.

For getting around town, mainly.

69.2 QUESTIONS YOU MAY HEAR

What type of bike do you want?

What's your budget?

Would you like a test ride?

Will you be taking it on public transport?

69.3 HIRING A BIKE

How do I hire this city bike?

Where can we park after our ride?

You just need to download the app!

There are parking bays all over town!

69.4 BIKE PROBLEMS

What's up with the bike?

The chain is broken.

The front tyre is flat.

The brakes are loose.

The battery needs charging.

69.5 VOCABULARY PARTS OF A BICYCLE

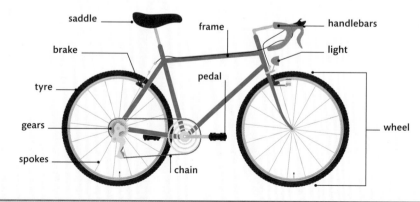

saddle
frame
handlebars
brake
light
tyre
pedal
gears
wheel
spokes
chain

helmet

to repair

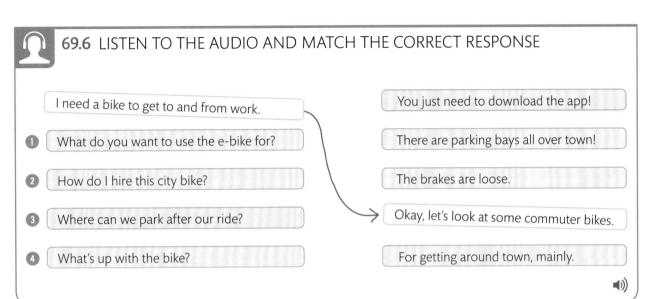

69.6 LISTEN TO THE AUDIO AND MATCH THE CORRECT RESPONSE

I need a bike to get to and from work.

You just need to download the app!

1. What do you want to use the e-bike for?

There are parking bays all over town!

2. How do I hire this city bike?

The brakes are loose.

3. Where can we park after our ride?

Okay, let's look at some commuter bikes.

4. What's up with the bike?

For getting around town, mainly.

69.7 LISTEN AND NUMBER THE PICTURES IN THE ORDER THEY ARE DESCRIBED

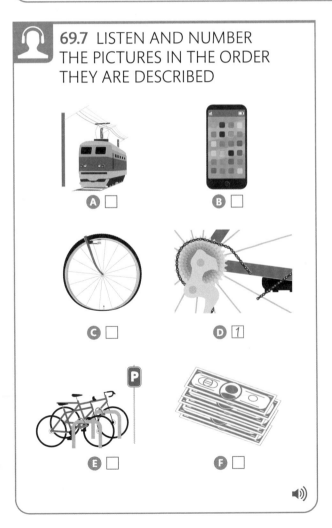

A ☐

B ☐

C ☐

D ☐ 1

E ☐

F ☐

69.8 SAY THE SENTENCES OUT LOUD, FILLING IN THE GAPS USING THE WORDS IN THE PANEL

brakes	tyre	battery	work
bike	app	test ride	bays

1. What type of _____ do you want?

2. The _____ needs charging.

3. The front _____ is flat.

4. Would you like a _____ ?

5. I need a bike to get to and from _____ .

6. There are parking _____ all over town!

7. You just need to download the _____ !

8. The _____ are loose.

70.1 TAKING A TAXI

Where's the nearest taxi rank?

The cabs wait just there, across the street.

Can you take me to this address?

No problem. Let me put your case in the boot.

Can you drop me here, please?

Sure, that will be £19.10.

70.2 BOOKING IN ADVANCE

Hello, can I book a taxi from the airport?

For how many people and when do you need it?

Tomorrow at 11am. There are four of us.

Where are you travelling to?

To Evergreen Avenue.

How many pieces of luggage have you got?

One small suitcase and one large one.

Okay. That's all booked for you.

70.3 MORE PHRASES

How long will it take to get there?

Can we make an extra stop?

Keep the change.

Can I pay with contactless?

How soon will the cab be here?

I'll book a ride-share via the app.

I left my laptop in one of your taxis.

I'm travelling with my assistance dog.

A	B
① Where's the nearest taxi rank?	The cabs wait just there, across the street.
② For how many people and when do you need it?	Tomorrow at 11am. There are four of us.
③ How many pieces of luggage have you got?	One small suitcase and one large one.
④ Can you drop me here, please?	Sure, that will be £19.10.

70.5 LISTEN AND NUMBER THE SENTENCES IN THE ORDER YOU HEAR THEM

Ⓐ Keep the change. ☐

Ⓑ One small suitcase and one large one. ☐

Ⓒ Where's the nearest taxi rank? ☐1

Ⓓ Can you drop me here, please? ☐

Ⓔ How soon will the cab be here? ☐

Ⓕ Can you take me to this address? ☐

Ⓖ Let me put your case in the boot. ☐

Ⓗ I'll book a ride-share via the app. ☐

70.6 SAY THE SENTENCES OUT LOUD, FILLING IN THE GAPS USING THE WORDS IN THE PANEL

| long | pay | address | cab | drop | taxis | book | dog |

① Hello, can I _____ a taxi from the airport?

② How soon will the _____ be here?

③ Can you _____ me here, please?

④ I'm travelling with my assistance _____ .

⑤ I left my laptop in one of your _____ .

⑥ Can you take me to this _____ ?

⑦ How _____ will it take to get there?

⑧ Can I _____ with contactless?

71 At the garage

71.1 BOOKING A SERVICE

ABC Autos, how can I help?

Could I book my car in for a service, please?

When will my car be ready?

It should be ready to pick up at 5.30.

71.2 FAULTS AND REPAIRS

What does this warning light mean? It keeps flashing...

Looks like your oil level is too low. Let me check it.

So, what seems to be the problem?

I think the engine's overheating.

Okay, I'll take a look.

71.3 MORE PROBLEMS

The headlight isn't working.

The oil needs changing.

The steering wheel is jammed.

The windscreen is cracked.

The tyre keeps going down.

71.4 VOCABULARY CAR PARTS

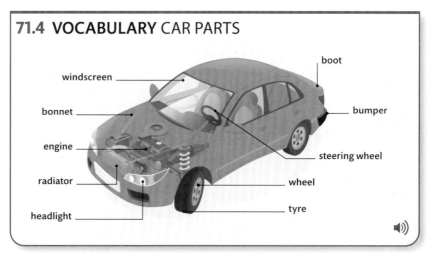

windscreen

bonnet

engine

radiator

headlight

boot

bumper

steering wheel

wheel

tyre

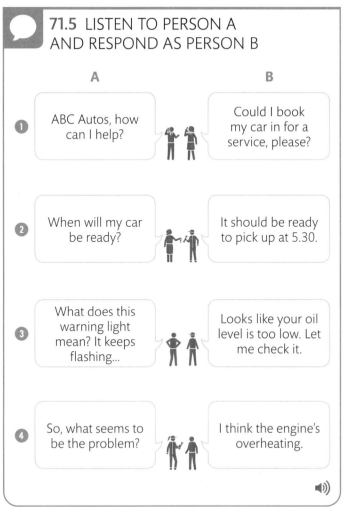

71.5 LISTEN TO PERSON A AND RESPOND AS PERSON B

A	B
❶ ABC Autos, how can I help?	Could I book my car in for a service, please?
❷ When will my car be ready?	It should be ready to pick up at 5.30.
❸ What does this warning light mean? It keeps flashing...	Looks like your oil level is too low. Let me check it.
❹ So, what seems to be the problem?	I think the engine's overheating.

71.6 LISTEN AND CIRCLE THE ITEM YOU HEAR

❶ Ⓐ B
❷ A B
❸ A B
❹ A B

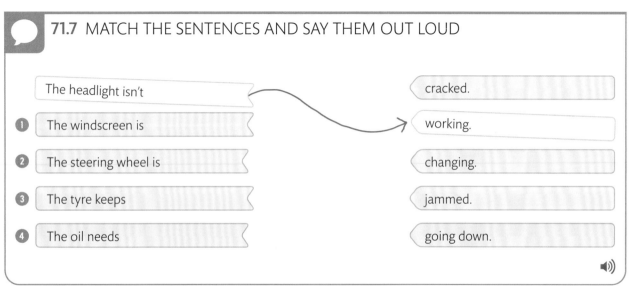

71.7 MATCH THE SENTENCES AND SAY THEM OUT LOUD

The headlight isn't → working.

❶ The windscreen is — cracked.

❷ The steering wheel is — changing.

❸ The tyre keeps — jammed.

❹ The oil needs — going down.

72.1 ACCOMMODATION

hotel   motel   bed and breakfast   hostel

chalet   cabin   campsite   caravan

accessible   pet-friendly   Wi-Fi   swimming pool

balcony   cot   room service   buffet

72.2 HOLIDAY ESSENTIALS

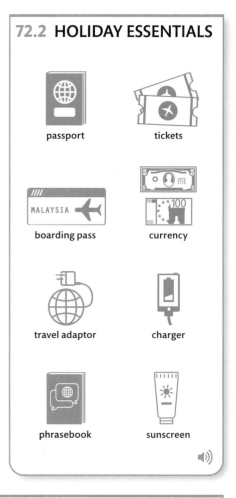

passport   tickets

boarding pass   currency

travel adaptor   charger

phrasebook   sunscreen

72.3 VERBS

to book a flight   to make a reservation   to go on holiday   to rent a cottage   to stay in a hotel   to book a pitch

to pack (a suitcase)   to change money   to go abroad   to hire a car   to check in   to check out

72.4 HOLIDAY ACTIVITIES

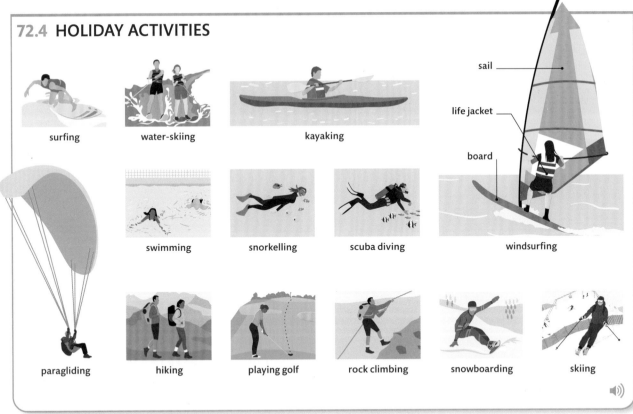

surfing

water-skiing

kayaking

sail

life jacket

board

swimming

snorkelling

scuba diving

windsurfing

paragliding

hiking

playing golf

rock climbing

snowboarding

skiing

72.5 SIGHTSEEING AND ATTRACTIONS

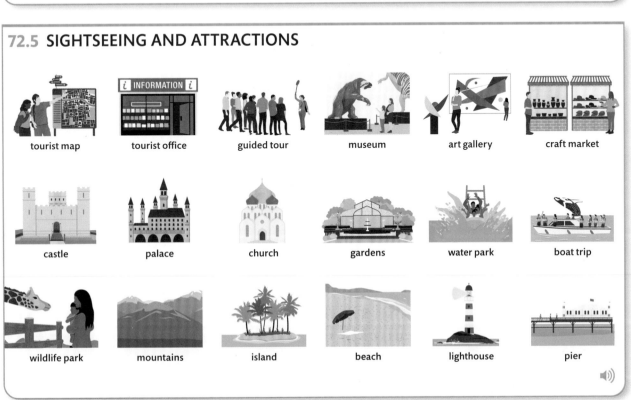

tourist map

i INFORMATION *i*

tourist office

guided tour

museum

art gallery

craft market

castle

palace

church

gardens

water park

boat trip

wildlife park

mountains

island

beach

lighthouse

pier

73 Booking a holiday

73.1 TALKING TO THE TRAVEL AGENT

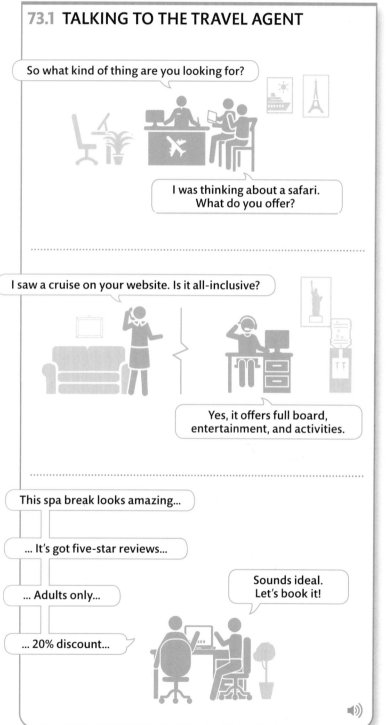

So what kind of thing are you looking for?

I was thinking about a safari. What do you offer?

I saw a cruise on your website. Is it all-inclusive?

Yes, it offers full board, entertainment, and activities.

This spa break looks amazing...

... It's got five-star reviews...

... Adults only...

... 20% discount...

Sounds ideal. Let's book it!

73.2 MORE QUESTIONS

What facilities are there?

What's your cancellation policy?

Do I need a visa?

Is it suitable for young children?

Can I bring my guide dog?

73.3 VOCABULARY
TYPES OF HOLIDAY

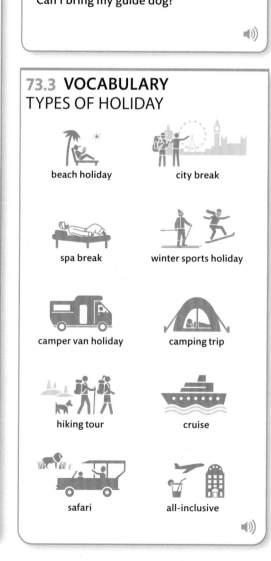

beach holiday

city break

spa break

winter sports holiday

camper van holiday

camping trip

hiking tour

cruise

safari

all-inclusive

73.4 LISTEN AND NUMBER THE SENTENCES IN THE ORDER YOU HEAR THEM

A I was thinking about a safari. What do you offer? ☐

B I saw a cruise on your website. Is it all-inclusive? ☐

C So what kind of thing are you looking for? ☑ 1

D Yes, it offers full board, entertainment, and activities. ☐

E What's your cancellation policy? ☐

F Sounds ideal. Let's book it! ☐

73.5 MATCH THE SENTENCES AND SAY THEM OUT LOUD

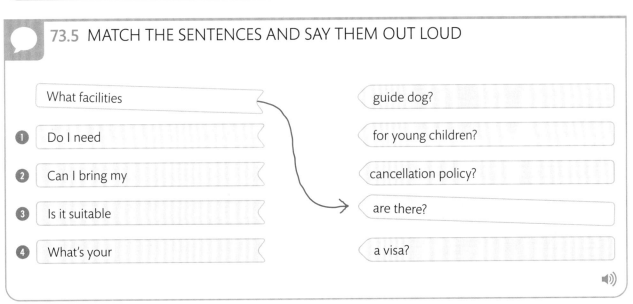

What facilities		guide dog?
1 Do I need		for young children?
2 Can I bring my		cancellation policy?
3 Is it suitable		are there?
4 What's your		a visa?

73.6 USE THE CHART TO CREATE 12 SENTENCES AND SAY THEM OUT LOUD

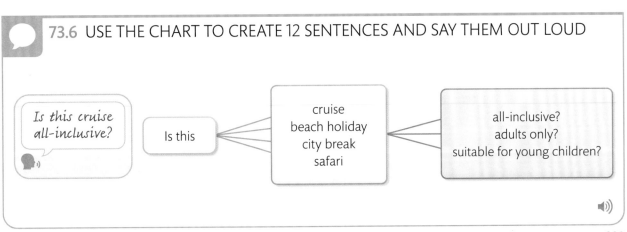

Is this cruise all-inclusive?

Is this → cruise / beach holiday / city break / safari → all-inclusive? / adults only? / suitable for young children?

74 Staying in a hotel

74.1 ARRIVAL AND CHECK-IN

74.3 LISTEN TO PERSON A AND RESPOND AS PERSON B

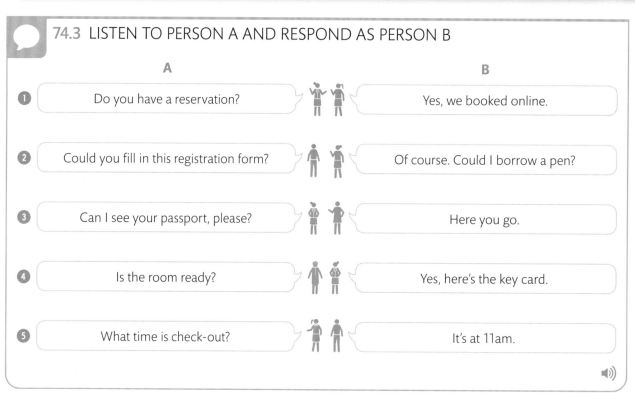

Is the room ready?

Yes, here's the key card.

What time is check-out?

It's at 11am.

74.2 MORE PHRASES

I paid in advance on the booking site.

Do you have a double room available?

We'd like a room with twin beds, please.

The restaurant serves dinner until 10pm.

The swimming pool opens again at 6am.

Your room is on the second floor.

Breakfast is from 7.30am to 10am.

74.4 LISTEN AND CIRCLE THE ITEM YOU HEAR

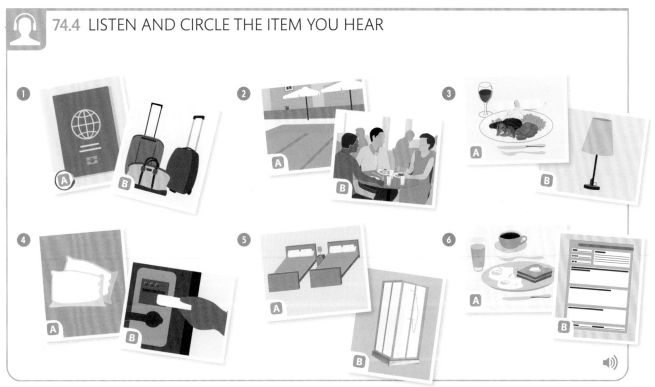

74.5 ASKING FOR THINGS

"Could I have some fresh towels, please?"

"Yes, I'll have some sent up right away."

74.6 MORE PHRASES

I'd like...

... a hairdryer brought to my room.

... a club sandwich sent up, please.

... two extra pillows.

... a 7am wake-up call.

74.7 DESCRIBING PROBLEMS

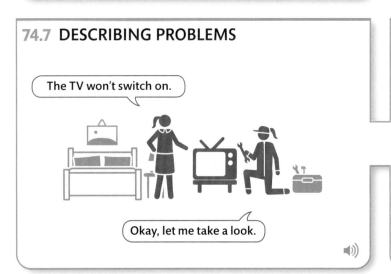

"The TV won't switch on."

"Okay, let me take a look."

74.8 MORE PROBLEMS

The Wi-Fi password is wrong.

The lamp is broken.

The room is too hot.

My window doesn't close properly.

The shower is leaking.

My key card isn't working.

74.9 VOCABULARY AT THE HOTEL

passport

registration form

double room

twin beds

club sandwich

shower

key card

luggage

pillows

lamp

towels

hairdryer

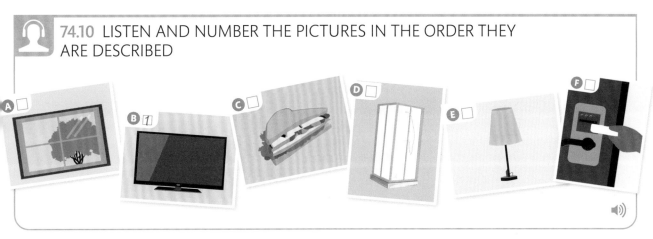

74.10 LISTEN AND NUMBER THE PICTURES IN THE ORDER THEY ARE DESCRIBED

A ☐ B 1 C ☐ D ☐ E ☐ F ☐

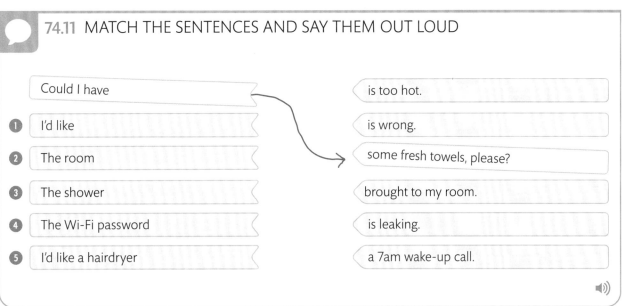

74.11 MATCH THE SENTENCES AND SAY THEM OUT LOUD

Could I have   is too hot.

1 I'd like   is wrong.

2 The room   some fresh towels, please?

3 The shower   brought to my room.

4 The Wi-Fi password   is leaking.

5 I'd like a hairdryer   a 7am wake-up call.

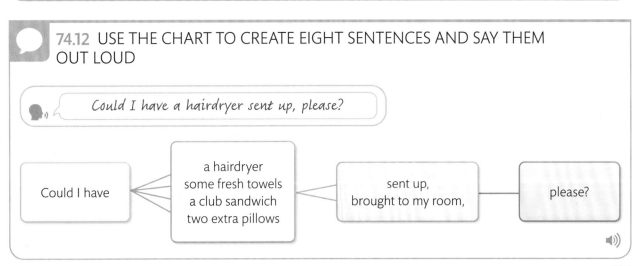

74.12 USE THE CHART TO CREATE EIGHT SENTENCES AND SAY THEM OUT LOUD

Could I have a hairdryer sent up, please?

| Could I have | a hairdryer
some fresh towels
a club sandwich
two extra pillows | sent up,
brought to my room, | please? |

187

74.13 AT BREAKFAST

Am I too late for breakfast?

No, you're just in time.

Can I take your room number?

Can we sit anywhere we like?

Yes, and do help yourselves at the buffet.

Could I have some more coffee?

Sure, I'll bring it to your table.

74.14 CHECKING OUT

Did you enjoy your stay?

It was lovely, thanks.

The room was a bit noisy.

Here's your bill if you'd like to check it.

That all looks fine.

Are you paying by card?

74.15 MORE PHRASES

Dinner was delicious.

Our breakfast was a bit cold.

The bed was a little bit hard.

Is it possible to stay an extra night?

Can I leave my luggage here?

Could you call me a taxi, please?

🌐 GOOD TO KNOW

In spoken English, we often use **a bit** or **a little bit** – instead of more formal **quite**, **a little**, or **rather** – when we want to describe something negative. For example, we wouldn't say our breakfast was **a bit** delicious, but we might say it was **a bit** bland or **a little bit** cold.

74.16 MATCH THE SENTENCES AND SAY THEM OUT LOUD

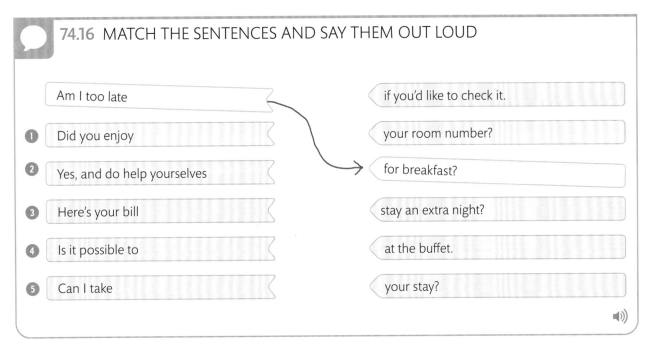

Am I too late ——————→ for breakfast?

1. Did you enjoy → your stay?
2. Yes, and do help yourselves → at the buffet.
3. Here's your bill → if you'd like to check it.
4. Is it possible to → stay an extra night?
5. Can I take → your room number?

74.17 SAY THE SENTENCES OUT LOUD, REPLACING THE PICTURES WITH WORDS

1. Could I have some more ☕ ?
2. Are you paying by 💳 ?
3. Could you call me a 🚕 , please?
4. The 🛏 was a little bit hard.
5. Can I leave my 👜 here?

74.18 SAY THE SENTENCES OUT LOUD, FILLING IN THE GAPS USING THE WORDS IN THE PANEL

room   check-out   floor

delicious   restaurant   twin beds

passport   double

1. Can I see your _____ , please?
2. What time is _____ ?
3. We'd like a room with _____ , please.
4. The _____ was a bit noisy.
5. Dinner was _____ .
6. Do you have a _____ room available?
7. The _____ serves dinner until 10pm.
8. Your room is on the second _____ .

75 City sightseeing

75.1 VISITING THE SIGHTS

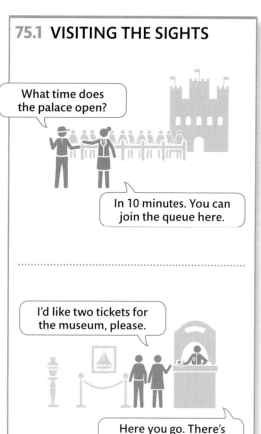

What time does the palace open?

In 10 minutes. You can join the queue here.

I'd like two tickets for the museum, please.

Here you go. There's a guided tour at 10.30.

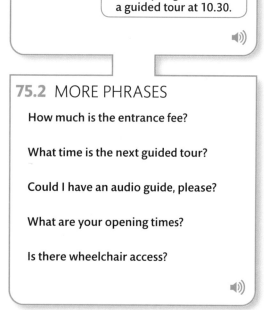

75.2 MORE PHRASES

How much is the entrance fee?

What time is the next guided tour?

Could I have an audio guide, please?

What are your opening times?

Is there wheelchair access?

75.3 ON A TOUR BUS

On your right, you'll see the oldest building in the city.

Look – we're here on the map and there's our hotel!

Wow! Check that out!

Quick! Take a picture!

Shall we get off at the next stop?

75.4 VOCABULARY TOURIST ESSENTIALS

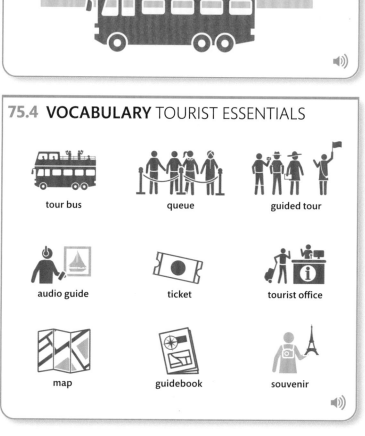

tour bus

queue

guided tour

audio guide

ticket

tourist office

map

guidebook

souvenir

75.5 LISTEN AND CIRCLE THE ITEM YOU HEAR

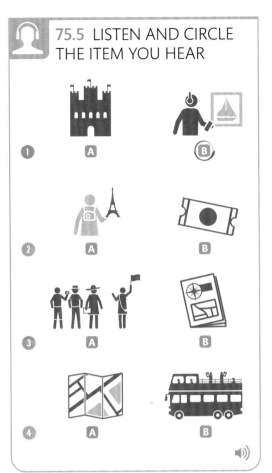

75.6 LISTEN TO PERSON A AND RESPOND AS PERSON B

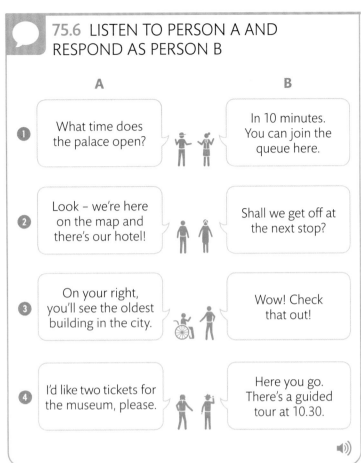

75.7 MATCH THE SENTENCES AND SAY THEM OUT LOUD

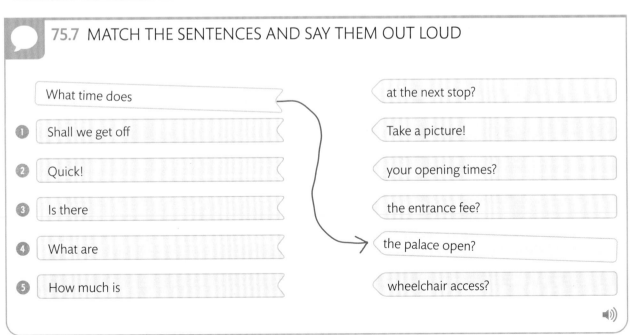

What time does — the palace open?

1 Shall we get off — at the next stop?

2 Quick! — Take a picture!

3 Is there — wheelchair access?

4 What are — your opening times?

5 How much is — the entrance fee?

76 Going camping

76.1 ARRIVING AT THE CAMPSITE

Hello, how can I help you?

Hi, we've booked a pitch for two nights.

Where can we pitch our tent?

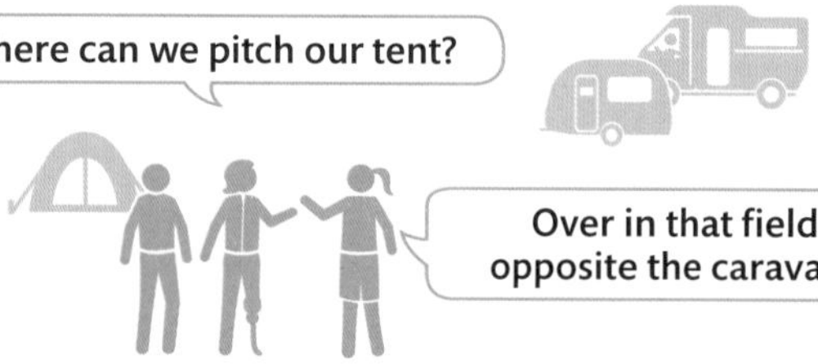

Over in that field, opposite the caravans.

Can we park our camper van near the site shop?

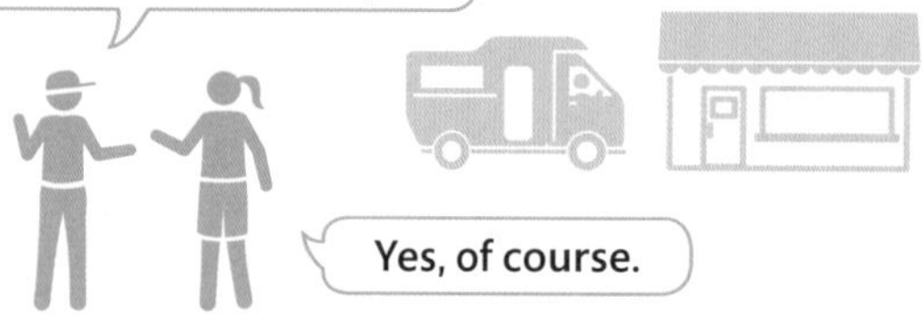

Yes, of course.

There's loads to do here! The beach is just over there...

Great! We'll set up camp then head out to explore.

76.2 AT THE SITE SHOP

Can we light a campfire?

Yes, you can. Do you need firewood?

We forgot to bring camping gas! Have you got any?

Sure, on that shelf over there. Anything else?

Yes, I'll take a box of matches, too.

76.3 VOCABULARY CAMPING

tent

campfire

shower block

caravan

camper van

site shop

matches

camping stove

camping gas

76.4 LISTEN TO PERSON A AND RESPOND AS PERSON B

A

1. Hello, how can I help you?

2. Where can we pitch our tent?

3. There's loads to do here!

4. Can we light a campfire?

5. Sure, on that shelf over there. Anything else?

B

Hi, we've booked a pitch for two nights.

Over in that field, opposite the caravans.

Great! We'll set up camp then head out to explore.

Yes, you can. Do you need firewood?

Yes, I'll take a box of matches, too.

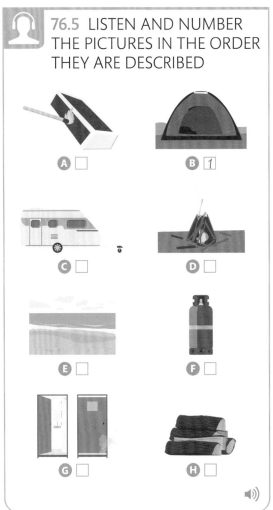

76.5 LISTEN AND NUMBER THE PICTURES IN THE ORDER THEY ARE DESCRIBED

A ☐

B 1

C ☐

D ☐

E ☐

F ☐

G ☐

H ☐

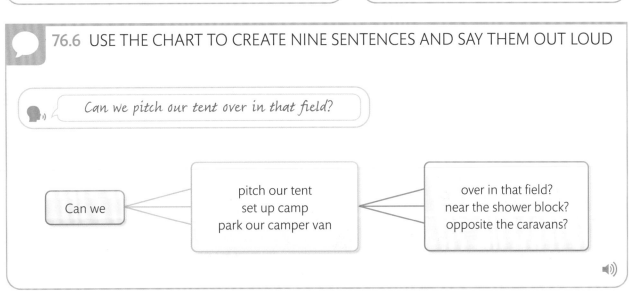

76.6 USE THE CHART TO CREATE NINE SENTENCES AND SAY THEM OUT LOUD

Can we pitch our tent over in that field?

Can we

pitch our tent
set up camp
park our camper van

over in that field?
near the shower block?
opposite the caravans?

77 At the beach

77.1 ARRIVING AT THE BEACH

Wow, I can't wait to go swimming!

There's a nice shady spot just over there.

Is it safe to swim today?

Yes, but you must stay between the flags.

77.2 BEACH ACTIVITIES

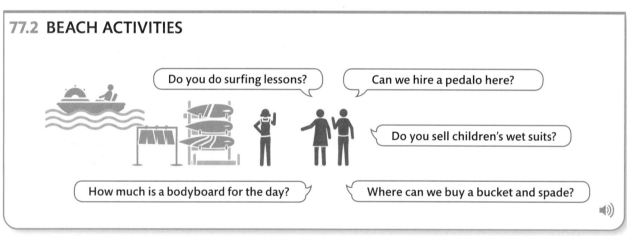

Do you do surfing lessons?

Can we hire a pedalo here?

Do you sell children's wet suits?

How much is a bodyboard for the day?

Where can we buy a bucket and spade?

77.3 VOCABULARY AT THE BEACH

wet suit

bodyboard

paddleboard

pedalo

flag

lifeguard

surfboard

beach ball

deck chair

spade

sun lounger

bucket

77.4 LISTEN AND NUMBER THE SENTENCES IN THE ORDER YOU HEAR THEM

A Can we hire a pedalo here? ☐

B Wow, I can't wait to go swimming! ☐

C There's a nice shady spot just over there. ☐

D Is it safe to swim today? ☐

E How much is a bodyboard for the day? ☑1

F Yes, but you must stay between the flags. ☐

G Do you do surfing lessons? ☐

H Where can we buy a bucket and spade? ☐

77.5 SAY THE SENTENCES OUT LOUD, REPLACING THE PICTURES WITH WORDS

1 Can we hire a 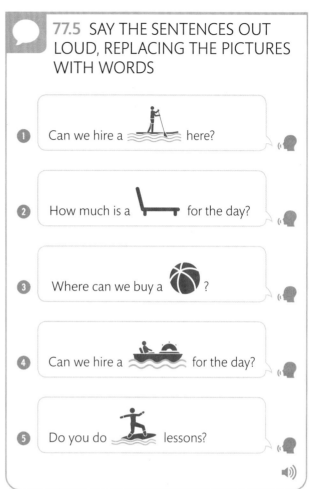 here?

2 How much is a ⌐ for the day?

3 Where can we buy a ⬤ ?

4 Can we hire a 🚣 for the day?

5 Do you do 🏄 lessons?

77.6 MATCH THE SENTENCES AND SAY THEM OUT LOUD

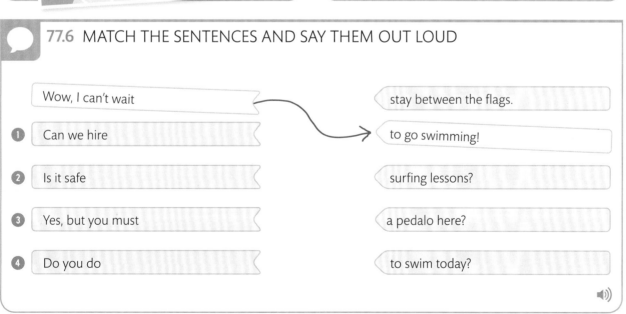

Wow, I can't wait — to go swimming!

stay between the flags.

1 Can we hire — a pedalo here?

2 Is it safe — surfing lessons?

3 Yes, but you must — to swim today?

4 Do you do

78 Finding your way

78.1 ASKING FOR DIRECTIONS

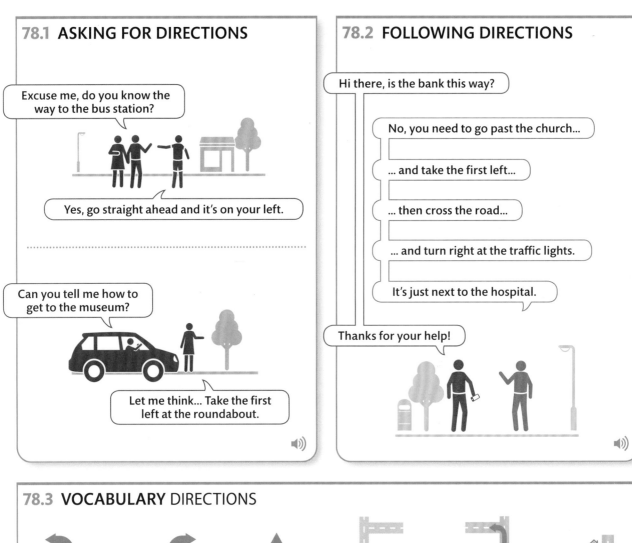

Excuse me, do you know the way to the bus station?

Yes, go straight ahead and it's on your left.

Can you tell me how to get to the museum?

Let me think... Take the first left at the roundabout.

78.2 FOLLOWING DIRECTIONS

Hi there, is the bank this way?

No, you need to go past the church...

... and take the first left...

... then cross the road...

... and turn right at the traffic lights.

It's just next to the hospital.

Thanks for your help!

78.3 VOCABULARY DIRECTIONS

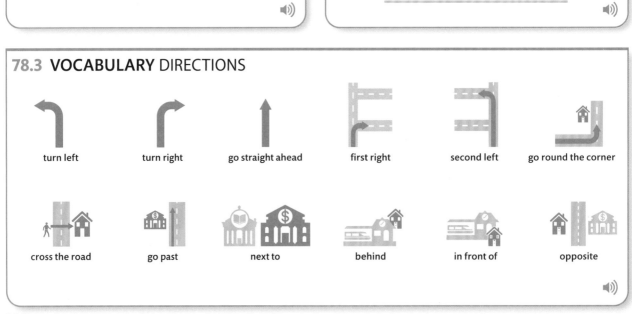

turn left

turn right

go straight ahead

first right

second left

go round the corner

cross the road

go past

next to

behind

in front of

opposite

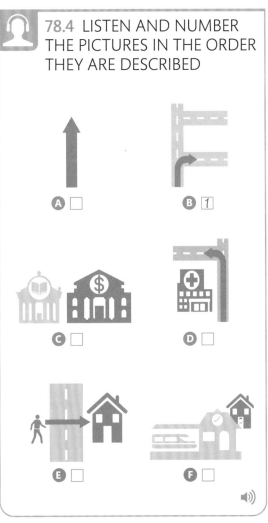

78.4 LISTEN AND NUMBER THE PICTURES IN THE ORDER THEY ARE DESCRIBED

Ⓐ ☐

Ⓑ 1

Ⓒ ☐

Ⓓ ☐

Ⓔ ☐

Ⓕ ☐

🔊

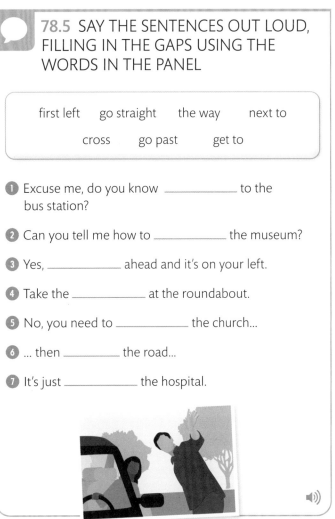

78.5 SAY THE SENTENCES OUT LOUD, FILLING IN THE GAPS USING THE WORDS IN THE PANEL

first left   go straight   the way   next to

cross   go past   get to

1 Excuse me, do you know ＿＿＿＿ to the bus station?

2 Can you tell me how to ＿＿＿＿ the museum?

3 Yes, ＿＿＿＿ ahead and it's on your left.

4 Take the ＿＿＿＿ at the roundabout.

5 No, you need to ＿＿＿＿ the church...

6 ... then ＿＿＿＿ the road...

7 It's just ＿＿＿＿ the hospital.

🔊

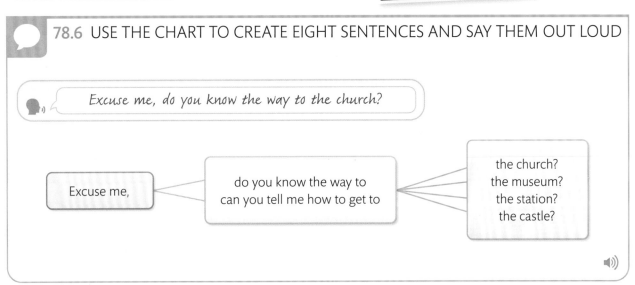

78.6 USE THE CHART TO CREATE EIGHT SENTENCES AND SAY THEM OUT LOUD

🗣 *Excuse me, do you know the way to the church?*

| Excuse me, | do you know the way to
can you tell me how to get to | the church?
the museum?
the station?
the castle? |

🔊

79 Holiday problems

79.1 LOST BELONGINGS

My bag's been stolen with my passport inside!

Okay, I'll need to take some details.

Excuse me, my suitcase hasn't shown up.

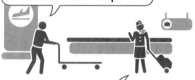

The airline desk can help you.

Hello, you left your phone behind!

Oh gosh, thank you so much!

79.2 DELAYS AND CANCELLATIONS

I'm afraid your flight is delayed.

We'll let you know more as soon as we can.

I can't see our platform number anywhere...

Look at the board. Our train has been cancelled!

79.3 MORE PHRASES

Your luggage has an excess charge.

I'm afraid the gate has closed.

The baggage handlers are on strike.

The train is cancelled due to lack of available train crew.

79.4 ILLNESS AND INJURY

Wanna come hiking tomorrow?

I can't – I've put my back out!

You look awful!

Yeah, I won't make the beach, I've got a tummy bug!

Hello, I've had an accident on holiday and I can't fly home!

Your insurance should cover you if you get a doctor's note.

79.5 LISTEN TO PERSON A AND RESPOND AS PERSON B

A		B
1 My bag's been stolen with my passport inside!		Okay, I'll need to take some details.
2 Excuse me, my suitcase hasn't shown up.		The airline desk can help you.
3 Hello, you left your phone behind!		Oh gosh, thank you so much!
4 Wanna come hiking tomorrow?		I can't – I've put my back out!

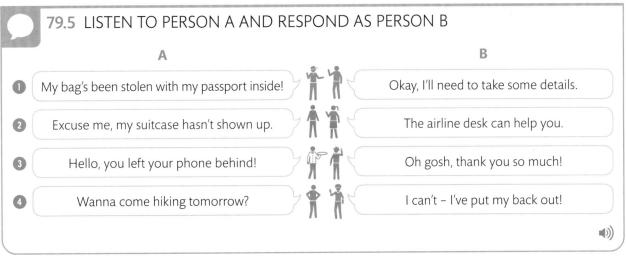

79.6 LISTEN AND NUMBER THE SENTENCES IN THE ORDER YOU HEAR THEM

A We'll let you know more as soon as we can. ☐

B Your luggage has an excess charge. ☐

C I'm afraid the gate has closed. ☑ 1

D I'm afraid your flight is delayed. ☐

E My bag's been stolen with my passport inside! ☐

F Your insurance should cover you if you get a doctor's note. ☐

G Okay, I'll need to take some details. ☐

H Hello, I've had an accident on holiday and I can't fly home! ☐

I The baggage handlers are on strike. ☐

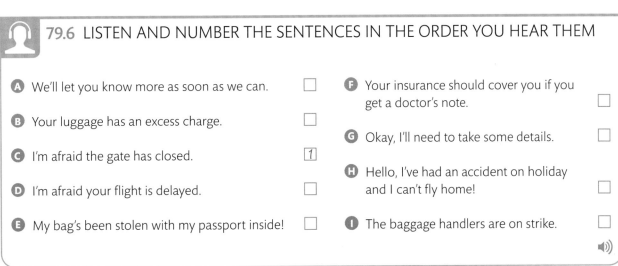

79.7 MATCH THE SENTENCES AND SAY THEM OUT LOUD

The baggage handlers	I've got a tummy bug!
1 The train is cancelled	if you get a doctor's note.
2 Yeah, I won't make the beach,	are on strike.
3 Look at the board.	due to lack of available train crew.
4 Your insurance should cover you	Our train has been cancelled!

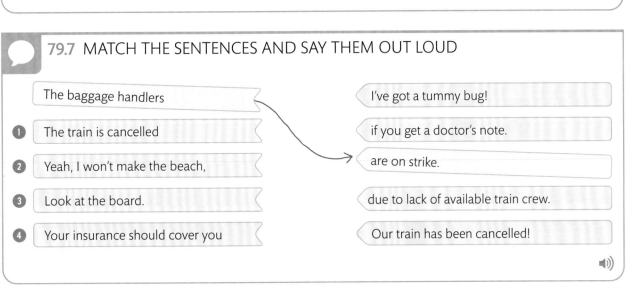

80.1 THE HUMAN BODY

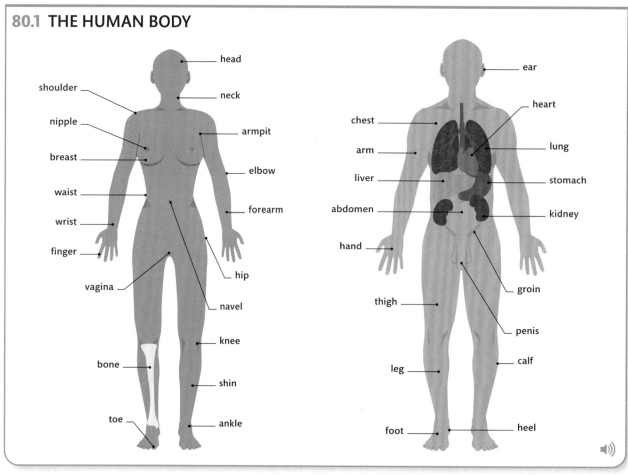

head
shoulder
neck
nipple
armpit
breast
elbow
waist
forearm
wrist
finger
vagina
hip
navel
knee
bone
shin
toe
ankle

ear
chest
heart
arm
lung
liver
stomach
abdomen
kidney
hand
groin
thigh
penis
leg
calf
foot
heel

80.2 MEDICAL PROFESSIONALS

doctor   nurse   surgeon   anaesthetist   paramedic   pharmacist

midwife   paediatrician   optician   physiotherapist   dentist   therapist

80.3 ILLNESSES AND INJURIES

 cough

 cold

 runny nose

 virus

 fever

 sore throat

 infection

 allergy

 headache

 earache

 nausea

 diarrhoea

 food poisoning

 upset stomach

 rash

 graze

 bruise

 bump

 cut

 burn

 bite

 cramp

 sprain

 broken bone

80.4 EMERGENCIES, DIAGNOSES, AND TREATMENT

 ambulance

 hospital

  A & E (accident and emergency)

 emergency

 accident

 hospital porter

 temperature

 blood pressure

 blood test

 heart rate

 X-ray

 scan

 check-up

 bandage

 stitches

 injection / jab

 medication

medication

antibiotics

201

81 At the pharmacy

81.1 DESCRIBING YOUR SYMPTOMS

I have a really sore eye.

It could be an infection.

I have an itchy rash on my arm.

Hmm... It looks like an allergy.

Really? What do you recommend?

This ointment should help.

81.2 MORE PHRASES

My knee really hurts.

I have a really bad headache.

My back is killing me.

🌐 GOOD TO KNOW

In spoken English, we frequently use **really** to emphasize something: I have a **really** sore eye; My eye **really** hurts. **Really** has a similar function to **very**, but it's a little more informal. We also use it to express interest or surprise: **Really? What do you recommend?**

81.3 QUESTIONS YOU MAY HEAR

Do you have any other symptoms?

Yes, I also have a runny nose.

Do you have any allergies?

Yes, I'm allergic to aspirin.

Are you taking any other medication?

Yes, I'm taking antibiotics.

How long have you had symptoms?

For about a week.

81.4 LISTEN AND NUMBER THE PICTURES IN THE ORDER THEY ARE DESCRIBED

A ☐

B ☐

C 1

D ☐

E ☐

F ☐

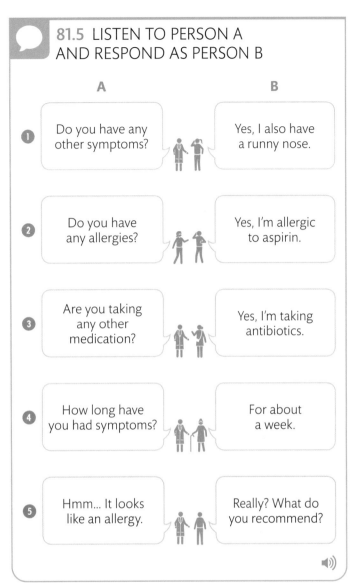

81.5 LISTEN TO PERSON A AND RESPOND AS PERSON B

	A	B
1	Do you have any other symptoms?	Yes, I also have a runny nose.
2	Do you have any allergies?	Yes, I'm allergic to aspirin.
3	Are you taking any other medication?	Yes, I'm taking antibiotics.
4	How long have you had symptoms?	For about a week.
5	Hmm... It looks like an allergy.	Really? What do you recommend?

81.6 USE THE CHART TO CREATE FIVE SENTENCES AND SAY THEM OUT LOUD

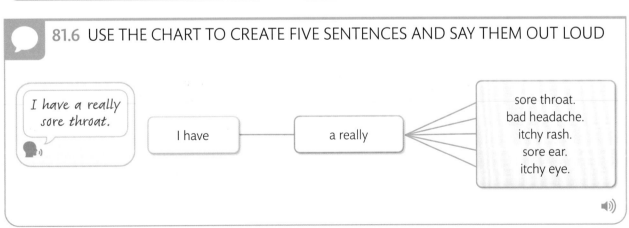

I have a really sore throat.

I have → a really →

sore throat.
bad headache.
itchy rash.
sore ear.
itchy eye.

81.7 TREATMENT AND DOSAGE

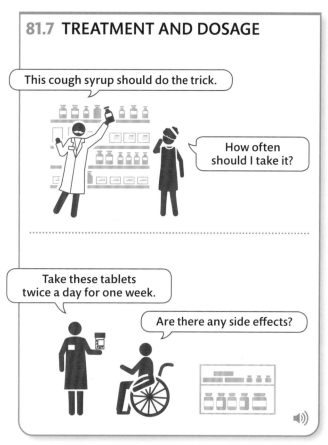

This cough syrup should do the trick.

How often should I take it?

Take these tablets twice a day for one week.

Are there any side effects?

81.8 PRESCRIPTIONS

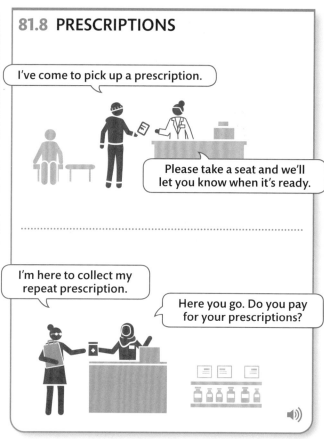

I've come to pick up a prescription.

Please take a seat and we'll let you know when it's ready.

I'm here to collect my repeat prescription.

Here you go. Do you pay for your prescriptions?

81.9 VOCABULARY IN A PHARMACY

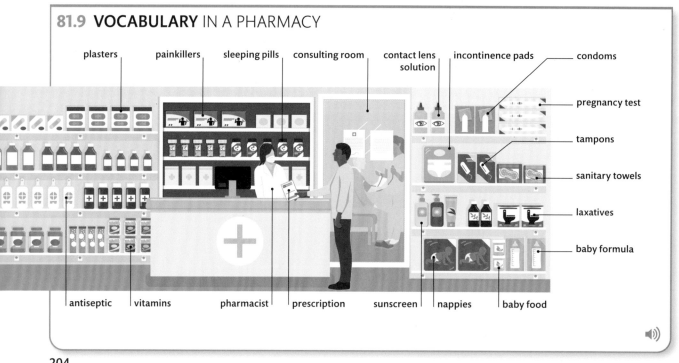

plasters

painkillers

sleeping pills

consulting room

contact lens solution

incontinence pads

condoms

pregnancy test

tampons

sanitary towels

laxatives

baby formula

antiseptic

vitamins

pharmacist

prescription

sunscreen

nappies

baby food

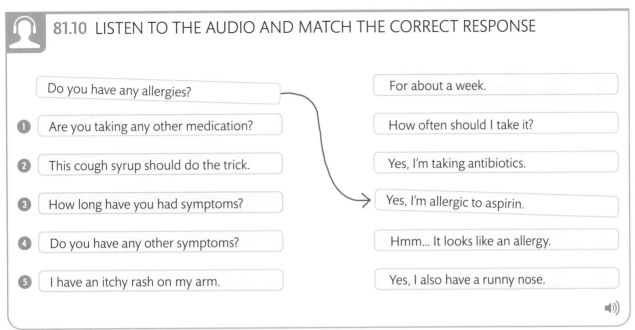

81.10 LISTEN TO THE AUDIO AND MATCH THE CORRECT RESPONSE

Do you have any allergies?

① Are you taking any other medication?

② This cough syrup should do the trick.

③ How long have you had symptoms?

④ Do you have any other symptoms?

⑤ I have an itchy rash on my arm.

For about a week.

How often should I take it?

Yes, I'm taking antibiotics.

Yes, I'm allergic to aspirin.

Hmm... It looks like an allergy.

Yes, I also have a runny nose.

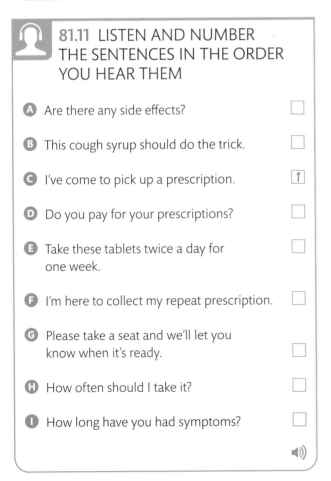

81.11 LISTEN AND NUMBER THE SENTENCES IN THE ORDER YOU HEAR THEM

Ⓐ Are there any side effects?

Ⓑ This cough syrup should do the trick.

Ⓒ I've come to pick up a prescription. `1`

Ⓓ Do you pay for your prescriptions?

Ⓔ Take these tablets twice a day for one week.

Ⓕ I'm here to collect my repeat prescription.

Ⓖ Please take a seat and we'll let you know when it's ready.

Ⓗ How often should I take it?

Ⓘ How long have you had symptoms?

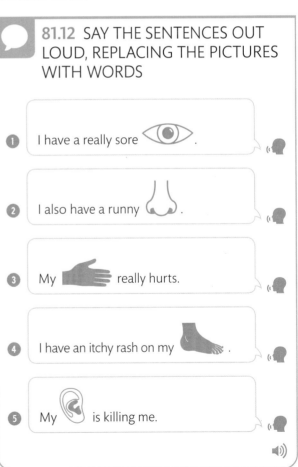

81.12 SAY THE SENTENCES OUT LOUD, REPLACING THE PICTURES WITH WORDS

① I have a really sore ⊙.

② I also have a runny 👃.

③ My 🖐 really hurts.

④ I have an itchy rash on my 🦶.

⑤ My 👂 is killing me.

82 Booking an appointment

82.1 AT THE DOCTOR'S SURGERY

Hi there, I'd like to book an appointment with Doctor Cole.

Can I ask what it's about?

I think I might have a chest infection.

We could squeeze you in later at 4.30?

That's great, thanks.

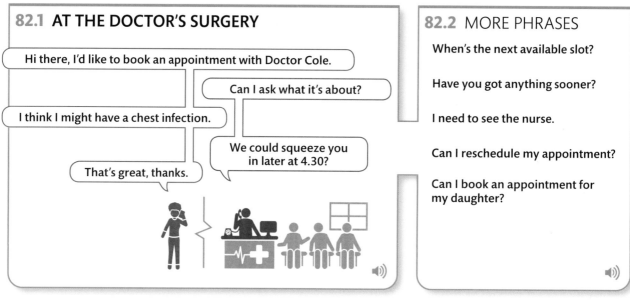

82.2 MORE PHRASES

When's the next available slot?

Have you got anything sooner?

I need to see the nurse.

Can I reschedule my appointment?

Can I book an appointment for my daughter?

82.3 AT THE DENTIST

I'd like to book a check-up, please.

Have you been with us before?

No, I haven't.

I'm afraid we're not taking on new patients.

I've got an appointment next week but I need to cancel it.

No problem, can I take your name?

SMILE Dental

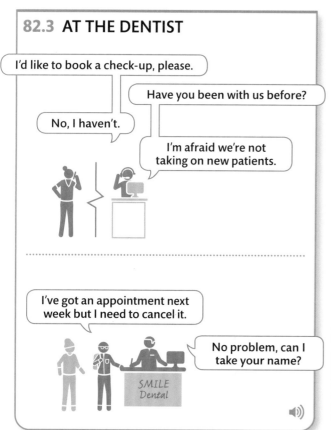

82.4 EMERGENCY APPOINTMENTS

I need an emergency appointment. I've got really bad toothache.

We've got a slot in half an hour if that's any good?

If you need an urgent appointment, we'll place you on the triage list...

... and the doctor will call you back as soon as possible.

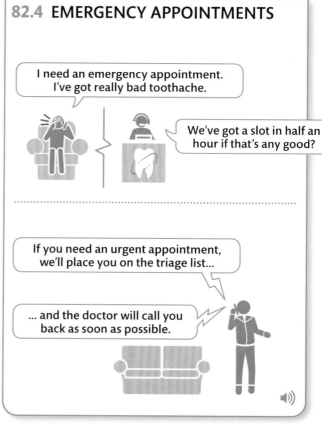

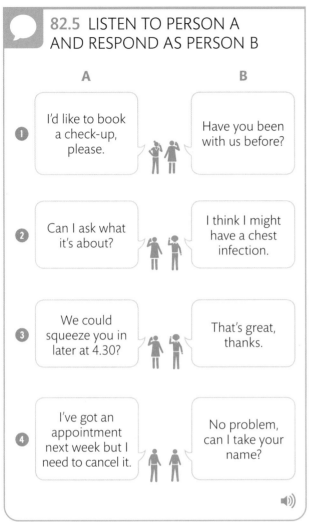

82.5 LISTEN TO PERSON A AND RESPOND AS PERSON B

A | B

1. I'd like to book a check-up, please. | Have you been with us before?

2. Can I ask what it's about? | I think I might have a chest infection.

3. We could squeeze you in later at 4.30? | That's great, thanks.

4. I've got an appointment next week but I need to cancel it. | No problem, can I take your name?

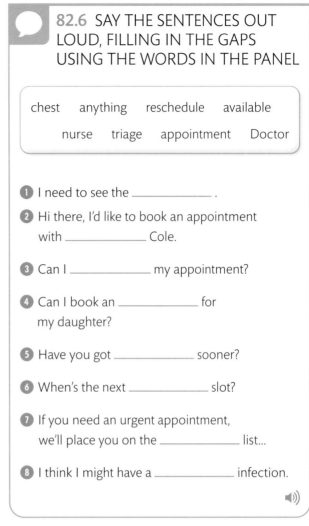

82.6 SAY THE SENTENCES OUT LOUD, FILLING IN THE GAPS USING THE WORDS IN THE PANEL

chest   anything   reschedule   available

nurse   triage   appointment   Doctor

1. I need to see the _____ .
2. Hi there, I'd like to book an appointment with _____ Cole.
3. Can I _____ my appointment?
4. Can I book an _____ for my daughter?
5. Have you got _____ sooner?
6. When's the next _____ slot?
7. If you need an urgent appointment, we'll place you on the _____ list...
8. I think I might have a _____ infection.

82.7 USE THE CHART TO CREATE 12 SENTENCES AND SAY THEM OUT LOUD

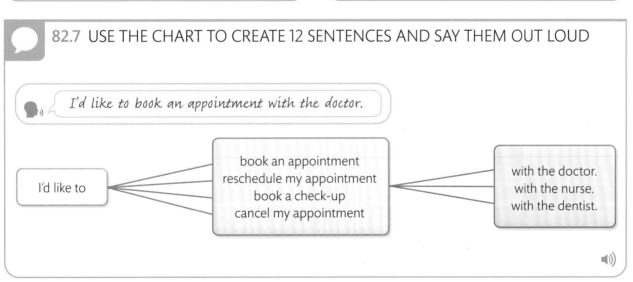

I'd like to book an appointment with the doctor.

| I'd like to | book an appointment / reschedule my appointment / book a check-up / cancel my appointment | with the doctor. / with the nurse. / with the dentist. |

207

83 Seeing the doctor

83.1 DESCRIBING SYMPTOMS

What seems to be the problem?

I've had a bad cough for a week and it's getting worse.

I keep getting splitting headaches.

Okay, let me listen to your chest.

83.2 MORE PHRASES

I've been throwing up all night.

My shoulder has been hurting.

My son's got a fever.

I've been under the weather.

I've found a lump in my breast.

83.3 GENERAL CARE

It seems to be healing up nicely...

Which arm would you like the injection in?

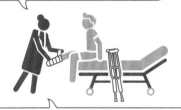

... I'll just change your bandage.

Right, please! I'm left-handed.

83.4 MORE PHRASES

I'll refer you for some tests.

Can I book a flu jab?

Let's take your temperature.

I'd like a repeat prescription.

I'm due a check-up.

83.5 ADVICE AND DIAGNOSIS

What do you advise?

It looks like a mild infection.

Come back in two weeks and we'll see how it's looking.

You need to rest and drink plenty of fluids.

Will I need antibiotics?

83.6 LISTEN TO PERSON A AND RESPOND AS PERSON B

A | | **B**

1. Which arm would you like the injection in? 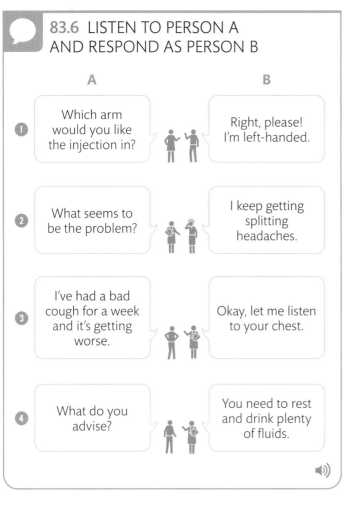 Right, please! I'm left-handed.

2. What seems to be the problem? I keep getting splitting headaches.

3. I've had a bad cough for a week and it's getting worse. Okay, let me listen to your chest.

4. What do you advise? You need to rest and drink plenty of fluids.

🔊

83.7 LISTEN AND NUMBER THE SENTENCES IN THE ORDER YOU HEAR THEM

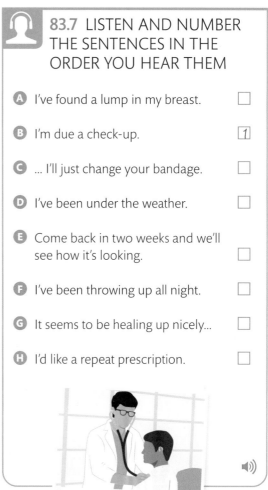

A I've found a lump in my breast. ☐

B I'm due a check-up. [1]

C ... I'll just change your bandage. ☐

D I've been under the weather. ☐

E Come back in two weeks and we'll see how it's looking. ☐

F I've been throwing up all night. ☐

G It seems to be healing up nicely... ☐

H I'd like a repeat prescription. ☐

🔊

83.8 MATCH THE SENTENCES AND SAY THEM OUT LOUD

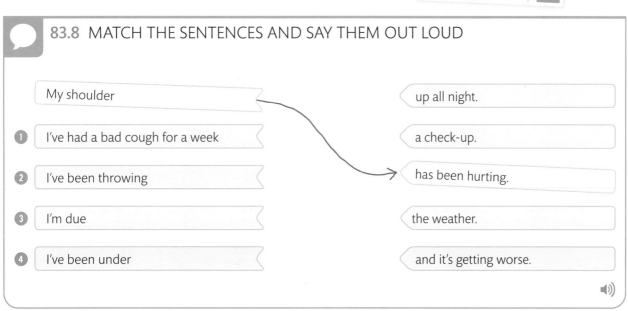

My shoulder ⟶ has been hurting.

1. I've had a bad cough for a week — up all night.

2. I've been throwing — a check-up.

3. I'm due — the weather.

4. I've been under — and it's getting worse.

🔊

84 Injuries and emergencies

84.1 IN AN EMERGENCY

Which service do you require?

I need an ambulance.

What's the emergency?

My husband has severe chest pains.

I'll send an ambulance for you right away.

84.2 MORE PHRASES

I've had an accident.

Please come quickly!

She's had a fall.

I need a doctor urgently.

He's having a fit.

84.3 MINOR INJURIES

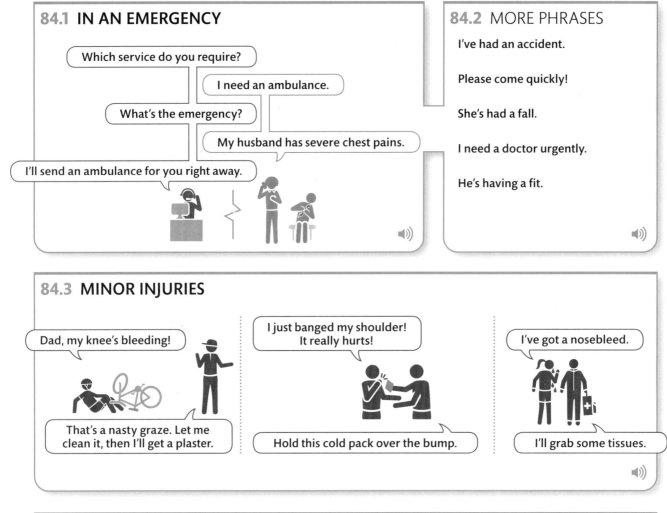

Dad, my knee's bleeding!

That's a nasty graze. Let me clean it, then I'll get a plaster.

I just banged my shoulder! It really hurts!

Hold this cold pack over the bump.

I've got a nosebleed.

I'll grab some tissues.

84.4 MORE SERIOUS INJURIES

Is my ankle broken or just sprained?

Not sure... I'm sending you for an X-ray.

My daughter's gashed her arm.

It looks like she may need stitches.

I burned my hand on the stove. It's really painful.

Let me take a look.

84.5 MATCH THE SENTENCES AND SAY THEM OUT LOUD

I've had → an accident.

❶ I need a — doctor urgently.

❷ I burned my hand on the — stove. It's really painful.

❸ I'll grab — some tissues.

❹ My husband has — severe chest pains.

❺ He's having — a fit.

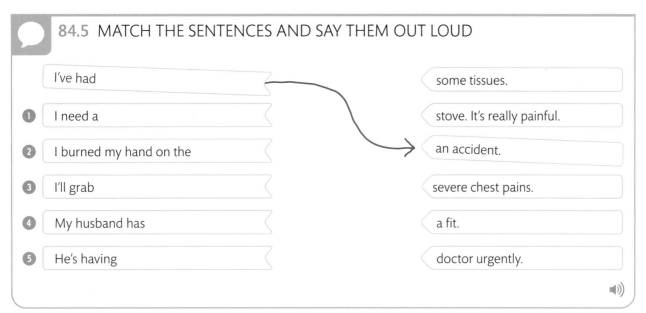

84.6 LISTEN AND CIRCLE THE ITEM YOU HEAR

❶ A   B

❷ A   B

❸ A   B

❹ A   B

84.7 RESPOND OUT LOUD TO THE AUDIO, FILLING IN THE GAPS USING THE WORDS IN THE PANEL

graze   bump   stitches   pains

❶ My daughter's gashed her arm.

It looks like she may need _____.

❷ I just banged my shoulder! It really hurts!

Hold this cold pack over the _____.

❸ What's the emergency?

My husband has severe chest _____.

❹ Dad, my knee's bleeding!

That's a nasty _____.

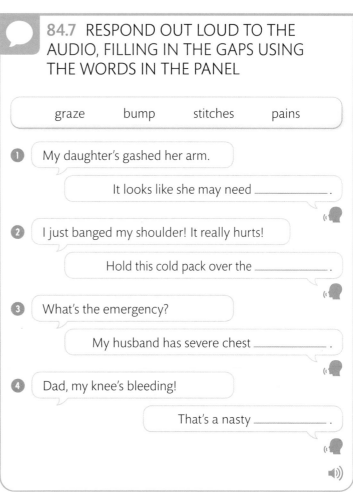

85 The hospital

85.1 AT THE HOSPITAL

We need to keep you overnight for observation.

I've got a check-up with the nurse at 4.30.

Ward 1 →

EXIT ↗

Waiting room →

I need to see someone urgently.

Do I need to have an operation?

Okay, could I see your appointment letter, please?

I'll take your details so we can get you seen.

Are you allergic to anything?

Yes, I'm allergic to penicillin.

85.3 LISTEN AND NUMBER THE PICTURES IN THE ORDER THEY ARE DESCRIBED

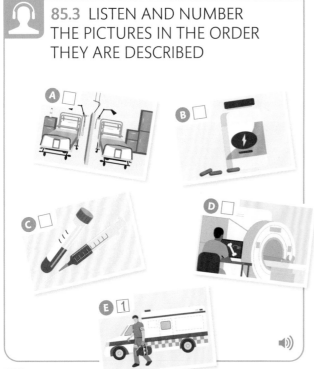

A ☐
B ☐
C ☐
D ☐
E 1

85.4 SAY THE SENTENCES OUT LOUD, FILLING IN THE GAPS USING THE WORDS IN THE PANEL

check-up   urgently   examine

doctor   operation   medical

1 I need to see someone _____ .

2 We have a _____ emergency.

3 How soon will I be seen by a _____ ?

4 I've got a _____ with the nurse at 4.30.

5 Do I need to have an _____ ?

6 I'm going to need to _____ you.

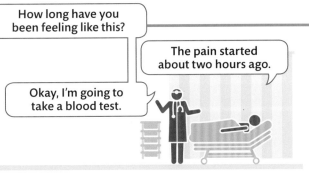

How long have you been feeling like this?

The pain started about two hours ago.

Okay, I'm going to take a blood test.

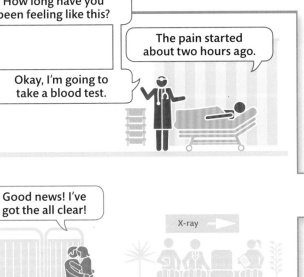

Good news! I've got the all clear!

That's such a relief!

X-ray →

85.2 MORE PHRASES

We have a medical emergency.

Are you taking any regular medications?

Have you got someone you'd like to call?

We'll follow up in three months.

I'm going to need to examine you.

I'm here for my scan.

How soon will I be seen by a doctor?

We'll move you to another ward for observation.

🔊

85.5 LISTEN TO PERSON A AND RESPOND AS PERSON B

A		B
① I need to see someone urgently.		I'll take your details so we can get you seen.
② Are you allergic to anything?		Yes, I'm allergic to penicillin.
③ How long have you been feeling like this?		The pain started about two hours ago.
④ Good news! I've got the all clear!		That's such a relief!
⑤ I've got a check-up with the nurse at 4.30.		Okay, could I see your appointment letter, please?
⑥ The pain started about two hours ago.		Okay, I'm going to take a blood test.

🔊

85.6 HAVING AN OPERATION

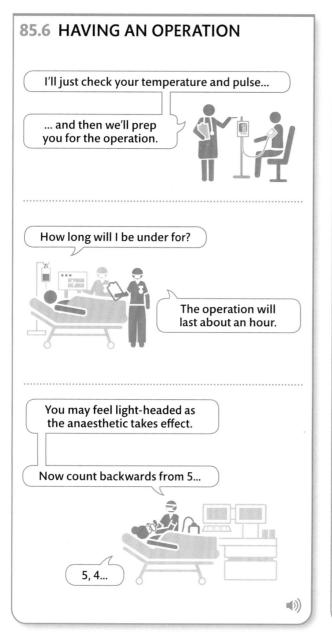

I'll just check your temperature and pulse...

... and then we'll prep you for the operation.

How long will I be under for?

The operation will last about an hour.

You may feel light-headed as the anaesthetic takes effect.

Now count backwards from 5...

5, 4...

85.7 RECOVERING FROM TREATMENT

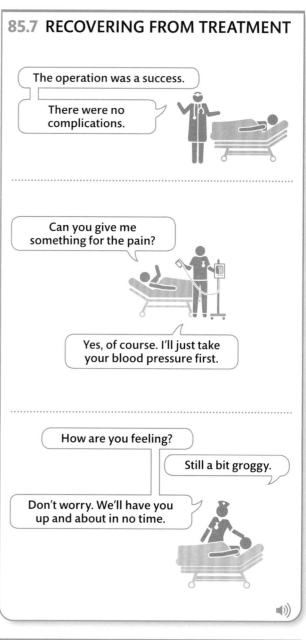

The operation was a success.

There were no complications.

Can you give me something for the pain?

Yes, of course. I'll just take your blood pressure first.

How are you feeling?

Still a bit groggy.

Don't worry. We'll have you up and about in no time.

85.8 VOCABULARY HOSPITAL TREATMENT

operation

operating theatre

anaesthetic

ward

intensive care unit

visiting hours

85.9 LISTEN TO PERSON A AND RESPOND AS PERSON B

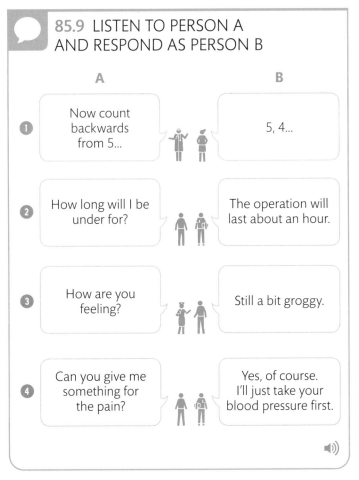

A	B
1 Now count backwards from 5...	5, 4...
2 How long will I be under for?	The operation will last about an hour.
3 How are you feeling?	Still a bit groggy.
4 Can you give me something for the pain?	Yes, of course. I'll just take your blood pressure first.

85.10 LISTEN AND NUMBER THE SENTENCES IN THE ORDER YOU HEAR THEM

Ⓐ How long will I be under for? ☐

Ⓑ Now count backwards from 5... ☐

Ⓒ There were no complications. ☐

Ⓓ ... and then we'll prep you for the operation. ☐

Ⓔ Still a bit groggy. ☐

Ⓕ I'll just check your temperature and pulse... ☐

Ⓖ How are you feeling? ☐ 1

Ⓗ The operation was a success. ☐

85.11 SAY THE SENTENCES OUT LOUD, FILLING IN THE GAPS USING THE WORDS IN THE PANEL

complications	pressure	groggy	about
under	backwards	anaesthetic	temperature

1 I'll just take your blood _____ first.

2 Still a bit _____ .

3 Don't worry. We'll have you up and _____ in no time.

4 I'll just check your _____ and pulse...

5 You may feel light-headed as the _____ takes effect.

6 How long will I be _____ for?

7 Now count _____ from 5...

8 There were no _____ .

86 Dental care

86.1 TALKING TO THE DENTIST

I've got bad toothache.

Do I need braces?

I think my crown has come loose.

My filling has come out.

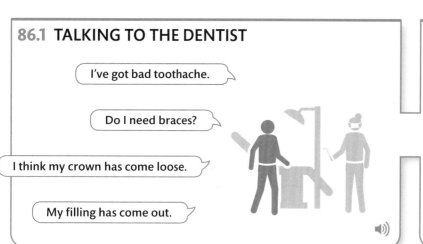

86.2 MORE PHRASES

Can I have my teeth whitened?

I brush my teeth twice a day.

I need to see the hygienist.

My son's first teeth are coming through.

86.3 ADVICE AND DIAGNOSIS

Remember to floss regularly.

It looks like you need a small filling.

Would you like to rinse your mouth out?

Make sure you don't brush too hard.

86.4 MORE PHRASES

Open a bit wider for me, please.

You've got a build-up of plaque.

You'll need this tooth taken out.

Let me know if you feel any pain.

You've got a small cavity.

86.5 VOCABULARY AT THE DENTIST

dentist

whitening

toothache

to floss

to brush

to rinse

cavity

filling

plaque

crown

toothbrush

braces

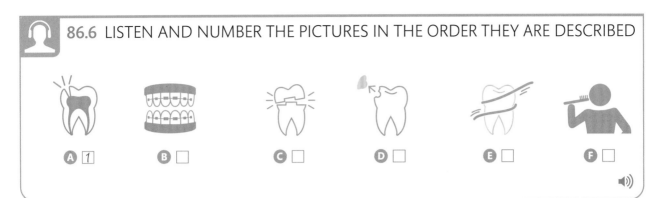

A 1   B ☐   C ☐   D ☐   E ☐   F ☐

86.7 LISTEN AND NUMBER THE SENTENCES IN THE ORDER YOU HEAR THEM

A I've got bad toothache. ☐
B You've got a small cavity. ☐
C Remember to floss regularly. 1
D You've got a build-up of plaque. ☐
E Open a bit wider for me, please. ☐

F I need to see the hygienist. ☐
G Let me know if you feel any pain. ☐
H Make sure you don't brush too hard. ☐
I You'll need this tooth taken out. ☐
J It looks like you need a small filling. ☐

86.8 MATCH THE SENTENCES AND SAY THEM OUT LOUD

It looks like you need   are coming through.

1 I brush my teeth   my teeth whitened?

2 I need to see   a small filling.

3 I think my crown   twice a day.

4 Can I have   the hygienist.

5 My son's first teeth   has come loose.

Mental health support

87.1 ASKING FOR THERAPY

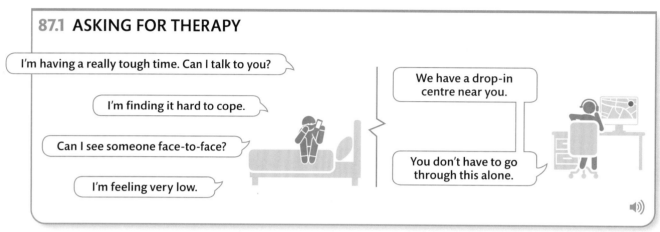

I'm having a really tough time. Can I talk to you?

I'm finding it hard to cope.

Can I see someone face-to-face?

I'm feeling very low.

We have a drop-in centre near you.

You don't have to go through this alone.

87.2 THERAPY QUESTIONS

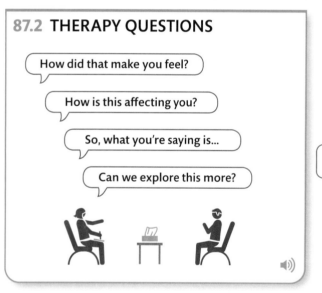

How did that make you feel?

How is this affecting you?

So, what you're saying is...

Can we explore this more?

87.3 GROUP THERAPY

Let's go round the group and say how we're feeling.

I've been a bit up and down.

I'm doing better this week.

These sessions are really helping me.

I'm anxious all the time.

87.4 MORE PHRASES

How are you feeling today?

That's a real trigger for me.

Your feelings are valid.

Talking about it really helps.

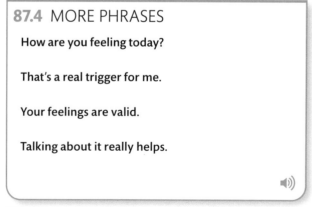

87.5 VOCABULARY EMOTIONS

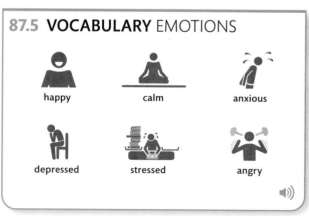

happy

calm

anxious

depressed

stressed

angry

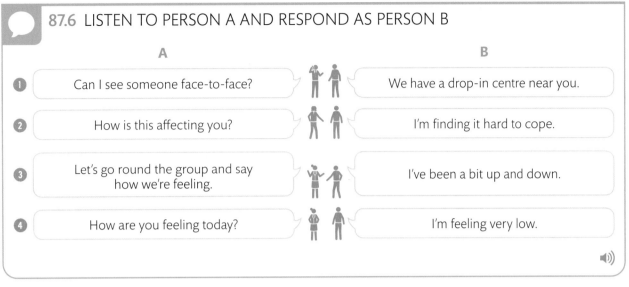

87.6 LISTEN TO PERSON A AND RESPOND AS PERSON B

	A	B
1	Can I see someone face-to-face?	We have a drop-in centre near you.
2	How is this affecting you?	I'm finding it hard to cope.
3	Let's go round the group and say how we're feeling.	I've been a bit up and down.
4	How are you feeling today?	I'm feeling very low.

87.7 USE THE CHART TO CREATE 12 SENTENCES AND SAY THEM OUT LOUD

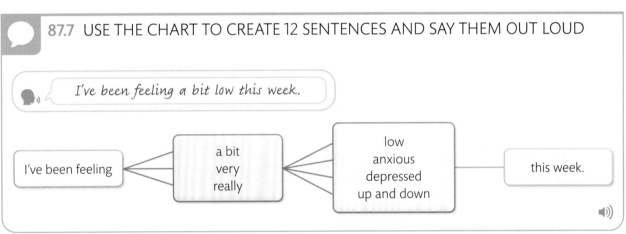

I've been feeling a bit low this week.

I've been feeling → a bit / very / really → low / anxious / depressed / up and down → this week.

87.8 SAY THE SENTENCES OUT LOUD, FILLING IN THE GAPS USING THE WORDS IN THE PANEL

explore	better	helping	feel	trigger	cope	valid	affecting

1 How is this _____ you?

2 These sessions are really _____ me.

3 I'm finding it hard to _____ .

4 Your feelings are _____ .

5 How did that make you _____ ?

6 That's a real _____ for me.

7 Can we _____ this more?

8 I'm doing _____ this week.

88 Media and communications

88.1 PHONE CALLS, TEXTS, AND EMAILS

to call

to leave a voicemail

to take a message

to put on hold

to transfer a call

to put on speaker

text / message

video call

email

email address

to click

to tap

88.2 DEVICES

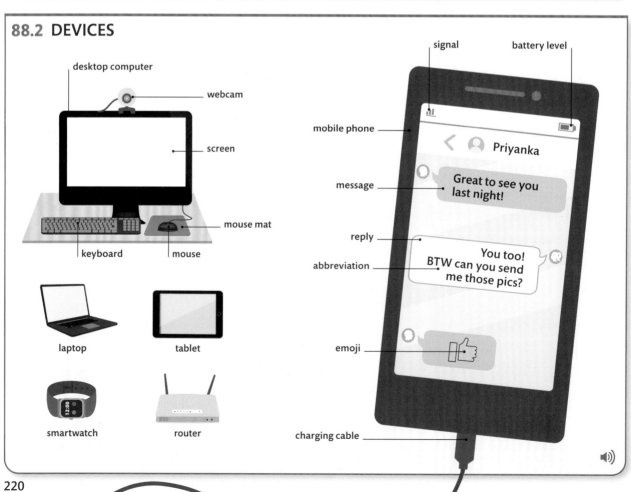

desktop computer

webcam

screen

mouse mat

keyboard

mouse

laptop

tablet

smartwatch

router

signal

battery level

mobile phone

Priyanka

message

Great to see you last night!

reply

You too! BTW can you send me those pics?

abbreviation

emoji

charging cable

88.3 THE INTERNET

website

Wi-Fi

broadband

internet provider

data

account

settings

network

signal

hotspot

virus

password

menu

app

cookies

link

to browse

to stream

88.4 SOCIAL MEDIA

to follow

to like

to go viral

to trend

to DM someone

to livestream

to troll

to scroll

to share

to block

podcast

post

influencer

follower

hashtag

selfie

88.5 READING

book

e-reader

magazine

subscription

article

headline

GIRL RAISES MONEY FOR CHARITY

newspaper

221

89 Formal phone calls

89.1 MAKING A CALL

Hi, could I speak to...?

Hello, I wonder if you can help me...

I'm calling about...

I'm calling you regarding...

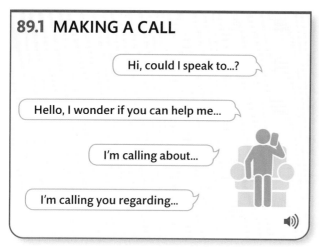

89.2 CALLING CUSTOMER SERVICE

Hello, customer service, how can I help?

I'll just put you on hold while I transfer you.

Thank you for waiting.

Thanks for calling.

89.3 LEAVING MESSAGES AND CALLING BACK

Janos isn't available right now. Can I take a message?

Yes. Please ask him to call Ash at ABC Tech as soon as possible.

89.4 MORE PHRASES

Can I leave a message?

He knows where to reach me.

She'll call you back shortly.

We'll need to check our system and get back to you.

89.5 ENDING A CALL

Is there anything else I can help with?

No, that's all. Thanks for your help. Goodbye.

I appreciate the call, thank you.

My pleasure.

89.6 MORE PHRASES

Thanks for your call.

Thank you so much for calling.

Let's speak again soon.

You've been a great help.

Have a nice evening.

89.7 LISTEN TO PERSON A AND RESPOND AS PERSON B

A	B

1 Janos isn't available right now. Can I take a message? | Yes. Please ask him to call Ash at ABC Tech as soon as possible.

2 I appreciate the call, thank you. | My pleasure.

3 Thank you so much for calling. | Let's speak again soon.

4 Is there anything else I can help with? | No, that's all. Thanks for your help. Goodbye.

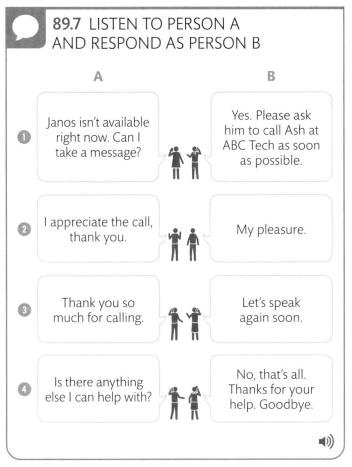

🔊

89.8 LISTEN AND NUMBER THE SENTENCES IN THE ORDER YOU HEAR THEM

A I appreciate the call, thank you. ☐

B Hi, could I speak to...? ☐ 1

C I'm calling you regarding... ☐

D Have a nice evening. ☐

E Let's speak again soon. ☐

F She'll call you back shortly. ☐

G You've been a great help. ☐

H Thanks for your call. ☐

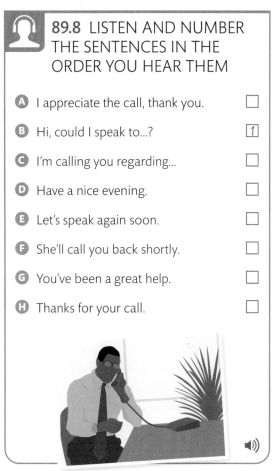

🔊

89.9 MATCH THE SENTENCES AND SAY THEM OUT LOUD

Hello, customer service, → how can I help?

1 We'll need to check our system — to reach me.

2 Is there anything else — if you can help me...

3 He knows where — I can help with?

4 Hello, I wonder — and get back to you.

5 Thank you so much — for calling.

🔊

90 Informal phone calls

90.1 MAKING AND RECEIVING CALLS

Hi, Mum. How's it going?

Good, thank you. I'm just checking in about tonight.

Hey mate, whereabouts are you?

Hiya, I'm right here!

90.2 MORE PHRASES

You okay?

Lovely to hear from you!

Sorry, I can't talk now.

I'll message you back.

I'll put you on speaker.

90.3 PHONE PROBLEMS

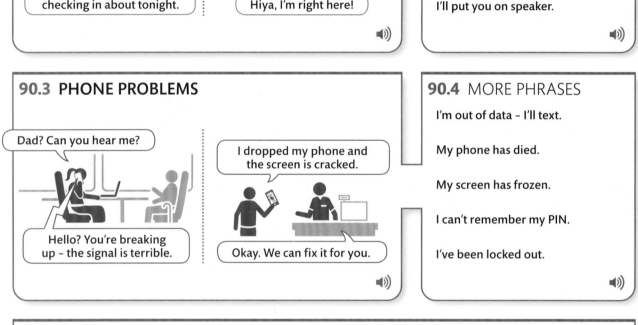

Dad? Can you hear me?

Hello? You're breaking up – the signal is terrible.

I dropped my phone and the screen is cracked.

Okay. We can fix it for you.

90.4 MORE PHRASES

I'm out of data – I'll text.

My phone has died.

My screen has frozen.

I can't remember my PIN.

I've been locked out.

90.5 ENDING A CALL

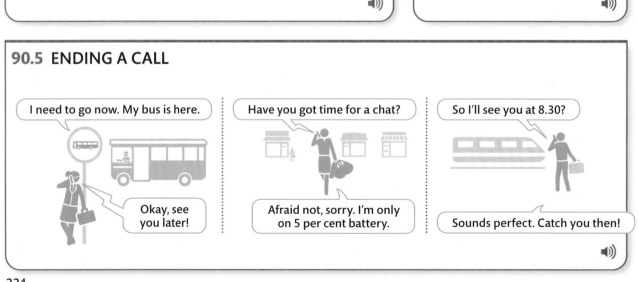

I need to go now. My bus is here.

Okay, see you later!

Have you got time for a chat?

Afraid not, sorry. I'm only on 5 per cent battery.

So I'll see you at 8.30?

Sounds perfect. Catch you then!

90.6 LISTEN TO PERSON A AND RESPOND AS PERSON B

	A		B
1	Hi, Mum. How's it going?		Good, thank you. I'm just checking in about tonight.
2	Hey mate, whereabouts are you?		Hiya, I'm right here!
3	Have you got time for a chat?		Afraid not, sorry. I'm only on 5 per cent battery.
4	I dropped my phone and the screen is cracked.		Okay. We can fix it for you.

90.7 SAY THE SENTENCES OUT LOUD, FILLING IN THE GAPS USING THE WORDS IN THE PANEL

> PIN   talk   message   locked
> screen   died   speaker

1 Sorry, I can't _____ now.

2 I can't remember my _____ .

3 I'll _____ you back.

4 I'll put you on _____ .

5 My phone has _____ .

6 I've been _____ out.

7 My _____ has frozen.

90.8 RESPOND OUT LOUD TO THE AUDIO, FILLING IN THE GAPS USING THE WORDS IN THE PANEL

> Catch   breaking   fix   checking

1 Dad? Can you hear me?

   Hello? You're _____ up – the signal is terrible.

2 So I'll see you at 8.30?

   Sounds perfect. _____ you then!

3 Hi, Mum. How's it going?

   Good, thank you. I'm just _____ in about tonight.

4 I dropped my phone and the screen is cracked.

   Okay. We can _____ it for you.

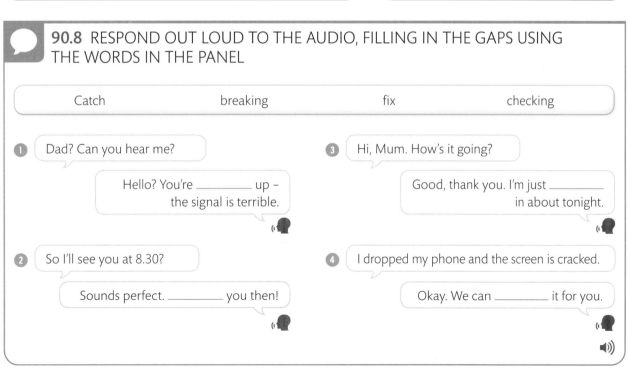

91 Using the internet

91.1 ACCESSING WI-FI

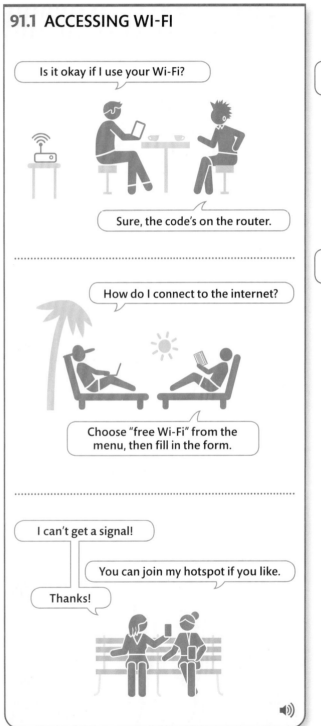

Is it okay if I use your Wi-Fi?

Sure, the code's on the router.

How do I connect to the internet?

Choose "free Wi-Fi" from the menu, then fill in the form.

I can't get a signal!

You can join my hotspot if you like.

Thanks!

91.2 STAYING SAFE

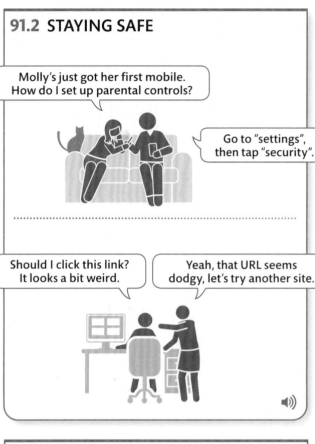

Molly's just got her first mobile. How do I set up parental controls?

Go to "settings", then tap "security".

Should I click this link? It looks a bit weird.

Yeah, that URL seems dodgy, let's try another site.

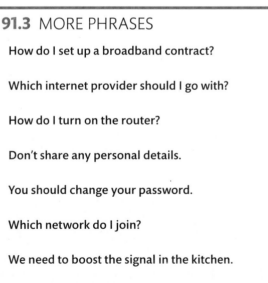

91.3 MORE PHRASES

How do I set up a broadband contract?

Which internet provider should I go with?

How do I turn on the router?

Don't share any personal details.

You should change your password.

Which network do I join?

We need to boost the signal in the kitchen.

91.4 LISTEN TO PERSON A AND RESPOND AS PERSON B

	A		B
1	Is it okay if I use your Wi-Fi?		Sure, the code's on the router.
2	How do I connect to the internet?		Choose "free Wi-Fi" from the menu, then fill in the form.
3	I can't get a signal!		You can join my hotspot if you like.
4	Should I click this link? It looks a bit weird.		Yeah, that URL seems dodgy, let's try another site.

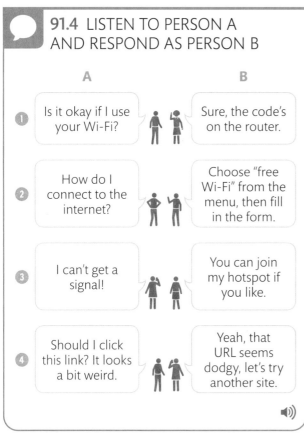

91.5 LISTEN AND NUMBER THE SENTENCES IN THE ORDER YOU HEAR THEM

A How do I set up a broadband contract? ☐

B Which internet provider should I go with? ☐

C How do I turn on the router? ☐

D Which network do I join? 1

E Don't share any personal details. ☐

F You should change your password. ☐

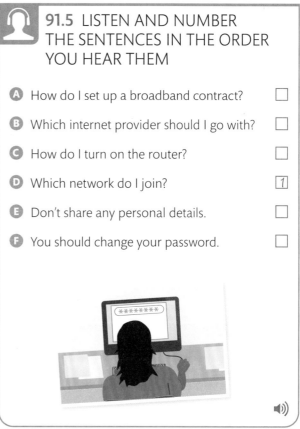

91.6 RESPOND OUT LOUD TO THE AUDIO, FILLING IN THE GAPS USING THE WORDS IN THE PANEL

site	hotspot	menu	security

1 How do I connect to the internet?

Choose "free Wi-Fi" from the _____ , then fill in the form.

2 Molly's just got her first mobile. How do I set up parental controls?

Go to "settings", then tap "_____".

3 I can't get a signal!

You can join my _____ if you like.

4 Should I click this link? It looks a bit weird.

Yeah, that URL seems dodgy, let's try another _____ .

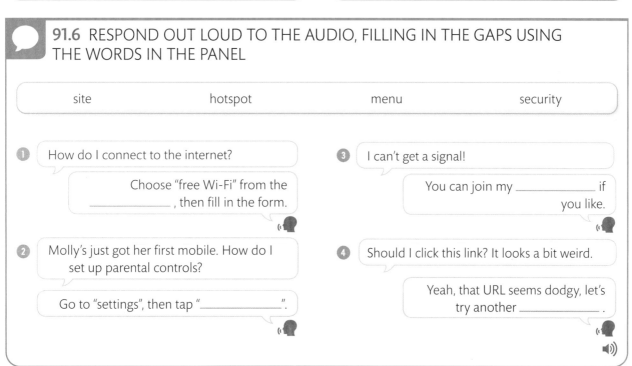

227

91.7 EVERYDAY TASKS

Hey, what's going on?

I'm setting up an online account for our energy bills.

I'm looking up some recipes for lunch.

I'm just tracking the grocery delivery.

91.8 MORE PHRASES

I'm booking a doctor's appointment.

I'm ordering more cat food.

I'm renewing my driving licence.

I'm cancelling my gym membership.

I'm transferring some money.

91.9 WORK AND STUDY

So, what's on your agenda for today?

Let's see... I need to check my emails...

... catch up on the latest research...

... watch the company livestream...

... and sign up for that online training course.

How's it going?

Not too bad, thanks. I'm just uploading my essay...

... then I've got a webinar this afternoon.

91.10 HAVING FUN

What are you all up to?

I'm putting some new tunes on my party playlist.

I'm messaging my friend.

I'm downloading our tickets for today...

... I'll share yours with you on our group chat.

I'm streaming a new series.

I'm scrolling through my socials.

We're gaming!

91.11 LISTEN AND NUMBER THE PICTURES IN THE ORDER THEY ARE DESCRIBED

A ☐ B ☐ 1
C ☐ D ☐
E ☐ F ☐

91.12 SAY THE SENTENCES OUT LOUD, FILLING IN THE GAPS USING THE WORDS IN THE PANEL

webinar	booking	online	ordering
streaming	tracking	check	scrolling

1 I'm _____ a doctor's appointment.

2 I need to _____ my emails...

3 I've got a _____ this afternoon.

4 I'm _____ a new series.

5 ... and sign up for that _____ training course.

6 I'm _____ more cat food.

7 I'm _____ through my socials.

8 I'm just _____ the grocery delivery.

91.13 MATCH THE SENTENCES AND SAY THEM OUT LOUD

I'm putting some new tunes → on my party playlist.

1 I'm downloading — our tickets for today...

2 ... I'll share yours with you — on our group chat.

3 I'm setting up an online account — ... then I've got a webinar this afternoon.

4 I'm just uploading my essay... — for our energy bills.

92.1 CONNECTION ISSUES

92.2 TROUBLESHOOTING

92.3 DIGITAL SECURITY

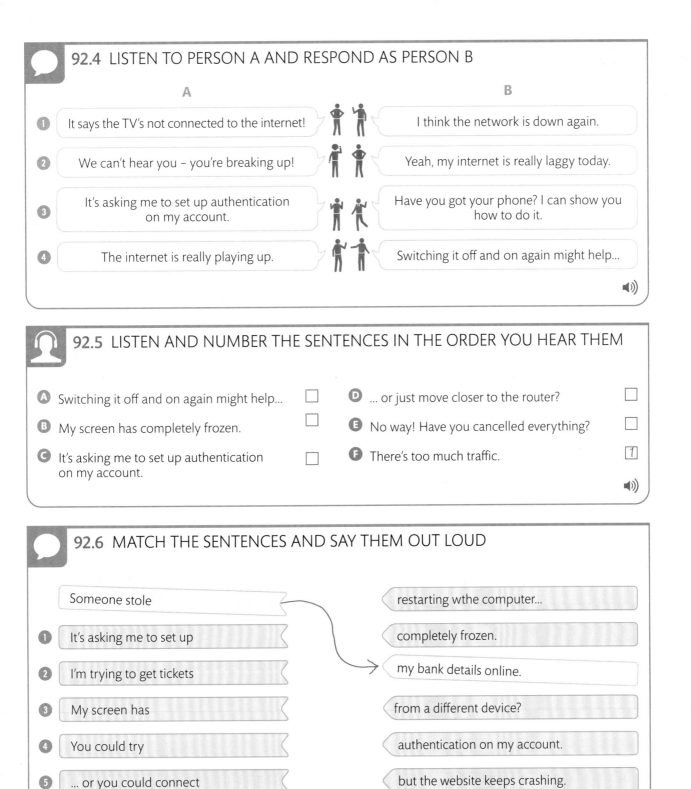

92.4 LISTEN TO PERSON A AND RESPOND AS PERSON B

A

1 It says the TV's not connected to the internet!

2 We can't hear you – you're breaking up!

3 It's asking me to set up authentication on my account.

4 The internet is really playing up.

B

I think the network is down again.

Yeah, my internet is really laggy today.

Have you got your phone? I can show you how to do it.

Switching it off and on again might help...

92.5 LISTEN AND NUMBER THE SENTENCES IN THE ORDER YOU HEAR THEM

A Switching it off and on again might help... ☐

B My screen has completely frozen. ☐

C It's asking me to set up authentication on my account. ☐

D ... or just move closer to the router? ☐

E No way! Have you cancelled everything? ☐

F There's too much traffic. ☐ 1

92.6 MATCH THE SENTENCES AND SAY THEM OUT LOUD

Someone stole

1 It's asking me to set up

2 I'm trying to get tickets

3 My screen has

4 You could try

5 ... or you could connect

restarting wthe computer...

completely frozen.

my bank details online.

from a different device?

authentication on my account.

but the website keeps crashing.

93.1 SENDING AND RECEIVING

Did you get my email?

I did, thanks. Sorry I haven't got back to you.

Has Anna sent you the trip details?

Yeah, I'll forward you her message.

93.2 MORE PHRASES

Your email went to my junk folder.

I've sent the file as an attachment.

Can you check this draft email?

I'm just updating my email signature.

How do I unsubscribe from updates?

93.3 EMAIL ISSUES

Does this attachment look okay to you?

It looks suspicious – I wouldn't download it.

I'm getting so much junk mail!

Okay, let's have a look at your filters.

I think I deleted the email with the concert tickets!

Check your trash. Maybe it's still there.

93.4 VOCABULARY SENDING EMAILS

inbox

outbox

junk / spam mail

trash

contact

draft

to send

to forward

to delete

to reply

to reply all

to download

to upload

attachment

93.5 LISTEN TO PERSON A AND RESPOND AS PERSON B

	A		B
1	Did you get my email?		I did, thanks. Sorry I haven't got back to you.
2	Has Anna sent you the trip details?		Yeah, I'll forward you her message.
3	Does this attachment look okay to you?		It looks suspicious – I wouldn't download it.
4	I'm getting so much junk mail!		Okay, let's have a look at your filters.

93.6 LISTEN AND CIRCLE THE ITEM YOU HEAR

1. **A** / B
2. A / B
3. A / B
4. A / B
5. A / B
6. A / B

93.7 RESPOND OUT LOUD TO THE AUDIO, FILLING IN THE GAPS USING THE WORDS IN THE PANEL

filters   download   forward   trash

1. I think I deleted the email with the concert tickets!

   Check your _____ . Maybe it's still there.

2. I'm getting so much junk mail!

   Okay, let's have a look at your _____ .

3. Has Anna sent you the trip details?

   Yeah, I'll _____ you her message.

4. Does this attachment look okay to you?

   It looks suspicious – I wouldn't _____ it.

94.1 TEXTING AND MESSAGING

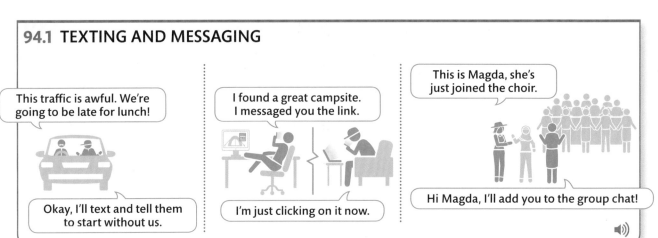

This traffic is awful. We're going to be late for lunch!

Okay, I'll text and tell them to start without us.

I found a great campsite. I messaged you the link.

I'm just clicking on it now.

This is Magda, she's just joined the choir.

Hi Magda, I'll add you to the group chat!

94.2 TEXT SPEAK

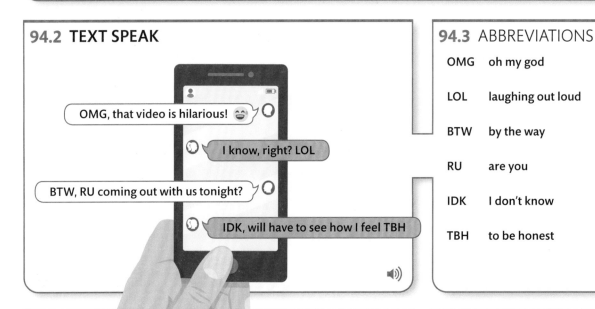

OMG, that video is hilarious! 😄

I know, right? LOL

BTW, RU coming out with us tonight?

IDK, will have to see how I feel TBH

94.3 ABBREVIATIONS

OMG	oh my god
LOL	laughing out loud
BTW	by the way
RU	are you
IDK	I don't know
TBH	to be honest

94.4 VIDEO CALLS

Hey, Mum. Can you see me okay?

I can, darling! Can you see me?

I can only see the top of your head! Try moving your tablet.

🌐 GOOD TO KNOW

In informal written English that people use in messaging apps and text messages, it is common to omit punctuation, particularly full stops at the end of messages. You may also see text speak abbreviations in lower case letters (e.g. **idk**) instead of in block capital letters (e.g. **IDK**).

LISTEN TO PERSON A AND RESPOND AS PERSON B

A	B
❶ This traffic is awful. We're going to be late for lunch!	Okay, I'll text and tell them to start without us.
❷ I found a great campsite. I messaged you the link.	I'm just clicking on it now.
❸ This is Magda, she's just joined the choir.	Hi Magda, I'll add you to the group chat!
❹ Hey, Mum. Can you see me okay?	I can, darling! Can you see me?

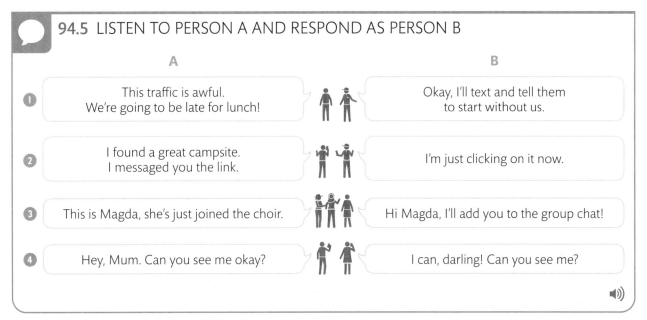

94.6 LISTEN AND NUMBER THE SENTENCES IN THE ORDER YOU HEAR THEM

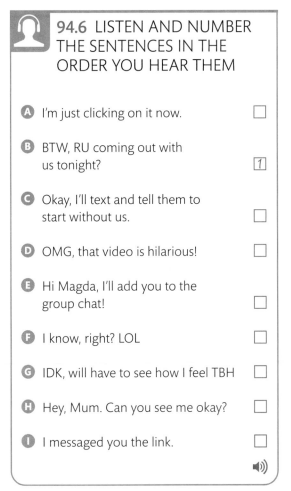

Ⓐ I'm just clicking on it now. ☐

Ⓑ BTW, RU coming out with us tonight? [1]

Ⓒ Okay, I'll text and tell them to start without us. ☐

Ⓓ OMG, that video is hilarious! ☐

Ⓔ Hi Magda, I'll add you to the group chat! ☐

Ⓕ I know, right? LOL ☐

Ⓖ IDK, will have to see how I feel TBH ☐

Ⓗ Hey, Mum. Can you see me okay? ☐

Ⓘ I messaged you the link. ☐

94.7 RESPOND OUT LOUD TO THE AUDIO, FILLING IN THE GAPS USING THE WORDS IN THE PANEL

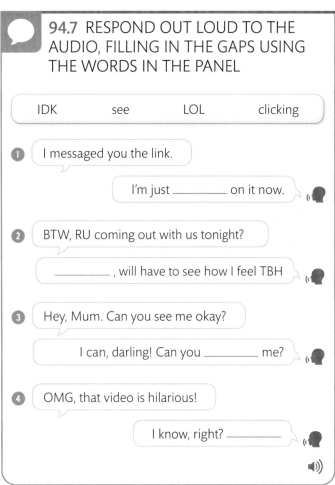

IDK	see	LOL	clicking

❶ I messaged you the link.

I'm just _____ on it now.

❷ BTW, RU coming out with us tonight?

_____ , will have to see how I feel TBH

❸ Hey, Mum. Can you see me okay?

I can, darling! Can you _____ me?

❹ OMG, that video is hilarious!

I know, right? _____

235

95 Social media

95.1 USING SOCIAL MEDIA

Did you get any good photos on your trip?

They're all up on my profile....

... check out this selfie I took at the Taj Mahal!

I've just given you a follow so we can stay in touch.

Cool, I can see you in my notifications.

Oh no! That boy I met just DM'd me.

Not him! Just block him.

95.2 GOING VIRAL

My dog-grooming videos have gone viral!

I saw! I think you've won the internet.

You've got loads of followers!

Yeah, a few big accounts have been sharing my posts.

Did you see that reel of Usha making a massive cake?

It's adorable, right! It's got hundreds of "likes"!

95.3 BUILDING A BUSINESS

So, we need to grow our social reach.

More video content would help.

Or how about a monthly podcast?

Maybe hook up with an influencer...

We could livestream the launch party.

95.4 MORE PHRASES

There are loads of comments on my post!

That's just a troll, I'm blocking them.

Click the follow button to get all our updates!

95.5 LISTEN TO PERSON A AND RESPOND AS PERSON B

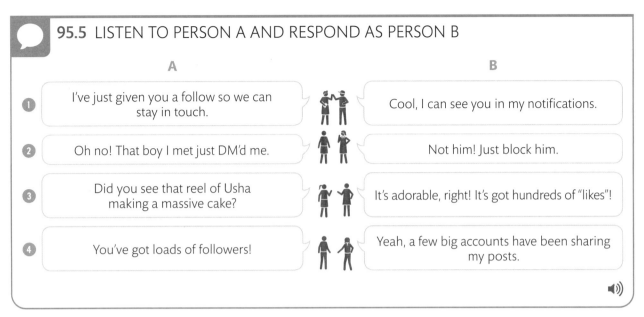

	A		B
1	I've just given you a follow so we can stay in touch.		Cool, I can see you in my notifications.
2	Oh no! That boy I met just DM'd me.		Not him! Just block him.
3	Did you see that reel of Usha making a massive cake?		It's adorable, right! It's got hundreds of "likes"!
4	You've got loads of followers!		Yeah, a few big accounts have been sharing my posts.

95.6 LISTEN TO THE AUDIO AND MATCH THE CORRECT RESPONSE

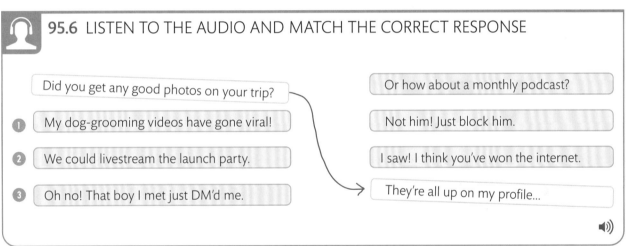

Did you get any good photos on your trip?

1 My dog-grooming videos have gone viral!

2 We could livestream the launch party.

3 Oh no! That boy I met just DM'd me.

Or how about a monthly podcast?

Not him! Just block him.

I saw! I think you've won the internet.

They're all up on my profile...

95.7 SAY THE SENTENCES OUT LOUD, FILLING IN THE GAPS USING THE WORDS IN THE PANEL

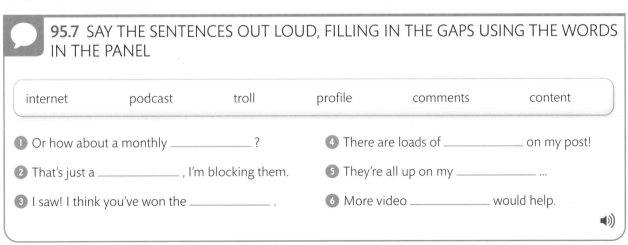

| internet | podcast | troll | profile | comments | content |

1 Or how about a monthly _____ ?

2 That's just a _____ , I'm blocking them.

3 I saw! I think you've won the _____ .

4 There are loads of _____ on my post!

5 They're all up on my _____ ...

6 More video _____ would help.

96.1 DISCUSSING BOOKS

It's the best book I've read in ages.

I agree. I couldn't put it down!

Yeah, it had me on the edge of my seat!

The ending was a bit of a letdown.

I found it quite hard-going, actually.

🌐 GOOD TO KNOW

English idioms are very common in everyday conversations, and phrases such as **a bit of a letdown** and **on the edge of my seat** can help make your spoken English sound more natural. Idioms don't always make sense literally, so you'll need to learn and practise each one individually.

96.2 AT THE BOOKSHOP

Can you recommend a good holiday read?

Yes, this one is a real page-turner.

Can I help at all?

No, thanks. I'm just browsing.

I'm afraid that book's out of stock.

Okay, could you order it in for me, please?

96.3 MAGAZINES AND NEWSPAPERS

Want a flick through *Fashion Monthly*?

Yes, please, if you've finished with it.

Have you seen today's headlines?

No, what's been going on?

Did you renew our subscription to *World Weekly*?

Sorry, not yet – I'll do it now!

96.4 LISTEN TO PERSON A AND RESPOND AS PERSON B

	A		B
1	Have you seen today's headlines?		No, what's been going on?
2	Want a flick through *Fashion Monthly*?		Yes, please, if you've finished with it.
3	Can you recommend a good holiday read?		Yes, this one is a real page-turner.
4	It's the best book I've read in ages.		I agree. I couldn't put it down!

96.5 LISTEN AND NUMBER THE SENTENCES IN THE ORDER YOU HEAR THEM

A The ending was a bit of a letdown. ☐

B Okay, could you order it in for me, please? ☐

C Yeah, it had me on the edge of my seat! ☐

D I found it quite hard-going, actually. ☑ 1

E No, thanks. I'm just browsing. ☐

F Sorry, not yet – I'll do it now! ☐

G Did you renew our subscription to *World Weekly*? ☐

96.6 MATCH THE SENTENCES AND SAY THEM OUT LOUD

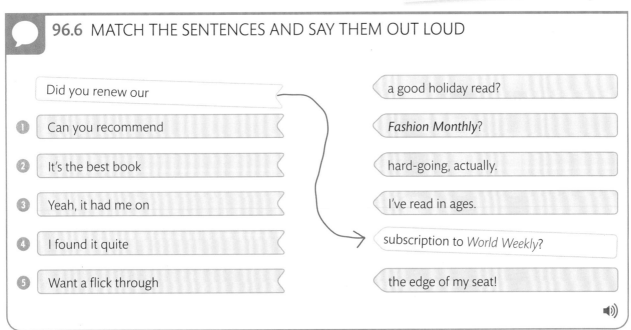

Did you renew our ⟶ subscription to *World Weekly*?

1 Can you recommend — a good holiday read?

2 It's the best book — *Fashion Monthly*?

3 Yeah, it had me on — hard-going, actually.

4 I found it quite — I've read in ages.

5 Want a flick through — the edge of my seat!

Answers

Audio recordings are available for you to listen to for all answers marked with the symbol 🔊. Please see pp.8–9 for more information on how to access all the supporting audio resources for this book.

01

1.7
- Ⓐ 2
- Ⓑ 6
- Ⓒ 7
- Ⓓ 3
- Ⓔ 8
- Ⓕ 4
- Ⓖ 1
- Ⓗ 5

1.8 🔊
1. How do you **do**?
2. **Good** evening.
3. It's good to **meet** you.
4. Good **afternoon**.
5. Hey, Jay, how's it **going**?
6. **Hey**, everyone!
7. How're you **doing**?
8. Long **time** no see!

02

2.6 🔊
1. This is my friend, Kit.
2. I'd like to introduce my friend, Kit.
3. I'd like you to meet my friend, Kit.
4. This is my partner, Kit.
5. I'd like to introduce my partner, Kit.
6. I'd like you to meet my partner, Kit.
7. This is my colleague, Kit.
8. I'd like to introduce my colleague, Kit.
9. I'd like you to meet my colleague, Kit.

2.7 🔊
1. Of course. I'm Samantha, but you can **call** me Sam.
2. It's a pleasure to **meet** you, Mr Ali.
3. I don't think so. **Great** to meet you!
4. **How's it going**? I'm Joe.

04

4.4
- Ⓐ 6
- Ⓑ 4
- Ⓒ 1
- Ⓓ 8
- Ⓔ 7
- Ⓕ 2
- Ⓖ 3
- Ⓗ 5

4.5 🔊
1. Sorry, my English **isn't great.**
2. Sorry, I didn't **catch that.**
3. I'm not quite sure **what you mean.**
4. Sorry, I'm not **with you.**
5. Can you repeat **that more slowly, please?**

4.6 🔊
1. Sorry? Could you say that again, please?
2. Sorry? Could you repeat that more slowly, please?
3. Sorry? Could you explain that one more time, please?
4. Sorry? Could you talk me through that again, please?
5. Excuse me? Could you say that again, please?
6. Excuse me? Could you repeat that more slowly, please?
7. Excuse me? Could you explain that one more time, please?
8. Excuse me? Could you talk me through that again, please?
9. Pardon? Could you say that again, please?
10. Pardon? Could you repeat that more slowly, please?
11. Pardon? Could you explain that one more time, please?
12. Pardon? Could you talk me through that again, please?

05

5.5 🔊
1. Yes, I'm really **into** it at the moment!
2. I absolutely **love** them!
3. I've **always** loved it.
4. I'm a big **fan**!
5. Yeah, it's **pretty** good!
6. It's so my **thing**!
7. This soup is **great**, isn't it?
8. What do you **think**?

5.6 🔊
1. I'm not much of **a curry fan.**
2. Skateboarding isn't really **my thing.**
3. No way! I can't **stand them.**
4. I couldn't think of **anything worse!**

5.12
- Ⓐ 4
- Ⓑ 3
- Ⓒ 8
- Ⓓ 1
- Ⓔ 2
- Ⓕ 5
- Ⓖ 10
- Ⓗ 7
- Ⓘ 9
- Ⓙ 6

5.13 🔊
1. I'd prefer sushi.
2. I'd rather have sushi.
3. I'd much rather have sushi.
4. I'd definitely go for sushi.
5. I'd prefer pizza.
6. I'd rather have pizza.
7. I'd much rather have pizza.
8. I'd definitely go for pizza.

06

6.5 🔊
1. Yeah, I know what you mean.
2. Yeah, I hear you.
3. Yeah, I couldn't agree more.
4. Yeah, I totally agree.
5. Absolutely, I know what you mean.
6. Absolutely, I hear you.
7. Absolutely, I couldn't agree more.
8. Absolutely, I totally agree.
9. Exactly, I know what you mean.
10. Exactly, I hear you.
11. Exactly, I couldn't agree more.
12. Exactly, I totally agree.

6.6 🔊
1. Absolutely, I couldn't **agree more.**
2. I don't think **so, either...**
3. I know **what you mean.**
4. We might have to agree **to disagree on this!**
5. Sorry, I'm not **with you on this one.**

07

7.6 🔊
1. **How** about cycling to the park?
2. I **think** I'll give it a miss.
3. **Count** me in!
4. I know! **Let's** go swimming!
5. I'd **like** that.
6. I'm not that **keen**, to be honest.
7. **Sounds** good.
8. I don't really **feel** like it, sorry.

7.7 🔊
1. Is anyone going to Juan's party tomorrow?
2. Is anyone going to the beach tomorrow?
3. Is anyone going to the castle tomorrow?
4. How about coming to Juan's party tomorrow?
5. How about coming to the beach tomorrow?
6. How about coming to the castle tomorrow?
7. Are you up for Juan's party tomorrow?
8. Are you up for the beach tomorrow?
9. Are you up for the castle tomorrow?

08

8.4
- Ⓐ 2
- Ⓔ 6
- Ⓑ 8
- Ⓕ 5
- Ⓒ 1
- Ⓖ 3
- Ⓓ 7
- Ⓗ 4

8.5 🔊
1. Don't **mention** it.
2. Thank you so **much**!
3. My **pleasure**!
4. I can't thank you **enough**!
5. Thank you, I really **appreciate** it.

09

9.5
- Ⓐ 7
- Ⓔ 5
- Ⓑ 2
- Ⓕ 8
- Ⓒ 1
- Ⓖ 3
- Ⓓ 6
- Ⓗ 4

9.6 🔊
1. Thanks, I appreciate **you saying that.**
2. That's okay, **it was nothing.**
3. I'm really sorry **I forgot your birthday!**
4. Thank you, that **means a lot.**

10

10.4
- Ⓐ 4
- Ⓔ 6
- Ⓑ 1
- Ⓕ 8
- Ⓒ 7
- Ⓖ 3
- Ⓓ 5
- Ⓗ 2

10.5 🔊
1. Thank you **for your time.**
2. It was a pleasure **meeting you.**
3. Good talking **with you.**
4. Speak to **you soon.**
5. Bye! Have **a safe trip!**
6. Great to **catch up!**

10.6 🔊
1. It was a pleasure meeting you.
2. It was lovely meeting you.
3. It was good meeting you.
4. It was a pleasure to see you.
5. It was lovely to see you.
6. It was good to see you.
7. It was a pleasure talking with you.
8. It was lovely talking with you.
9. It was good talking with you.

12

12.4 🔊
1. No worries, shall we do Sunday instead?
2. Let's make it quarter past, just to be sure.
3. Friday works for me…
4. It's at 10.

12.6 🔊
1. Which day **suits** you for lunch this week?
2. Friday **works** for me...
3. Shall I order the taxi for half **three**?
4. Hey, are you free for a drink **on Tuesday**?
5. Sorry, we can't come over **next** Saturday.
6. Keep it **free**!
7. We've set the date for **May the 31st** next year!

13

13.6
- Ⓐ 4
- Ⓔ 5
- Ⓑ 1
- Ⓕ 6
- Ⓒ 3
- Ⓖ 8
- Ⓓ 2
- Ⓗ 7

13.7 🔊
1. It's really windy today, isn't it?
2. It's freezing today, isn't it?
3. It's boiling today, isn't it?
4. It's a bit chilly today, isn't it?
5. It's lovely weather today, isn't it?
6. It's really windy out there!
7. It's freezing out there!
8. It's boiling out there!
9. It's a bit chilly out there!
10. It's lovely weather out there!

15

15.4
- Ⓐ 5
- Ⓓ 2
- Ⓑ 1
- Ⓔ 4
- Ⓒ 6
- Ⓕ 3

15.6 🔊
1. Yes, I've got a **brother and two stepsisters.**
2. I'm an **only child.**
3. I've got two **younger sisters.**
4. We grew up **in Birmingham.**

16

16.5
- Ⓐ 6
- Ⓕ 1
- Ⓑ 2
- Ⓖ 4
- Ⓒ 3
- Ⓗ 5
- Ⓓ 8
- Ⓘ 10
- Ⓔ 7
- Ⓙ 9

16.6 🔊
1. **Happy** birthday!
2. I hear **congratulations** are in order?
3. We're really **proud** of you!
4. All the **best** for your retirement.
5. Well **done**!
6. I'll **miss** you all!

17

17.3 🔊
1. I'm good! How are things with you?
2. I didn't know you were coming!
3. At a charity shop – for 10 quid!
4. I'm an English teacher. How about you?

18

18.6 🔊
1. Do you fancy going for a coffee this Saturday?
2. Do you fancy going for a coffee next Friday?
3. Do you fancy going for a coffee sometime?
4. Do you fancy going out this Saturday?
5. Do you fancy going out next Friday?
6. Do you fancy going out sometime?
7. I was wondering if you'd like to go for a coffee this Saturday?
8. I was wondering if you'd like to go for a coffee next Friday?
9. I was wondering if you'd like to go for a coffee sometime?
10. I was wondering if you'd like to go out this Saturday?
11. I was wondering if you'd like to go out next Friday?
12. I was wondering if you'd like to go out sometime?

18.7 🔊
1. I was hoping **you'd ask me.**
2. You took **your time!**
3. That would be **really nice.**
4. I just like you **as a friend.**

18.12
A 7	F 6
B 1	G 2
C 3	H 10
D 4	I 5
E 8	J 9

18.13 🔊
1. It was nice to **hang** with you.
2. What kind of things are you **into**?
3. I'd really like to see you **again.**
4. I'd better **head** off. Early start tomorrow!
5. How long have you been **single**?
6. I'm just **booking** a cab.

19

19.4
A 5	E 2
B 1	F 7
C 6	G 4
D 3	

19.6 🔊
1. Anything you need, just **ask.**
2. Let me know if I can do **anything.**
3. I know things are **tough**, but we're here for you.
4. You've been a lot of **help.**
5. That's really **kind**. I will!
6. I'm very **grateful.**
7. I know this hasn't been **easy.**
8. Thank you, I really **appreciate** it.

21

21.3
1. A
2. B
3. B
4. A
5. B
6. A

22

22.5
A 3	D 6
B 1	E 2
C 4	F 5

22.6 🔊
1. Can I check if you **deliver** to this address?
2. Two burgers to **go**, please.
3. I'll **pick** it up on my way home.
4. Okay, I'll **order** it on the app.
5. We've got no food. **Let's** get a pizza in!
6. Our fried chicken order still hasn't **arrived.**
7. Let me **check** what's happening.
8. Do you **want** fries with that?

23

23.6
A 5	E 6
B 3	F 8
C 7	G 2
D 1	H 4

23.7 🔊
1. Can I get a **beer**, please?
2. Do you serve **mocktails**?
3. A glass of **wine** for me, please!
4. What **cocktails** can you recommend?
5. What **soft drinks** are there?

24

24.7
A 2	D 6
B 3	E 4
C 1	F 5

24.8 🔊
1. I'll bring you the **menu.**
2. I'll have the **steak**, please.
3. Could you bring us a **jug of water**, please?
4. I think I'll go for the **fish.**
5. I'll bring you the **black pepper.**
6. Could I have the **salad**?

24.13
1. A
2. B
3. B
4. A

24.14 🔊
1. Nothing **special**, to be honest.
2. No, I'll **get this.**
3. It's a bit too salty, **actually.**
4. **Really tasty**. How's yours?

24.15 🔊
1. This chicken is a bit too salty, actually.
2. This chicken is a bit too cold, actually.
3. This chicken is nothing special, actually.
4. This chicken is really tasty, actually.
5. This chicken is a bit too salty, to be honest.
6. This chicken is a bit too cold, to be honest.
7. This chicken is nothing special, to be honest.
8. This chicken is really tasty, to be honest.

25

25.5
(A) 4   (D) 5
(B) 3   (E) 6
(C) 1   (F) 2

25.7 ◄))
1. I'll start **weighing** the flour.
2. **Chop** the butter into cubes.
3. **Preheat** the oven to 250°C (480°F).
4. Turn it down and **simmer** for 20 minutes.
5. I'm **roasting** a chicken for our lunch.
6. **Mix** the ingredients together.
7. I've **baked** you a birthday cake!
8. Okay, I'll **set** the timer!

25.13
(A) 4   (E) 8
(B) 5   (F) 6
(C) 1   (G) 3
(D) 2   (H) 7

25.14 ◄))
1. I think I'll start **with a mushroom kebab.**
2. I'd love **a bit of everything!**
3. I'm allergic **to shellfish.**
4. Shall I do some **garlic bread to go with it?**
5. Thanks for **having us over.**
6. Something **smells good!**

25.15 ◄))
1. This is so delicious.
2. This is really delicious.
3. This is absolutely delicious.
4. This is so amazing!
5. This is really amazing!
6. This is absolutely amazing!
7. This is so fantastic!
8. This is really fantastic!
9. This is absolutely fantastic!
10. This is so yummy.
11. This is really yummy.
12. This is absolutely yummy.

27

27.6
(A) 5   (D) 2
(B) 1   (E) 6
(C) 3   (F) 4

27.7 ◄))
1. The **3D glasses** made it so realistic!
2. Which **screen** is it showing at?
3. Can we have **seats** at the back?
4. I wasn't **keen** on the ending.
5. Is there time to get **popcorn**?
6. How long is the **film**?
7. Is this the **subtitled** screening?
8. Is the film okay for **kids** under 10?

28

28.6
1. A
2. B
3. A
4. A
5. B
6. B

28.7 ◄))
1. I've booked seats **in the stalls.**
2. Is there **an interval?**
3. Can I see **your tickets, please?**
4. Where is **the cloakroom?**

28.8 ◄))
1. Follow me, you're in the front row.
2. Follow me, you're in the stalls.
3. Follow me, you're in Box 5.
4. I've booked seats in the front row.
5. I've booked seats in the stalls.
6. I've booked seats in Box 5.

29

29.5
(A) 4   (E) 1
(B) 2   (F) 7
(C) 5   (G) 3
(D) 6   (H) 8

29.6 ◄))
1. Here's **the line-up** for the whole weekend.
2. I'll meet you back in **the main arena.**
3. No, we can just **turn up.**
4. 9pm, but the support band has just **come on.**
5. What an amazing **performance**!

30

30.6
(A) 3   (E) 8
(B) 5   (F) 2
(C) 1   (G) 7
(D) 4   (H) 6

30.7 ◄))
1. Have you been to this yoga class before?
2. Have you been to this Pilates class before?
3. Have you been to this fitness class before?
4. Have you been to this spin class before?
5. Have you been to this dance class before?

31

31.4 ◄))
1. Yes, we run them on Saturdays.
2. Of course. What time would you like?
3. Over here!
4. No, I sprained my ankle last week!

31.6 ◄))
1. Wanna join us for a game of **badminton**?
2. Are you coming to **ice hockey** practice?
3. Do you give **golf** lessons here?
4. I'd like to book a **tennis** lesson, please.
5. We run **football** practice on Mondays.

32

32.5
(A) 6   (D) 5
(B) 1   (E) 2
(C) 4   (F) 3

① Any seats left for the golf tournament today?
② Any seats left for the tennis final today?
③ Any seats left for the athletics today?
④ Any seats left for the football today?
⑤ Fancy going to watch the golf tournament today?
⑥ Fancy going to watch the tennis final today?
⑦ Fancy going to watch the athletics today?
⑧ Fancy going to watch the football today?

33

33.4
① B
② A
③ B
④ A
⑤ B

33.5 ◄))
① I'm giving **pottery** a go!
② I've taken up **knitting** recently.
③ I only started learning **karate** a year ago.
④ I usually play **tennis** at the weekend.
⑤ I've just started learning the **piano**.
⑥ I've been playing the **guitar** for six years.

33.6 ◄))
① I've been doing karate for two years.
② I've been playing the guitar for two years.
③ I've been learning the piano for two years.
④ I've been playing tennis for two years.
⑤ I've been doing karate since I was 12.
⑥ I've been playing the guitar since I was 12.
⑦ I've been learning the piano since I was 12.
⑧ I've been playing tennis since I was 12.

35

35.6
① A
② A
③ A
④ B
⑤ A

35.7 ◄))
① Can I have a jar of honey, please?
② Can I have a bunch of grapes, please?
③ Can I have a loaf of bread, please?
④ Can I have a punnet of strawberries, please?
⑤ Can I have a box of eggs, please?
⑥ Could I have a jar of honey, please?
⑦ Could I have a bunch of grapes, please?
⑧ Could I have a loaf of bread, please?
⑨ Could I have a punnet of strawberries, please?
⑩ Could I have a box of eggs, please?

36

36.2
Ⓐ 3		Ⓓ 6	
Ⓑ 5		Ⓔ 2	
Ⓒ 1		Ⓕ 4	

36.3
① B
② A
③ B
④ B
⑤ B
⑥ A

36.9
Ⓐ 3		Ⓓ 5	
Ⓑ 6		Ⓔ 4	
Ⓒ 1		Ⓕ 2	

36.10 ◄))
① Excuse me, where's the **frozen food** aisle?
② Would you like to use the **self-checkout**?
③ Where can I find the **pet food**?
④ Do you stock **baby products** here?
⑤ I can't find the **fruit** and **vegetables**.

37

37.5
Ⓐ 2		Ⓓ 3	
Ⓑ 1		Ⓔ 6	
Ⓒ 4		Ⓕ 5	

37.6 ◄))
① Will it **survive** the winter?
② When is the best time to plant these **seeds**?
③ How much **sunlight** do they need?
④ Does it need much **looking** after?
⑤ How often should I **feed** it?
⑥ How do I get rid of **weeds**?

37.7 ◄))
① We need some advice **on starting up a vegetable garden.**
② What's a good **compost to use?**
③ I don't really mind, but **my flat doesn't get much light.**
④ What kind of houseplants **are you after?**
⑤ How do I **get rid of weeds?**

38

38.6
Ⓐ 5		Ⓕ 4	
Ⓑ 7		Ⓖ 6	
Ⓒ 1		Ⓗ 3	
Ⓓ 8		Ⓘ 10	
Ⓔ 2		Ⓙ 9	

38.7 ◄))
① I'm looking for a **screwdriver**.
② Where can I find a **hammer**?
③ Have you got any **drills**?
④ Who can I ask about **saws**?
⑤ What kind of **nails** do you sell?
⑥ Where are the **screws**?

38.8 ◄))
① What do I need for plastering walls?
② What would you recommend for plastering walls?
③ What's best for plastering walls?
④ What do I need for tiling my bathroom?
⑤ What would you recommend for tiling my bathroom?
⑥ What's best for tiling my bathroom?
⑦ What do I need for filling a crack?
⑧ What would you recommend for filling a crack?
⑨ What's best for filling a crack?

39

39.4
Ⓐ 1 Ⓓ 2
Ⓑ 6 Ⓔ 4
Ⓒ 3 Ⓕ 5

39.6 🔊
1 Have you got this jumper in a size 10, please?
2 Have you got this jacket in a size 10, please?
3 Have you got this suit in a size 10, please?
4 Have you got this shirt in a size 10, please?
5 Have you got this jumper in a larger size, please?
6 Have you got this jacket in a larger size, please?
7 Have you got this suit in a larger size, please?
8 Have you got this shirt in a larger size, please?
9 Have you got this jumper in the next size down, please?
10 Have you got this jacket in the next size down, please?
11 Have you got this suit in the next size down, please?
12 Have you got this shirt in the next size down, please?

40

40.5 🔊
1 The **boots** are too tight.
2 Where can I return these **shoes**?
3 This **dress** is too small.
4 I have to return this, but I lost my **receipt**.
5 The **trousers** don't fit properly.
6 I need to return this **bag**.

41

41.6 🔊
1 Can you do **Thursday at 3pm?**
2 Is Saturday afternoon **any good?**
3 I just need **a quick trim.**
4 We're fully booked **on Thursday, I'm afraid.**
5 Can you come in **on Monday?**

41.7 🔊
1 Can you fit me in on Monday?
2 Can you fit me in on Tuesday afternoon?
3 Can you fit me in on Wednesday morning?
4 Can you fit me in on Thursday at 3pm?
5 Can you do Monday?
6 Can you do Tuesday afternoon?
7 Can you do Wednesday morning?
8 Can you do Thursday at 3pm?

41.11
Ⓐ 5 Ⓕ 7
Ⓑ 1 Ⓖ 2
Ⓒ 8 Ⓗ 6
Ⓓ 9 Ⓘ 3
Ⓔ 4

41.12 🔊
1 I feel like a change, but I don't know what to **go for.**
2 Just **my usual**, I think.
3 I'll have some **styling** gel on it, please.
4 What colour would be **best** for me?
5 Could you cut the fringe **a bit more**?
6 I think a shorter style would really **suit you.**
7 Leave it longer **on top**, please.

41.13 🔊
1 What style would be best for me?
2 What colour would be best for me?
3 What highlights would be best for me?
4 What style would suit me?
5 What colour would suit me?
6 What highlights would suit me?
7 What style should I go for?
8 What colour should I go for?
9 What highlights should I go for?

42

42.6
Ⓐ 3 Ⓓ 5
Ⓑ 1 Ⓔ 6
Ⓒ 2 Ⓕ 4

42.7 🔊
1 How many would you **like**?
2 Can you **pop** it on the scales, please?
3 How much does it **cost** to send this to Japan?
4 I've come to **collect** a parcel.
5 Can you **sign** for this, please?
6 How soon will my parcel **arrive**?
7 Can I **send** this letter to France?
8 Sure. I've been **waiting** for it to arrive!

43

43.5
1 A
2 B
3 A
4 B

43.6 🔊
1 I'd like to open a bank account, please.
2 I'd like to withdraw £300 in cash, please.
3 I'd like to open a savings account, please.
4 I'd like to transfer money into my bank account, please.
5 I'd like to pay money into my savings account, please.

43.12 🔊
1 You can transfer **your share later.**
2 I've just ordered **our holiday money!**
3 The cash machine has just **swallowed my card!**
4 Shall we split it **three ways?**
5 Let me know **your bank details.**

44

44.5
Ⓐ 1 Ⓓ 2
Ⓑ 5 Ⓔ 3
Ⓒ 4 Ⓕ 6

44.6 🔊
1 Do you run computing **courses** here?
2 Have you got this as an **audiobook**?
3 I need to renew these **books**, please.
4 How do I join the **library**?
5 Where is the children's **section**?
6 Can I see your **newspaper** archive?

46.7
① A
② A
③ A
④ B

46.8 ◄))
① Is there a maths club?
② Is there a science club?
③ Is there a history club?
④ Is there an after-school club?
⑤ Is there an art club?

47.6
Ⓐ 4   Ⓓ 3
Ⓑ 1   Ⓔ 2
Ⓒ 6   Ⓕ 5

47.7 ◄))
① What are your entry **requirements**?
② Sure, it's a two-year, **full-time** programme.
③ I've just signed up for the French **class**.
④ The **teacher** is amazing!
⑤ The **website** also has lots of information.
⑥ What **qualifications** do I need?
⑦ Is there a chance to study **abroad**?
⑧ Students work once a week in a **salon**.

47.12
Ⓐ 2   Ⓓ 4
Ⓑ 5   Ⓔ 6
Ⓒ 1   Ⓕ 3

47.13 ◄))
① Do you know where the art school is?
② Do you know where the humanities department is?
③ Do you know where the physics lecture is?
④ Do you know where the café is?
⑤ Can you tell me where the art school is?
⑥ Can you tell me where the humanities department is?
⑦ Can you tell me where the physics lecture is?
⑧ Can you tell me where the café is?
⑨ Any idea where the art school is?

⑩ Any idea where the humanities department is?
⑪ Any idea where the physics lecture is?
⑫ Any idea where the café is?

47.19
① A
② B
③ B
④ A

47.20 ◄))
① I'm finding it hard to **make friends**.
② I'd **rather not**, actually.
③ Not **too bad**!
④ I'd be **up for that**!

47.21 ◄))
① How are you finding **your first week**?
② I'm feeling **a bit homesick**.
③ I think I'll **give it a miss**.
④ Sounds like **fun**!

48.5
Ⓐ 2   Ⓔ 6
Ⓑ 4   Ⓕ 1
Ⓒ 3   Ⓖ 7
Ⓓ 5

48.6 ◄))
① Okay, let me take some **details** about you.
② This **job** looks interesting…
③ I'm looking for a **part-time** sales job.
④ What **hours** can you work?
⑤ Have you used this job search **website**?
⑥ Yes, could you email us your **CV**?
⑦ What **skills** have you got?
⑧ Is the job in the **window** still vacant?

49.5
① A
② B
③ B

49.6 ◄))
① I really want to apply for **this job**.
② I just need to fill in **my personal details and it'll be ready**.
③ Don't forget to send **your covering letter, too**!
④ Have you finished **your application yet**?

50.5 ◄))
① I'm used to working under pressure.
② I'm a quick learner.
③ I enjoy solving problems.
④ I'm really keen to use my planning skills.

50.6 ◄))
① What can you bring to our **company**?
② What **salary** are you expecting?
③ What's the **notice** period in your current job?
④ How soon could you **start**?
⑤ I'm used to **working** under pressure.
⑥ I'm good with **customers**.

50.7 ◄))
① I've got the experience you're looking for.
② I've got the skills you're looking for.
③ I've got the qualifications you're looking for.
④ I've got the enthusiasm you're looking for.
⑤ I've got the strengths you're looking for.

51.7
Ⓐ 3   Ⓔ 2
Ⓑ 1   Ⓕ 4
Ⓒ 5   Ⓖ 6
Ⓓ 7

51.8 ◄))
① Your first **break** is at 12.30.
② And always wear your **hard hat**!
③ It's great to have you on the **team**.
④ I've set up your **email** account.
⑤ Shall we grab some **lunch**?
⑥ How's your **morning** been?
⑦ Have you got **everything** you need?
⑧ Can you type in a **password**?

52

52.5
1. A
2. A
3. B
4. A

52.6 🔊
1. It's in half an hour. **How about** yours?
2. Not again! Okay, **let's call** the supervisor.
3. I'm **down for** the morning shift.
4. Thanks. I'll **put it in** my diary.

53

53.4
A 3		E 8	
B 1		F 6	
C 4		G 5	
D 2		H 7	

53.5 🔊
1. Now let's turn to **the subject of...**
2. The focus of **my presentation is...**
3. Lastly, **I'd like to finish by saying...**
4. Does anyone have **anything to add?**
5. Now I'd like to **talk about...**
6. Firstly, **I'd like to begin by saying...**

53.6 🔊
1. Today, I'd like to talk about…
2. Firstly, I'd like to talk about…
3. Now I'd like to talk about…
4. Lastly, I'd like to talk about…
5. Finally, I'd like to talk about…
6. Today, I'm going to talk about…
7. Firstly, I'm going to talk about…
8. Now I'm going to talk about…
9. Lastly, I'm going to talk about…
10. Finally, I'm going to talk about…

54

54.5 🔊
1. Could I just jump in? **I totally agree.**
2. If I can just add… **It will be a slow process.**
3. So that's the situation. **Let's hear your thoughts.**
4. Just to clarify… **Which changes exactly?**
5. Can I go first? **For me, these changes are important.**

54.7 🔊
1. Let's hear from James on this **point.**
2. I think we're all here, so let's get **started.**
3. If you **ask** me, it's a non-starter.
4. I see where you're **coming** from, so…
5. Could I just **jump** in? I totally agree.
6. Just to **clarify**… Which changes exactly?
7. Let's go round the table and see where we all **stand.**

54.11
A 5		E 7	
B 4		F 2	
C 1		G 6	
D 8		H 3	

54.12 🔊
1. You, too. Let's stay **in touch.**
2. That's right. Sorry, I didn't catch **your name.**
3. Me too. Let's **follow it up** in the office.

55

55.6
A 6		E 3	
B 5		F 7	
C 4		G 2	
D 1			

55.7 🔊
1. Sorry for interrupting, **please carry on.**
2. Shall we put in **another meeting?**
3. My connection **keeps dropping out.**
4. Would you like to **speak first?**
5. Can you enlarge it **on your screen?**
6. Right, I'll run through **the key points.**

57

57.7 🔊
1. We'd need to **put in a new kitchen.**
2. I want a property **close to the station.**
3. I quite like **the layout.**
4. I think **it's too small for us.**

57.8 🔊
1. We'd like a house with a garden.
2. We'd like a flat with a garden.
3. We'd like a property with a garden.
4. We'd like a house close to the station.
5. We'd like a flat close to the station.
6. We'd like a property close to the station.
7. We'd like a house near a school.
8. We'd like a flat near a school.
9. We'd like a property near a school.

57.13
A 3		D 5	
B 1		E 2	
C 6		F 4	

57.14 🔊
1. How much is the **rent?**
2. Are **utility bills** included?
3. Can I put this **picture** up?
4. The **washing machine** is leaking.
5. Are **pets** allowed?
6. As soon as you've signed the **tenancy agreement!**

57.15 🔊
1. Can I rent it **unfurnished?**
2. One year, with an option to **renew.**
3. Are utility **bills** included?
4. Do you need a **deposit?**
5. Do I **pay** the rent monthly?
6. What **references** do you need?

58

58.5
A 1		D 5	
B 3		E 6	
C 4		F 2	

58.6 🔊
1. Is everything packed and **ready?**
2. Hope **the move** goes well!
3. Do you have any spare **boxes?**
4. I've told everyone our **moving** date.
5. We have to move out by the **weekend.**
6. I've **packed** up the bedroom.
7. Let's **load** the removal van!
8. We can **unpack** in the morning.

58.7 🔊
1. Hope the move **goes well!**
2. Let's load **the removal van!**
3. Where do you want us **to start?**
4. I've packed up **the bedroom.**
5. I'm here to pick up **the keys to my flat.**

59

59.7
A) 3   E) 8
B) 4   F) 6
C) 1   G) 2
D) 7   H) 5

59.8 🔊
1. Are you free for drinks later?
2. Are you free for lunch later?
3. Are you free for coffee later?
4. Are you free for drinks tomorrow?
5. Are you free for lunch tomorrow?
6. Are you free for coffee tomorrow?
7. Are you free for drinks on Sunday?
8. Are you free for lunch on Sunday?
9. Are you free for coffee on Sunday?

60

60.5
1. A
2. B
3. B
4. A

60.6 🔊
1. Whose turn is it to empty **the dishwasher?**
2. I've cleaned the worktops **and the oven.**
3. Great job! The kitchen **was in a right state.**
4. Phew! That was **a proper spring clean!**

61

61.5
A) 7   F) 9
B) 6   G) 4
C) 1   H) 5
D) 3   I) 8
E) 2

61.6 🔊
1. Could you give us a quote for fixing our fence?
2. Could you give us a quote for putting up some shelves?
3. Could you give us a quote for fitting a carpet?
4. Could you give us a quote for painting our kitchen walls?
5. Are you able to give us a quote for fixing our fence?
6. Are you able to give us a quote for putting up some shelves?
7. Are you able to give us a quote for fitting a carpet?
8. Are you able to give us a quote for painting our kitchen walls?

62

62.7
A) 1   D) 5
B) 4   E) 3
C) 2   F) 6

62.8 🔊
1. Is she good **with children?**
2. I think he's got **a broken leg.**
3. She's lost weight **and gone off her food.**
4. Hi, I'd like to **adopt a cat.**
5. We have to get him microchipped **and book his vaccinations!**

63

63.6
A) 4   E) 8
B) 5   F) 2
C) 7   G) 3
D) 1   H) 6

63.7 🔊
1. The power has **gone off.**
2. The power is **back on!**
3. The tap has been **dripping** for days.
4. When was the boiler last **serviced?**

64

64.6
A) 2   E) 3
B) 1   F) 6
C) 5   G) 8
D) 4   H) 7

64.7 🔊
1. Shall we play **the next level?**
2. Can you turn on **the subtitles?**
3. Is the console **plugged in?**
4. What shall we **watch tonight?**

66

66.5 🔊
1. We're almost there – it's the next stop.
2. Yes, via the train station.
3. Yes, they're right at the back.
4. Yup, just log on to our network.

66.6 🔊
1. Excuse me, does this bus go to the library?
2. Excuse me, are we nearly at the library?
3. Excuse me, is this the right stop for the library?
4. Excuse me, does this bus go to the town centre?
5. Excuse me, are we nearly at the town centre?
6. Excuse me, is this the right stop for the town centre?
7. Excuse me, does this bus go to the shopping centre?
8. Excuse me, are we nearly at the shopping centre?
9. Excuse me, is this the right stop for the shopping centre?

67

67.7
A) 6   D) 1
B) 4   E) 2
C) 3   F) 5

67.8 🔊
1 Can I reserve a **seat**?
2 What time is the next **train** to Newcastle?
3 There's a massive **queue** for tickets!
4 Does this train **stop** at Birmingham?
5 Let's wait in the **waiting** room.
6 Hello, can we **book** two return tickets to Leeds, please?
7 Do I **tap** in at the ticket barrier?

67.13
Ⓐ 3
Ⓑ 1
Ⓒ 4
Ⓓ 5
Ⓔ 2

67.14 🔊
1 Excuse me, how do I get to Leeds?
2 Excuse me, how many stops is it to Leeds?
3 Excuse me, how much is a return to Leeds?
4 Excuse me, how much is a single to Leeds?
5 Excuse me, how do I get to Cardiff?
6 Excuse me, how many stops is it to Cardiff?
7 Excuse me, how much is a return to Cardiff?
8 Excuse me, how much is a single to Cardiff?

68.4 🔊
1 What **time** is boarding?
2 Can I change to a window **seat**?
3 What's the gate **number**?
4 How long is the **delay**?
5 Any chance of an **upgrade**?
6 What time does the **gate** close?
7 Place your bag in the **tray**, please!
8 Where is the **check-in** desk?

68.9
Ⓐ 6   Ⓓ 3
Ⓑ 1   Ⓔ 4
Ⓒ 5   Ⓕ 2

68.10
Ⓐ 3   Ⓓ 1
Ⓑ 4   Ⓔ 6
Ⓒ 5   Ⓕ 2

68.11 🔊
1 I'll put our stuff **in the overhead locker.**
2 Please switch your digital devices **to "airplane" mode.**
3 We'll shortly be passing through **the cabin with snacks and drinks.**
4 Your tray tables **should be securely fastened.**
5 Make sure your seat **is in the upright position.**

68.14
1 B
2 A
3 B
4 A

68.16 🔊
1 Where do we meet our **taxi**?
2 I can't see our **suitcases** anywhere!
3 It's Belt 3. I'll grab a **trolley**.
4 Yes, I need to change some **Euros**.
5 I'm here to pick up a hire **car**.

69

69.6 🔊
1 For getting around town, mainly.
2 You just need to download the app!
3 There are parking bays all over town!
4 The brakes are loose.

69.7
Ⓐ 6   Ⓓ 1
Ⓑ 5   Ⓔ 4
Ⓒ 3   Ⓕ 2

69.8 🔊
1 What type of **bike** do you want?
2 The **battery** needs charging.
3 The front **tyre** is flat.
4 Would you like a **test ride**?
5 I need a bike to get to and from **work**.
6 There are parking **bays** all over town!
7 You just need to download the **app**!
8 The **brakes** are loose.

70

70.5
Ⓐ 7   Ⓔ 6
Ⓑ 4   Ⓕ 3
Ⓒ 1   Ⓖ 2
Ⓓ 8   Ⓗ 5

70.6 🔊
1 Hello, can I **book** a taxi from the airport?
2 How soon will the **cab** be here?
3 Can you **drop** me here, please?
4 I'm travelling with my assistance **dog**.
5 I left my laptop in one of your **taxis**.
6 Can you take me to this **address**?
7 How **long** will it take to get there?
8 Can I **pay** with contactless?

71

71.6
1 A
2 A
3 B
4 A

71.7 🔊
1 The windscreen is **cracked**.
2 The steering wheel is **jammed**.
3 The tyre keeps **going down**.
4 The oil needs **changing**.

73

73.4
Ⓐ 2   Ⓓ 4
Ⓑ 3   Ⓔ 6
Ⓒ 1   Ⓕ 5

73.5 🔊
1 Do I need **a visa**?
2 Can I bring my **guide dog**?
3 Is it suitable **for young children**?
4 What's your **cancellation policy**?

73.6 🔊
1 Is this cruise all-inclusive?
2 Is this beach holiday all-inclusive?
3 Is this city break all-inclusive?
4 Is this safari all-inclusive?
5 Is this cruise adults only?
6 Is this beach holiday adults only?
7 Is this city break adults only?
8 Is this safari adults only?
9 Is this cruise suitable for young children?
10 Is this beach holiday suitable for young children?
11 Is this city break suitable for young children?
12 Is this safari suitable for young children?

74.4
1 A
2 A
3 A
4 B
5 A
6 B

74.10
A 4   D 2
B 1   E 5
C 6   F 3

74.11 🔊
1 I'd like **a 7am wake-up call.**
2 The room **is too hot.**
3 The shower **is leaking.**
4 The Wi-Fi password **is wrong.**
5 I'd like a hairdryer **brought to my room.**

74.12 🔊
1 Could I have a hairdryer sent up, please?
2 Could I have some fresh towels sent up, please?
3 Could I have a club sandwich sent up, please?
4 Could I have two extra pillows sent up, please?
5 Could I have a hairdryer brought to my room, please?
6 Could I have some fresh towels brought to my room, please?

7 Could I have a club sandwich brought to my room, please?
8 Could I have two extra pillows brought to my room, please?

74.16 🔊
1 Did you enjoy **your stay?**
2 Yes, and do help yourselves **at the buffet.**
3 Here's your bill **if you'd like to check it.**
4 Is it possible to **stay an extra night?**
5 Can I take **your room number?**

74.17 🔊
1 Could I have some more **coffee?**
2 Are you paying by **card?**
3 Could you call me a **taxi**, please?
4 The **bed** was a little bit hard.
5 Can I leave my **luggage** here?

74.18 🔊
1 Can I see your **passport**, please?
2 What time is **check-out?**
3 We'd like a room with **twin beds**, please.
4 The **room** was a bit noisy.
5 Dinner was **delicious.**
6 Do you have a **double** room available?
7 The **restaurant** serves dinner until 10pm.
8 Your room is on the second **floor.**

75.5
1 B
2 B
3 A
4 A

75.7 🔊
1 Shall we get off **at the next stop?**
2 Quick! **Take a picture!**
3 Is there **wheelchair access?**
4 What are **your opening times?**
5 How much is **the entrance fee?**

76.5
A 3   E 6
B 1   F 5
C 2   G 4
D 7   H 8

76.6 🔊
1 Can we pitch our tent over in that field?
2 Can we set up camp over in that field?
3 Can we park our camper van over in that field?
4 Can we pitch our tent near the shower block?
5 Can we set up camp near the shower block?
6 Can we park our camper van near the shower block?
7 Can we pitch our tent opposite the caravans?
8 Can we set up camp opposite the caravans?
9 Can we park our camper van opposite the caravans?

77.4
A 5   E 1
B 8   F 2
C 7   G 6
D 4   H 3

77.5 🔊
1 Can we hire a **paddleboard** here?
2 How much is a **sun lounger** for the day?
3 Where can we buy a **beach ball?**
4 Can we hire a **pedalo** for the day?
5 Do you do **surfing** lessons?

77.6 🔊
1 Can we hire **a pedalo here?**
2 Is it safe **to swim today?**
3 Yes, but you must **stay between the flags.**
4 Do you do **surfing lessons?**

78.4
Ⓐ 4   Ⓓ 2
Ⓑ 1   Ⓔ 3
Ⓒ 6   Ⓕ 5

78.5 ◀))
❶ Excuse me, do you know **the way** to the bus station?
❷ Can you tell me how to **get to** the museum?
❸ Yes, **go straight** ahead and it's on your left.
❹ Take the **first left** at the roundabout.
❺ No, you need to **go past** the church…
❻ … then **cross** the road…
❼ It's just **next to** the hospital.

78.6 ◀))
❶ Excuse me, do you know the way to the church?
❷ Excuse me, can you tell me how to get to the church?
❸ Excuse me, do you know the way to the museum?
❹ Excuse me, can you tell me how to get to the museum?
❺ Excuse me, do you know the way to the station?
❻ Excuse me, can you tell me how to get to the station?
❼ Excuse me, do you know the way to the castle?
❽ Excuse me, can you tell me how to get to the castle?

79.6
Ⓐ 2   Ⓕ 8
Ⓑ 5   Ⓖ 3
Ⓒ 1   Ⓗ 7
Ⓓ 6   Ⓘ 4
Ⓔ 9

79.7 ◀))
❶ The train is cancelled **due to lack of available train crew.**
❷ Yeah, I won't make the beach, **I've got a tummy bug!**
❸ Look at the board. **Our train has been cancelled!**
❹ Your insurance should cover you **if you get a doctor's note.**

81.4
Ⓐ 6   Ⓓ 3
Ⓑ 2   Ⓔ 4
Ⓒ 1   Ⓕ 5

81.6 ◀))
❶ I have a really sore throat.
❷ I have a really bad headache.
❸ I have a really itchy rash.
❹ I have a really sore ear.
❺ I have a really itchy eye.

81.10 ◀))
❶ Yes, I'm taking antibiotics.
❷ How often should I take it?
❸ For about a week.
❹ Yes, I also have a runny nose.
❺ Hmm… It looks like an allergy.

81.11
Ⓐ 8   Ⓕ 9
Ⓑ 5   Ⓖ 6
Ⓒ 1   Ⓗ 2
Ⓓ 7   Ⓘ 4
Ⓔ 3

81.12 ◀))
❶ I have a really sore **eye.**
❷ I also have a runny **nose.**
❸ My **hand** really hurts.
❹ I have an itchy rash on my **foot.**
❺ My **ear** is killing me.

82.6 ◀))
❶ I need to see the **nurse.**
❷ Hi there, I'd like to book an appointment with **Doctor** Cole.
❸ Can I **reschedule** my appointment?
❹ Can I book an **appointment** for my daughter?
❺ Have you got **anything** sooner?
❻ When's the next **available** slot?
❼ If you need an urgent appointment, we'll place you on the **triage** list…
❽ I think I might have a **chest** infection.

82.7 ◀))
❶ I'd like to book an appointment with the doctor.
❷ I'd like to reschedule my appointment with the doctor.
❸ I'd like to book a check-up with the doctor.
❹ I'd like to cancel my appointment with the doctor.
❺ I'd like to book an appointment with the nurse.
❻ I'd like to reschedule my appointment with the nurse.
❼ I'd like to book a check-up with the nurse.
❽ I'd like to cancel my appointment with the nurse.
❾ I'd like to book an appointment with the dentist.
❿ I'd like to reschedule my appointment with the dentist.
⓫ I'd like to book a check-up with the dentist.
⓬ I'd like to cancel my appointment with the dentist.

83.7
Ⓐ 3   Ⓔ 4
Ⓑ 1   Ⓕ 7
Ⓒ 8   Ⓖ 6
Ⓓ 5   Ⓗ 2

83.8 🔊
1 I've had a bad cough for a week **and it's getting worse.**
2 I've been throwing **up all night.**
3 I'm due **a check-up.**
4 I've been under **the weather.**

84

84.5 🔊
1 I need a **doctor urgently.**
2 I burned my hand on the **stove. It's really painful.**
3 I'll grab **some tissues.**
4 My husband has **severe chest pains.**
5 He's having **a fit.**

84.6
1 B
2 A
3 A
4 B

84.7 🔊
1 It looks like she may need **stitches.**
2 Hold this cold pack over the **bump.**
3 My husband has severe chest **pains.**
4 That's a nasty **graze.**

85

85.3
A 4
B 3
C 5
D 2
E 1

85.4 🔊
1 I need to see someone **urgently.**
2 We have a **medical** emergency.
3 How soon will I be seen by a **doctor?**
4 I've got a **check-up** with the nurse at 4.30.
5 Do I need to have an **operation?**
6 I'm going to need to **examine** you.

85.10
A 7   E 2
B 8   F 3
C 6   G 1
D 4   H 5

85.11 🔊
1 I'll just take your blood **pressure** first.
2 Still a bit **groggy.**
3 Don't worry. We'll have you up and **about** in no time.
4 I'll just check your **temperature** and pulse…
5 You may feel light-headed as the **anaesthetic** takes effect.
6 How long will I be **under** for?
7 Now count **backwards** from 5…
8 There were no **complications.**

86

86.6
A 1   D 2
B 6   E 3
C 4   F 5

86.7
A 6   F 10
B 2   G 9
C 1   H 4
D 7   I 3
E 8   J 5

86.8 🔊
1 I brush my teeth **twice a day.**
2 I need to see **the hygienist.**
3 I think my crown **has come loose.**
4 Can I have **my teeth whitened?**
5 My son's first teeth **are coming through.**

87

87.7 🔊
1 I've been feeling a bit low this week.
2 I've been feeling very low this week.
3 I've been feeling really low this week.
4 I've been feeling a bit anxious this week.
5 I've been feeling very anxious this week.
6 I've been feeling really anxious this week.
7 I've been feeling a bit depressed this week.
8 I've been feeling very depressed this week.
9 I've been feeling really depressed this week.
10 I've been feeling a bit up and down this week.
11 I've been feeling very up and down this week.
12 I've been feeling really up and down this week.

87.8 🔊
1 How is this **affecting** you?
2 These sessions are really **helping** me.
3 I'm finding it hard to **cope.**
4 Your feelings are **valid.**
5 How did that make you **feel?**
6 That's a real **trigger** for me.
7 Can we **explore** this more?
8 I'm doing **better** this week.

89

89.8
A 4   E 7
B 1   F 6
C 8   G 5
D 3   H 2

89.9 🔊
1 We'll need to check our system **and get back to you.**
2 Is there anything else **I can help with?**
3 He knows where **to reach me.**
4 Hello, I wonder **if you can help me…**
5 Thank you so much **for calling.**

90

90.7 🔊
1 Sorry, I can't **talk** now.
2 I can't remember my **PIN.**
3 I'll **message** you back.
4 I'll put you on **speaker.**
5 My phone has **died.**
6 I've been **locked** out.
7 My **screen** has frozen.

90.8 🔊
1. Hello? You're **breaking** up – the signal is terrible.
2. Sounds perfect. **Catch** you then!
3. Good, thank you. I'm just **checking** in about tonight.
4. Okay. We can **fix** it for you.

91

91.5
Ⓐ 5 Ⓓ 1
Ⓑ 2 Ⓔ 4
Ⓒ 6 Ⓕ 3

91.6 🔊
1. Choose "free Wi-Fi" from the **menu**, then fill in the form.
2. Go to "settings", then tap "**security**".
3. You can join my **hotspot** if you like.
4. Yeah, that URL seems dodgy, let's try another **site**.

91.11
Ⓐ 6 Ⓓ 3
Ⓑ 1 Ⓔ 2
Ⓒ 4 Ⓕ 5

91.12 🔊
1. I'm **booking** a doctor's appointment.
2. I need to **check** my emails…
3. I've got a **webinar** this afternoon.
4. I'm **streaming** a new series.
5. … and sign up for that **online** training course.
6. I'm **ordering** more cat food.
7. I'm **scrolling** through my socials.
8. I'm just **tracking** the grocery delivery.

91.13 🔊
1. I'm downloading **our tickets for today...**
2. … I'll share yours with you **on our group chat.**
3. I'm setting up an online account **for our energy bills.**
4. I'm just uploading my essay… **then I've got a webinar this afternoon.**

92

92.5
Ⓐ 6 Ⓓ 3
Ⓑ 5 Ⓔ 4
Ⓒ 2 Ⓕ 1

92.6 🔊
1. It's asking me to set up **authentication on my account.**
2. I'm trying to get tickets **but the website keeps crashing.**
3. My screen has **completely frozen.**
4. You could try **restarting the computer…**
5. … or you could connect **from a different device?**

93

93.6
1. A
2. A
3. B
4. B
5. A
6. B

93.7 🔊
1. Check your **trash**. Maybe it's still there.
2. Okay, let's have a look at your **filters**.
3. Yeah, I'll **forward** you her message.
4. It looks suspicious – I wouldn't **download** it.

94

94.6
Ⓐ 7 Ⓕ 8
Ⓑ 1 Ⓖ 6
Ⓒ 5 Ⓗ 2
Ⓓ 3 Ⓘ 4
Ⓔ 9

94.7 🔊
1. I'm just **clicking** on it now.
2. **IDK**, will have to see how I feel TBH
3. I can, darling! Can you **see** me?
4. I know, right? **LOL**

95

95.6 🔊
1. I saw! I think you've won the internet.
2. Or how about a monthly podcast?
3. Not him! Just block him.

95.7 🔊
1. Or how about a monthly **podcast**?
2. That's just a **troll**, I'm blocking them.
3. I saw! I think you've won the **internet**.
4. There are loads of **comments** on my post!
5. They're all up on my **profile**…
6. More video **content** would help.

96

96.5
Ⓐ 7 Ⓔ 6
Ⓑ 2 Ⓕ 4
Ⓒ 5 Ⓖ 3
Ⓓ 1

96.6 🔊
1. Can you recommend **a good holiday read?**
2. It's the best book **I've read in ages.**
3. Yeah, it had me on **the edge of my seat!**
4. I found it quite **hard-going, actually.**
5. Want a flick through *Fashion Monthly*?

Index

Main topics are shown in **bold** module numbers.

Acknowledgments

The publisher would like to thank:

Sophie Adam and Elizabeth Blakemore for editorial assistance; Amy Child, Mark Lloyd, and Collette Sadler for design assistance; Jane Ewart for project management support; Sonia Charbonnier for fonts; Oliver Drake for proofreading; Elizabeth Wise for indexing; Christine Stroyan for audio recording management; and ID Audio for audio recording and production.

All images are copyright DK. For more information, please visit **www.dkimages.com**.